P9-CCW-676

THE BOOK OF General Ignorance

Also by John Lloyd (with Douglas Adams)

The Meaning of Liff

The Deeper Meaning of Liff

THE BOOK OF General Ignorance

John Lloyd and John Mitchinson

Harmony Books
New York

Published in the United States by Harmony Books, an imprint of the Crown Publishing Group, a division of Random House, Inc., New York.
www.crownpublishing.com

Originally published in Great Britian by Faber and Faber Limited, London, in 2006.

Library of Congress Cataloging-in-Publication Data
Mitchinson, John, 1963–
The book of general ignorance / John Mitchinson and John Lloyd.
p. cm.
ISBN 978-0-307-39491-0
1. Questions and answers. I. Lloyd, John, 1951– II. Title.
AG 195.M58 2007
031.02–dc22 2007013231

ISBN 978-0-307-39491-0

Printed in the United States of America

Design by Lauren Dong

20 19 18 17 16 15

First Edition

Contents

Foreword | *Stephen Fry*

People sometimes accuse me of knowing a lot. "Stephen," they say, accusingly, "you know a lot." This is a bit like telling a person who has a few grains of sand clinging to him that he owns much sand. When you consider the vast amount of sand there is in the world such a person is, to all intents and purposes, sandless. We are all sandless. We are all ignorant. There are beaches and deserts and dunes of knowledge whose existence we have never even guessed at, let alone visited.

It's the ones who think they know what there is to be known that we have to look out for. "All is explained in this text—there is nothing else you need to know," they tell us. For thousands of years we put up with this kind of thing. Those who said, "Hang on, I think we might be ignorant, let's see . . ." were made to drink poison, or had their eyes put out and their bowels drawn out through their botties.

We are perhaps now more in danger of thinking we know everything than we were even in those dark times of religious superstition (if indeed they have gone away). Today we have the whole store of human knowledge a mouse-click away, which is all very fine and dandy, but it's in danger of becoming just another sacred text. What we need is a treasure house, not of knowledge, but of ignorance. Something that gives not answers but questions. Something that shines light, not on already garish facts, but into the dark, damp corners of ignorance. And the volume you have in your hands is just such a blazing torch which can help us embark upon the journey of dumbing up.

Read it wisely, Little One, for the power of ignorance is great.

Four Words | *Alan Davies*

Will this do, Stephen?

Introduction | *John Lloyd*

There's an idea going about that the human race basically understands how the universe works. Not you and me, obviously, but scientists perhaps, or experts. Regrettably, this is not the case. In the words of Thomas Edison, the man who didn't invent the lightbulb, "We don't know a millionth of one percent about anything."

This book is for the people who know they don't know very much. It contains hundreds of things that the average person doesn't know. But it doesn't begin to scratch the surface of human ignorance, because it's the kind of stuff that has answers. The really interesting questions aren't like that. What is life? Nobody knows. What is light? Or love? Or laughter?

It's a very well kept secret, which they don't teach you at school, that nobody has the faintest notion what gravity is. Or consciousness or electricity or viruses. We don't know why there is something and not nothing, and we do not know either how, or why, the universe began. Worse, 96 percent of the universe appears to be missing. The world is not solid; it is made of empty space and energy. But nobody knows what energy is, and they're beginning to suspect there is no such thing as emptiness.

One of the many things we don't understand is What is interestingness? The Romans, interestingly, had no word for "interesting." Nobody has ever successfully defined what interestingness actually is—or worked out why what you don't know is much more interesting than what you do know.

Biologists say our primal drives are food, sex, and shelter, no different from the animals. We say there is a fourth drive which makes us uniquely human—curiosity. Porcupines do not worry about the meaning of existence. Moths and aardvarks do not look up at the night sky and wonder what the twinkly bits are. People do. In the words of W. H. Auden, "Those who run to the apes to explain our behavior are chuckleheads too dumb to know their arse from a hole in the ground."

The human brain is the most complex single object in the cosmos. It can make more connections than there are positively charged particles in the visible universe. Nobody knows why it is so massively complicated, or what we are supposed to do with all that astonishing computing power.

We think we know the answer: Ask more questions.

Here are 230 of them.

THE BOOK OF General Ignorance

By ignorance the truth is known.

Henry Suso (1300–65),
The Little Book of Truth

What's the name of the tallest mountain in the world?

Mauna Kea, the highest point on the island of Hawaii.

The inactive volcano is a modest 13,799 feet above sea level, but when measured from the seabed to its summit, it is 33,465 feet high—about three-quarters of a mile taller than Mount Everest.

As far as mountains are concerned, the current convention is that "highest" means measured from sea level to summit; "tallest" means measured from the bottom of the mountain to the top.

So, while Mount Everest at 29,029 feet is the highest mountain in the world, it is not the tallest.

Measuring mountains is trickier than it looks. It's easy enough to see where the top is, but where exactly is the bottom of a mountain?

For example, some argue that Mount Kilimanjaro in Tanzania—at 19,340 feet—is taller than Everest because it rises straight out of the African plain, whereas Everest is merely one of many peaks topping the enormous base of the Himalayas, shared by the world's next thirteen highest mountains.

Others claim that the most logical measure ought to be the distance of a mountain's peak from the center of the Earth.

Because the Earth is a flattened rather than a perfect sphere, the equator is about thirteen miles further from the center of the Earth than the poles.

This is good news for the reputation of those mountains that are very close to the equator—like Mount Chimborazo in the Andes—but it also means accepting that even the beaches in Ecuador are higher than the Himalayas.

Though massive, the Himalayas are surprisingly young. When they were formed, the dinosaurs had been dead for twenty-five million years.

In Nepal, Everest is known as *Chomolungma* (Mother of the

Universe). In Tibet, it is called *Sagamartha* (Forehead of the Sky). Like any healthy youngster, it is still growing, at the not very exciting rate of less than a quarter of an inch a year.

How do moths feel about flames?

They're not attracted to them. They are disoriented by them.

Apart from the odd forest fire, artificial light sources have been in existence for an extremely short time in comparison with the age of the relationship between moths and the sun and moon. Many insects use these light sources to navigate by day and night.

Because the moon and sun are a long way away, insects have evolved to expect the light from them to strike their eyes in the same place at different times of day or night, enabling them to calculate how to fly in a straight line.

When people come along with their portable miniature suns and moons and a moth flies past, the light confuses it. It assumes it must somehow be moving in a curved path, because its position in relation to the stationary sun or moon, has unexpectedly changed.

The moth then adjusts its course until it sees the light as stationary again. With a light source so close, the only way this is possible is to fly around and around it in circles.

Moths do not eat clothes. (It's their caterpillars that do it.)

Where is the driest place on earth?

Antarctica. Parts of the continent have seen no rain for two million years.

A desert is technically defined as a place that receives less than ten inches of rain a year.

The Sahara gets just one inch of rain a year.

Antarctica's average annual rainfall is about the same, but 2 percent of it, known as the Dry Valleys, is free of ice and snow and it never rains there at all.

The next-driest place in the world is the Atacama Desert in Chile. In some areas, no rain has fallen for four hundred years and its average annual rainfall is a tiny 0.004 inch. Taken as a whole, this makes it the world's driest desert, 250 times as dry as the Sahara.

As well as the driest place on earth, Antarctica can also claim to be the wettest and the windiest. Seventy percent of the world's fresh water is found there in the form of ice, and its wind speeds are the fastest ever recorded.

The unique conditions in the Dry Valleys of Antarctica are caused by so-called katabatic winds (from the Greek word for "going down"). These occur when cold, dense air is pulled downhill simply by the force of gravity. The winds can reach speeds of 200 mph, evaporating all moisture—water, ice, and snow—in the process.

Though Antarctica is a desert, these completely dry parts of it are called, somewhat ironically, oases. They are so similar to conditions on Mars that NASA used them to test the *Viking* mission.

Where are you most likely to get caught in a hailstorm?

The Western Highlands of Kenya, in Africa.

In terms of annual average, Kericho, Kenya, has more hail than anywhere else on earth, with hail falling on 132 days each year. By comparison, the United Kingdom averages only 15 hail days in a year and the worst affected area in the United States, the eastern Rockies, experiences an average of 45 hail days a year.

What causes the abundance of hail is not fully understood. Kericho is the home of Kenya's tea plantations, and a 1978 study showed that organic litter from the tea plants gets stirred into the atmosphere, where it acts as a nucleus around which hailstones can grow.

Another theory is that the high altitude of the region could be to blame, as the shape of the terrain causes a large uplift of warm air that quickly condenses. This, and the reduced distance between the freezing level (about three miles up) and the ground, reduces the chance of hailstones' melting.

The average hailstone is about a quarter of an inch across, but they can grow large enough to dent cars, shatter greenhouses, and even injure people.

The largest single hailstone ever recorded in the United States was 7 inches in diameter, 18.75 inches in circumference, and weighed in at just under a pound. It fell into the backyard of a house in Aurora, Nebraska, in June 2003. This is off the end of the official U.S. scale for describing hailstones, which starts at "pea" and rises progressively through mothball, walnut, and teacup to softball. The Aurora hailstone was the size of a small melon and would have hit the ground at 100 mph.

THERE IS REALLY NO SUCH THING AS BAD WEATHER, ONLY DIFFERENT KINDS OF GOOD WEATHER.

JOHN RUSKIN

Hail costs the United States $1 billion each year in damage to property and crops. A hailstorm that struck Munich, Germany, in July 1984 caused an estimated $1 billion worth of damage to trees, buildings, and motor vehicles in a single afternoon. Trees were stripped of their bark, and whole fields of crops were destroyed. More than 70,000 buildings and 250,000 cars were damaged, and more than 400 people were injured.

However, the world's worst hailstorm occurred in the Gopalanj district of Bangladesh on April 14, 1986. Some of the hailstones weighed more than two pounds, and at least 92 people were killed.

What's the largest living thing?

It's a mushroom.

And it's not even a particularly rare one. You've probably got the honey fungus (*Armillaria ostoyae*) in your garden, growing on a dead tree stump.

For your sake, let's hope it doesn't reach the size of the largest recorded specimen, in Malheur National Forest in Oregon. It covers 2,200 acres and is between two thousand and eight thousand years old. Most of it is underground in the form of a massive mat of tentacle-like white mycelia (the mushroom's equivalent of roots). These spread along tree roots, killing the trees and peeping up through the soil occasionally as innocent-looking clumps of honey mushrooms.

> I CONFESS THAT NOTHING FRIGHTENS ME MORE THAN THE APPEARANCE OF MUSHROOMS ON THE TABLE, ESPECIALLY IN A SMALL PROVINCIAL TOWN.
>
> ALEXANDRE DUMAS

The giant honey fungus of Oregon was initially thought to grow in separate clusters throughout the forest, but researchers have now confirmed it is the world's single biggest organism, connected under the soil.

What's the biggest thing a blue whale can swallow?

a. A very large mushroom
b. A small family car
c. A grapefruit
d. A sailor

A grapefruit.

Quite interestingly, a blue whale's throat is almost exactly the same diameter as its belly button (which is about the size of a salad plate), but a little smaller than its eardrum (which is more the size of a dinner plate).

For eight months of the year, blue whales eat virtually nothing, but during the summer they feed almost continuously, scooping up three tons of food a day. As you may remember from biology lessons, their diet consists of tiny, pink, shrimplike crustaceans called krill, which go down like honey. Krill come conveniently served in huge swarms that can weigh more than 100,000 tons.

The word *krill* is Norwegian. It comes from the Dutch word *kriel*, meaning "small fry" but now also used to mean both pygmies and "small potatoes." Krill sticks have been marketed with reasonable success in Chile but krill mince was a bit of a disaster in Russia, Poland, and South Africa owing to dangerously high levels of fluoride. It came from the krill's shells, which were too small to pick off individually before mincing.

The narrow gauge of a blue whale's throat means it couldn't have swallowed Jonah. The only whale with a throat wide enough to swallow a person whole is the sperm whale and, once inside, the intense acidity of the sperm whale's stomach juices would make survival impossible. The celebrated case of the "Modern Jonah" in 1891, in which James Bartley claimed to have been swallowed by a sperm whale and rescued by his crewmates fifteen hours later, has been nailed as a fraud.

Aside from its throat, everything else about the blue whale is *big*. At 105 feet in length, it is the largest creature that has ever lived—three times the size of the biggest dinosaur and equivalent in weight to 2,700 people. Its tongue weighs more than an elephant; its heart is the size of a family car; its stomach can hold more than a ton of food. It also makes the loudest noise of any individual animal: a low-frequency hum that can be detected by other whales more than 10,000 miles away.

Which bird lays the smallest egg for its size?

The ostrich.

Although it is the largest single cell in nature, an ostrich egg is less than 1.5 percent of the weight of the mother. A wren's egg, by comparison, is 13 percent of its weight.

The largest egg in comparison with the size of the bird is that of the little spotted kiwi. Its egg accounts for 26 percent of its own weight: the equivalent of a woman giving birth to a six-year-old child.

An ostrich egg weighs as much as twenty-four hen's eggs; to soft-boil one takes forty-five minutes. Queen Victoria tucked into one for breakfast and declared it among the best meals she had ever eaten.

The largest egg laid by any animal—including the dinosaurs—belonged to the elephant bird of Madagascar, which became extinct in 1700. It was ten times the size of an ostrich egg, nine liters in volume and the equivalent of 180 chicken's eggs.

The elephant bird (*Aepyornis maximus*) is thought to be the basis for the legend of the fierce roc that Sinbad battles in the *Arabian Nights.*

How long can a chicken live without its head?

About two years.

On September 10, 1945, a plump young cockerel in Fruita, Colorado, had his head chopped off and lived. Incredibly, the axe had missed the jugular vein and left enough of the brain stem attached to the neck for him to survive, even thrive.

Mike, as he was known, became a national celebrity, touring the country and featuring in *Time* and *Life* magazines. His owner, Lloyd Olsen, charged twenty-five cents for a chance to meet "Mike the Headless Wonder Chicken" in sideshows across the United States. Mike would appear complete with a dried chicken's head purported to be his own—in fact, the Olsens' cat had made off with the original. At the height of his fame, Mike was making $4,500 a month, and was valued at $10,000. His success resulted in a wave of copycat chicken beheadings, though none of the unfortunate victims lived for more than a day or two.

Mike was fed and watered using an eyedropper. In the two years after he lost his head, he put on nearly six pounds and spent his time happily preening and "pecking" for food with his neck. One person who knew Mike well commented: "He was a big fat chicken who didn't know he didn't have a head."

Tragedy struck one night in a motel room in Phoenix, Arizona. Mike started to choke and Lloyd Olsen, to his horror, realized he'd left the eyedropper at the previous day's show. Unable to clear his airways, Mike choked to death.

Mike remains a cult figure in Colorado, and, every May since 1999, Fruita has marked his passing with a "Mike the Headless Chicken" Day.

What has a three-second memory?

Not a goldfish, for starters.

Despite its status as a proverbial fact, a goldfish's memory isn't a few seconds long.

Research by the School of Psychology at the University of Plymouth in 2003 demonstrated beyond a reasonable doubt that goldfish have a memory span of at least three months and can distinguish between different shapes, colors, and sounds. They were trained to push a lever to earn a food reward; when the lever was fixed to work only for an hour a day, the fish soon learned to activate it at the correct time. A number of similar studies have shown that farmed fish can easily be trained to feed at particular times and places in response to an audible signal.

Goldfish don't swim into the side of the bowl, not because they can see it, but because they are using a pressure-sensing system called the lateral line. Certain species of blind cave fish are able to navigate perfectly well in their lightless environment by using their lateral line system alone.

While we're dealing with goldfish myths, a pregnant goldfish isn't, hasn't, and can't be called a "twit." Goldfish don't get pregnant: they lay eggs that the males fertilize in the water.

In principle, there *could* be a word for a female fish with egg development, but none is listed in any proper dictionary.

What's the most dangerous animal that has ever lived?

Half the human beings who have ever died, perhaps as many as 45 billion people, have been killed by female mosquitoes (the males only bite plants).

Mosquitoes carry more than a hundred potentially fatal diseases, including malaria, yellow fever, dengue fever, encephalitis, filariasis, and elephantiasis. Even today, they kill one person every twelve seconds.

Amazingly, nobody had any idea that mosquitoes were dangerous until the end of the nineteenth century. In 1877 the British doctor Sir Patrick Manson—known as "Mosquito" Manson—proved that elephantiasis was caused by mosquito bites.

Seventeen years later, in 1894, it occurred to him that malaria might also be caused by mosquitoes. He

> IF YOU THINK YOU ARE TOO SMALL TO MAKE A DIFFERENCE, TRY SLEEPING IN A CLOSED ROOM WITH A MOSQUITO.
>
> AFRICAN PROVERB

encouraged his pupil Ronald Ross, then a young doctor based in India, to test the hypothesis.

Ross was the first person to show how female mosquitoes transmit the *Plasmodium* parasite through their saliva. He tested his theory using birds. Manson went one better. To show that the theory worked for humans, he infected his own son, using mosquitoes carried in the diplomatic bag from Rome. (Fortunately, after an immediate dose of quinine, the boy recovered.)

Ross won the Nobel Prize in Physiology or Medicine in 1902. Manson was elected a Fellow of the Royal Society, knighted, and founded the London School of Tropical Medicine.

There are 2,500 known species of mosquito; 400 of them are members of the *Anopheles* family, and, of these, 40 species are able to transmit malaria.

The females use the blood they suck to mature their eggs, which are laid on water. The eggs hatch into aquatic larvae, or wrigglers. Unlike most insects, the pupae of mosquitoes, known as tumblers, are active and swim about.

Male mosquitoes hum at a higher pitch than females: they can be sexually enticed by the note of a B-natural tuning fork.

Female mosquitoes are attracted to their hosts by moisture, milk, carbon dioxide, body heat, and movement. Sweaty people and pregnant women have a higher chance of being bitten.

Mosquito means "small fly" in Spanish and Portuguese.

Do marmots kill people?

Yes, they cough them to death.

Marmots are benign, pot-bellied members of the squirrel family. They are about the size of a cat and squeak loudly when alarmed. Less appealingly, the bobac variety, found on the Mongolian steppe, is particularly susceptible to a lung infection caused by the bacterium *Yersinia pestis*, commonly known as bubonic plague.

They spread it around by coughing on their neighbors, infecting fleas, rats, and, ultimately, humans. All the great plagues that swept through Eastern Asia to Europe came from marmots in Mongolia. The estimated death toll is more than a billion, making the marmot second only to the malarial mosquito as a killer of humans.

When marmots and humans succumb to plague, the lymph glands under the armpits and in the groin become black and swollen (these sores are called buboes, from the Greek *boubon* [groin], hence *bubonic*). Mongolians will never eat a marmot's armpits because "they contain the soul of a dead hunter."

The other parts of the marmot are a delicacy in Mongolia. Hunters have complicated rituals to stalk their prey that include wearing false rabbit ears, dancing, and waving the tail of a yak. The captured marmots are barbecued whole over hot stones. In Europe, the fat of the alpine marmot is valued as a salve for rheumatism.

Other species of marmot include the American prairie dog and the woodchuck, or groundhog. Groundhog Day is on February 2. Each year, a marmot known as Punxsutawney Phil is pulled out of his electrically heated burrow at Gobbler's Knob, in Punxsutawney, Pennsylvania, by his tuxedo-clad "keepers" who ask him if he can see his shadow. If he whispers "yes," it means winter has six weeks to go. Since 1887, Phil has never been wrong.

Bubonic plague is still with us today—the last serious outbreak occurred in India in 1994—and it is one of the three diseases listed in the United States as requiring quarantine (the other two being yellow fever and cholera).

How do lemmings die?

Not by mass suicide, if that's what you're thinking.

The suicide idea seems to have originated in the work of nineteenth-century naturalists who had witnessed (but not understood) the four-year boom-and-bust population cycle of the Norwegian lemming (*Lemmus lemmus*).

Lemmings have a phenomenal reproductive capacity. A single female can produce up to eighty offspring a year. Sudden surges in their numbers once led Scandinavians to think they were spontaneously generated by the weather.

What actually happens is that mild winters lead to overpopulation that in turn leads to overgrazing. The lemmings set off into unfamiliar territory in search of food until they pile up against natural obstacles like cliffs, lakes, and seas. The lemmings keep coming. Panic and violence ensue. Accidents happen. But it isn't suicide.

A secondary myth has evolved, which is that the whole idea of mass suicide was invented by the 1958 Walt Disney film *White Wilderness*. It's true that the film was a complete fake. It was filmed in landlocked, lemming-free Alberta, Canada: the lemmings had to be bused in from several hundred miles away in Manitoba. The shots of the "migration" were made using a few lemmings on a snow-covered turntable. The notorious final scene, where lemmings plunge into the sea to the doom-laden voice-over of Winston Hibbler—"This is the last chance to turn back, yet over they go, casting themselves out bodily into space"—was created by the filmmakers simply throwing the lemmings into a river.

But Disney was only guilty of trying to re-create an already entrenched story. Here it is described in the most influential children's reference book of the early twentieth century, Arthur Mee's *Children's Encyclopaedia*, published in 1908:

"They march straight forward, over hill and dell, through gardens, farms, villages, into wells and ponds to poison water and cause typhoid . . . on and on to the sea, then into the water to destruction. . . . It is sad and terrible, but if the dismal exodus did not occur lemmings would long ago have eaten Europe bare."

What do chameleons do?

They don't change color to match the background.

Never have; never will. Complete myth. Utter fabrication. Total lie.

They change color as a result of different emotional states. If they happen to match the background it's entirely coincidental.

Chameleons change color when frightened or picked up or when they beat another chameleon in a fight. They change color when a member of the opposite sex steps into view and they sometimes change color due to fluctuations in either light or temperature.

A chameleon's skin contains several layers of specialized cells called *chromataphores*—from Greek *chroma* (color) and *pherein* (to carry)—each with different colored pigments. Altering the balance between these layers causes the skin to reflect different kinds of light, making chameleons a kind of walking color wheel.

It's odd how persistent the belief that they change color to match the background is. The myth first appears in the work of a minor Greek writer of entertaining stories and potted biographies called Antigonus of Carystus in about 240 B.C. Aristotle, far more influential and writing a century earlier, had already, quite correctly, linked the color change to fear and by the Renaissance, the "background" theory had once again been almost entirely abandoned. But it's come back with a vengeance since and to this day is perhaps the only thing most people think they "know" about chameleons.

Chameleons can remain completely motionless for several hours at a time. Because of this, and the fact that they eat very little, they were, for many centuries, believed to live on air. This, of course, isn't true, either.

The word chameleon is Greek for "ground-lion." The smallest species is the *Brookesia minima*, which is an inch long; the largest is the *Chaemaeleo parsonnii*, which is more than two feet long. The Common Chameleon glories in the Latin name *Chamaeleo chamaeleon*, which sounds like the opening to a song.

Chameleons can rotate and focus either eye independently to look in two completely different directions at once, but they are stone deaf.

The Bible forbids the eating of chameleons.

How do polar bears disguise themselves?

They cover their black nose with their white paw, don't they?

Adorable but unfounded, unfortunately. And they're not left-handed, either. Naturalists have observed polar bears for many hundreds of hours and have never seen any evidence of discreet nose covering or of left-handedness.

They like toothpaste, though. There are regular reports of polar bears wreaking havoc in Arctic tourist camps, knocking over tents and trampling equipment, all in order to suck on a tube of Pepsodent.

This may be one of the reasons the town of Churchill in Manitoba has a large concrete polar bear jail. Any bear moseying into town is apprehended and incarcerated there. Some serve sentences of several months before being released back into the community, embittered, institutionalized, and jobless. Formerly the morgue for a military base, it is officially designated Building D-20. It can hold up to twenty-three bears. Polar bears don't eat during the summer, so some of the inmates aren't fed for months at a time. They're held until spring or the autumn—their hunting seasons—so that when they're released they go off fishing and don't just wander back to Churchill.

The earliest-known captive polar bear belonged to Ptolemy II of Egypt (308–246 B.C.), and was kept in his private zoo in Alexandria. In A.D. 57, the Roman writer Calpurnius Siculus wrote of polar bears pitted against seals in a flooded amphitheater. Viking hunters captured polar bear cubs by killing and skinning the mother, spreading her pelt on the snow, and nabbing the cubs when they came to lie on it.

The scientific names can be a bit misleading. *Ursus arctos* isn't the polar bear, it's the brown bear. *Ursus* means "bear" in Latin and *arctos* means "bear" in Greek. The Arctic is named after the bear, not the other way around; it was "the region of the bear," where bears lived and where the great bear in the sky, the constellation Ursa Major, pointed. The polar bear is *Ursus maritimus*—the sea bear.

The constellation Ursa Major has been identified as a bear by a number of cultures, including the Ainu of Japan in the East, the American Indians in the West, and ourselves in the middle. Even though all polar bears are born, literally, under the constellation of the Great Bear, astrologically they are all Capricorns, born in late December or early January.

The brown bear is the same species as the grizzly, which is the term applied to brown bears living in inland North America. Male and female bears are known as boars and sows, despite being about as closely related to pigs as koalas are to seals. Bears' closest relatives are actually dogs.

How many galaxies are visible to the naked eye?

Five thousand? Two million? Ten billion?

The answer is four—although from where you are sitting, you can only see two; and one of those is the Milky Way (the one we're in).

Given that there are estimated to be more than 100 billion

galaxies in the universe, each containing between 10 and 100 billion stars, it's a bit disappointing. In total, only four galaxies are visible from earth with the naked eye, only half of which can be seen at once (two from each hemisphere). In the Northern Hemisphere, you can see the Milky Way and Andromeda (M31), while in the Southern Hemisphere you can see the Large and Small Magellanic Clouds.

Some people with exceptional eyesight claim to be able to see three more—M33 in Triangulum, M81 in Ursa Major, and M83 in Hydra—but it's very hard to prove.

The number of stars supposedly visible to the naked eye varies wildly, but everyone agrees that the total is substantially less than 10,000. Most amateur-astronomy computer software uses the same database: it lists 9,600 stars as "naked-eye visible." But no one really believes this figure. Other estimates vary from around 8,000 down to fewer than 3,000.

It used to be said that there were more cinemas (around 5,200) in the former Soviet Union than there are stars visible in the night sky.

At the Canadian website www.starregistry.ca you can have a star named after yourself or a friend for $98 CDN (or $175 CDN with a framed certificate). They list 2,873 stars as being visible to the naked eye. None of these are available, as they already have historical or scientific names.

What man-made artifacts can be seen from the moon?

Deduct ten points if you said the Great Wall of China.

No human artifacts at all can be seen from the moon with the naked eye.

The idea that the Great Wall is the only man-made object that can be seen from the moon is all-pervasive, but it confuses the moon with space.

Space is quite close. It starts about 60 miles from the earth's surface. From there, many artificial objects are visible: motorways, ships on the sea, railways, cities, fields of crops, and even some individual buildings.

However, at an altitude of only a few thousand miles after leaving the earth's orbit, no man-made objects are visible at all. From the moon—more than 250,000 miles away—even the continents are barely visible.

And, despite *Trivial Pursuit* telling you otherwise, there is no point in between the two where only the Great Wall of China is visible.

Which of these are Chinese inventions?

a. Glass
b. Rickshaws
c. Chop suey
d. Fortune cookies

Chop suey. There are many fanciful stories about its American origin, but it is a Chinese dish.

In E. N. Anderson's definitive *The Food of China* (1988), chop suey is named as a dish local to Toisan, in southern Canton. They called it *tsap seui*, which means "miscellaneous scraps" in Cantonese. Most of the early immigrants to California came from this region, hence its early appearance in America.

Glass isn't Chinese: the earliest known glass artifacts are from ancient Egypt in 1350 B.C. The earliest Chinese porcelain dates from the Han dynasty (206 B.C.–A.D. 220). Ancient China built a whole culture on porcelain, but they never got to grips with transparent glass. This is sometimes used to explain the fact that they never had a scientific revolution comparable with the one in the West, which was made possible by the development of lenses and transparent glassware.

> SEEK KNOWLEDGE, EVEN IF IT BE IN CHINA.
>
> MUHAMMAD

The rickshaw was invented by an American missionary, Jonathan Scobie, who first used it to wheel his invalid wife through the streets of Yokohama, Japan, in 1869.

Fortune cookies are also American, though they were probably invented by a Japanese immigrant, Makato Hagiwara, a landscape designer who created the Japanese Tea Garden in Golden Gate Park, San Francisco. He served small, sweet Japanese buns with thank-you notes inside from about 1907 onward. Restaurant owners in the city's Chinatown copied them and the notes soon started to tell fortunes.

But who's complaining? Chinese resourcefulness has given us the abacus, bells, brandy, the calendar, the compass, the crossbow, the decimal system, drilling for oil, fireworks, the fishing reel, the flamethrower, the flush toilet, gunpowder, the helicopter, the horse collar, the iron plow, the kite, lacquer, magic mirrors, matches, the mechanical clock, miniature hot-air balloons, negative numbers, paper, parachutes, porcelain, printmaking, relief maps, rudders, seismographs, silk, stirrups, the suspension bridge, the umbrella, the water pump, and the wheelbarrow.

Where did Marco Polo come from?

Croatia.

Marco Polo (or Mark Chicken, in English) was born Marko Pilić in Korcula, Dalmatia, in 1254, then a protectorate of Venice.

We shall probably never know whether he really went to the Far East as a seventeen-year-old with his merchant uncles or if he simply recorded the tales of Silk Road traders who stopped off at their Black Sea trading post.

What is certain is that his famous book of travels was largely the work of a romance writer called Rustichello da Pisa, with whom he shared a cell after being captured by the Genoans in 1296. Polo dictated it; Rustichello wrote it in French, a language Polo didn't speak.

The result, which appeared in 1306, was designed to entertain, and it became a best seller in the era before printing. As an accurate history its status is less secure.

Its original title was *Il Milione* (the million) for reasons that are now obscure, although it quickly became nicknamed "the million lies," and Polo—now a rich and successful merchant—was known as "Mr Million." It was probably just a catchy thirteenth-century version of a title, like *Wonder Book of Wonders*. No original manuscripts survive.

Marco Polo is also supposed to have brought pasta and ice cream to Italy.

In fact, pasta was known in Arab countries in the ninth century and dried macaroni is mentioned in Genoa in 1279, twenty-five years before Polo claimed to have returned. According to the food historian Alan Davidson, the myth itself only dates back as far as 1929, when it was mentioned in an American pasta-trade journal.

Ice cream may well be a Chinese invention, but it seems unlikely to have been introduced to the West by Polo, as it doesn't get mentioned again until the middle of the seventeenth century.

What is Croatia's most lasting contribution to world business?

The necktie.

Hravat is the Croatian word for "Croat" and it's where we get the word *cravat*. So Croatia means "tie land."

In the seventeenth century, Louis XIII of France kept a regiment of Croatian mercenaries during the Thirty Years War. Part of their uniform was a broad, brightly colored neck cloth by which they became known. The flamboyant yet practical style became very popular in Paris, where military dress was much admired.

During the reign of Louis XIV, the cravat was replaced by a more restrained military *steinkirk*, tied about the neck in a loose knot, but it wasn't until the reintroduction of the flowing cravat by dandies (or "macaroni" as they were then known) in the late eighteenth century that individual styles of tying them became popular, the generic name then changing to "tie."

The relentless march of the tie through the twentieth century has made it the de rigueur dress item for men in all but the most casual of businesses. Bremer Communication, a U.S. image consultancy, has divided the now ubiquitous "business casual" into three levels: basic, standard, and executive. Only at the basic level is a tie not required, and they recommend that this is best restricted to "those days when you have little customer contact or are taking part in an informal activity."

In the late 1990s two researchers at Cambridge University used mathematical modeling to discover that it is topologically possible to tie eighty-five different knots with a conventional tie. They found that, in addition to the four well-known knots, six other knots produced aesthetically pleasing results.

Who invented the steam engine?

a. James Watt
b. George Stephenson
c. Richard Trevithick
d. Thomas Newcomen
e. A Heron from Egypt

Heron (sometimes called Hero) takes the prize, some sixteen hundred years before Newcomen's engine of 1711.

Heron lived in Alexandria around A.D. 62, and is best known as a mathematician and geometer. He was also a visionary inventor, and his *aeolopile* (wind ball) was the first working steam engine. Using the same principle as jet propulsion, a steam-driven metal sphere spun around at 1,500 rpm. Unfortunately for Heron, no one was able to see its practical function, so it was considered nothing more than an amusing novelty.

Amazingly, had Heron but known it, the railway had already been invented seven hundred years earlier by Periander, tyrant of Corinth. Called the Diolkos (slipway), it ran for four miles across the isthmus of Corinth in Greece, and consisted of a roadway paved with limestone blocks in which were cut parallel grooves five feet apart. Trolleys ran along these tracks, on to which ships were loaded. These were pushed by gangs of slaves, forming a sort of land canal that offered a shortcut between the Aegean and the Ionian seas.

The Diolkos was in use for some some fifteen hundred years until it fell into disrepair around A.D. 900. The principle of railways was then completely forgotten about for almost another five hundred years, until people had the idea of using them in mines in the fourteenth century.

The historian Arnold Toynbee wrote a brilliant essay speculating what would have happened if the two inventions had been combined to create a global Greek empire, based on a fast rail network, Athenian democracy, and a Buddhist-style religion founded on the teachings of Pythagoras. He briefly mentions a failed prophet who lived at 4 Railway Cuttings, Nazareth.

Heron also invented the vending machine—for four drachmas you got a shot of holy water—and a portable device to ensure that no one else could drink the wine you brought along to a bottle party.

Who invented the telephone?

Antonio Meucci.

An erratic, sometimes brilliant Florentine inventor, Meucci

arrived in the United States in 1850. In 1860 he first demonstrated a working model of an electric device he called the *teletrofono.* He filed a caveat (a kind of stopgap patent) in 1871, five years before Alexander Graham Bell's telephone patent.

In the same year, Meucci fell ill after he was badly scalded when the Staten Island ferry's boiler exploded. Unable to speak much English, and living on charity, he failed to send the $10 required to renew his caveat in 1874.

> ONE DAY THERE WILL BE A TELEPHONE IN EVERY MAJOR CITY IN THE USA.
>
> ALEXANDER GRAHAM BELL

When Bell's patent was registered in 1876, Meucci sued. He'd sent his original sketches and working models to the lab at Western Union. By an extraordinary coincidence, Bell worked in the very same lab, and the models had mysteriously disappeared.

Meucci died in 1889, while his case against Bell was still under way. As a result, it was Bell, not Meucci, who got the credit for the invention. In 2004 the balance was partly redressed by the U.S. House of Representatives, which passed a resolution that "the life and achievements of Antonio Meucci should be recognized, and his work in the invention of the telephone should be acknowledged."

Not that Bell was a complete fraud. As a young man he did teach his dog to say "How are you, grandmamma?" as a way of communicating with her when she was in a different room. And he made the telephone a practical tool.

Like his friend Thomas Edison, Bell was relentless in his search for novelty. And, like Edison, he wasn't always successful. His metal detector failed to locate the bullet in the body of the stricken President James Garfield. It seems Bell's machine was confused by the president's metal bedsprings.

Bell's foray into animal genetics was driven by his desire to increase the numbers of twin and triplet births in sheep. He noticed that sheep with more than two nipples produced more twins. All he managed to produce was sheep with more nipples.

On the plus side, he did help to invent a hydrofoil, the HP 4, which set the world water-speed record of 70.84 mph in 1919, which stood for ten years. Bell was eighty-two at the time and wisely refused to travel in it.

Bell always referred to himself first and foremost as a teacher of the deaf. His mother and wife were deaf, and he taught the young Helen Keller. She dedicated her autobiography to him.

Where do kilts, bagpipes, haggis, porridge, whisky, and tartan come from?

Not from Scotland.

In fact, not even Scotland is Scottish. Scotland is named after the *Scoti*, a Celtic tribe from Ireland, who arrived in what the Romans called Caledonia in the fifth or sixth century A.D. By the eleventh century they dominated the whole of mainland Scotland. Scots Gaelic is actually a dialect of Irish.

Kilts were invented by the Irish, but the word *kilt* is Danish (*kilte op*, "tuck up").

The bagpipes are ancient and were probably invented in Central Asia. They are mentioned in the Old Testament (Daniel 3:5–15) and in Greek poetry of the fourth century B.C. The Romans probably brought them to Britain but the earliest Pictish carvings date from the eighth century A.D.

Haggis was an ancient Greek sausage (Aristophanes mentions one exploding in *The Clouds* in 423 B.C.).

Oat porridge has been found in the stomachs of five-thousand-year-old Neolithic bog bodies in central Europe and Scandinavia.

Whisky was invented in ancient China. It arrived in Ireland before Scotland, first distilled by monks. The word derives from the Irish *uisge beatha*, from the Latin *aqua vitae* (water of life).

The elaborate system of clan tartans is a complete myth stemming from the early nineteenth century. All Highland dress, including what tartan or plaid there was, was banned after the 1745 rebellion. The English garrison regiments started designing their own tartans as an affectation, and to mark the state visit of King George IV to Edinburgh in 1822. Queen Victoria encouraged the trend, and it soon became a Victorian craze.

Hae'ing said a' that, they've nae been idle, ye ken. Scots inventions and discoveries include adhesive stamps, the Bank of England, bicycle pedals, Bovril, the breech-loading rifle, the cell nucleus, chloroform, the cloud chamber, color photography, corn flour, the cure for malaria, the decimal point, electromagnetism, the *Encyclopaedia Britannica*, fingerprinting, the fountain pen, hypnosis, hypodermic syringes, insulin, the kaleidoscope, the Kelvin scale, the lawn mower, lime cordial, logarithms, marmalade, motor insurance, the MRI scanner, the paddle steamer, paraffin, piano pedals, pneumatic tires, the postmark, radar, the raincoat, the reflecting telescope, savings banks, the screw propeller, the speedometer, the steam hammer, tarmac, the teleprinter, trucks, tubular steel, the typhoid vaccine, the ultrasound scanner, the U.S. Navy, Universal Standard Time, vacuum flasks, wave-powered electricity generators, and wire rope.

Where does chicken tikka masala come from?

Glasgow.

Britain exports chicken tikka masala to India.

Invented in Glasgow in the late 1960s, chicken tikka masala, or CTM, is Britain's most popular dish. There is no standard recipe. In a recent survey, the *Real Curry Guide* tested forty-eight different versions and found the only common ingredient was chicken.

Chicken tikka is a traditional Bangladeshi dish in which pieces of marinated chicken are cooked in a clay oven called a *tandoor*.

This ancient style of cooking originated in the Middle East, the word deriving from the Babylonian *tinuru*, meaning "fire."

The first chicken tandoori on a British restaurant menu was at the Gaylord in Mortimer Street, London, in 1966—the same restaurant where *Not the Nine O'Clock News* was invented in 1979. The recipe reached Glasgow shortly afterward and when, as the legend goes, a customer asked for some gravy to go with it, the chef improvised with tomato soup, spices, and cream.

Masala means "a mixture of spices," and the usual CTM contains ginger and garlic, tomatoes, butter, and cream, spiced with cardamom, cloves, cumin, nutmeg, mild red chili powder, paprika, fenugreek, and turmeric.

It is the turmeric that it gives it the bright yellow color, although the synthetic dye tartrazine is often substituted. (It is tartrazine, among other unpleasant things, that makes curry stains impossible to remove from clothing.) CTM doesn't have a standard style or color: it can be yellow, brown, red, or green and chili hot; creamy and mild; or very smooth and sweet.

In 2001 Foreign Secretary Robin Cook declared that: "Chicken tikka masala is now a true British national dish, not only because it is the most popular, but because it is a perfect illustration of the way Britain absorbs and adapts external influences."

One in seven curries sold in the United Kingdom are CTMs—23 million portions each year. Many of the schools and charities in the city of Sylhet, in Bangladesh, are funded by profits from the British chicken tikka masala boom.

There are now eight thousand Indian restaurants in Britain, turning over nearly $4 billion and employing seventy thousand workers.

Is French toast from France?

Yes and no. Dipping bread in eggs and frying it is a pretty universal solution to making stale bread go further.

The French certainly had a medieval version called *tostees dorees* (golden toast), and this later became *pain perdu* (lost bread), a name that has been enthusiastically adopted for the de luxe versions served in Cajun cooking.

The earliest recorded recipe for the dish occurs in the work of the Roman cook Apicius in the first century A.D. In his book *The Art of Cooking*, he writes rather casually that it's just "another sweet dish": "Break fine white bread, crust removed, into rather large pieces. Soak them in milk, fry in oil, cover in honey and serve."

There are references in early French documents to this recipe as *pain à la Romaine* (Roman bread). So that makes it Italian Toast. As ever, it depends where you are at the time, as there are records of German Toast, Spanish Toast, American Toast and even Nun's Toast being used.

French toast is first recorded in English in 1660 when it appears in *The Accomplisht Cook*, by Robert May. In the same year, Gervase Markham's influential *The English Huswife* has a rich and spicy version of "pamperdy" (*pain perdu*), so, as far as the English were concerned, French toast was French, in those days at least.

However, the dish was also sometimes referred to as "Poor Knights of Windsor." This finds its counterpart in the German (*arme Ritter*), Danish (*arme riddere*), Swedish (*fattiga riddare*) and Finnish (*köyhät ritarit*) versions—all of which mean "poor knights."

One theory offered in explanation is that the most expensive part of a medieval banquet was dessert—spices and nuts were costly imports. Although titled, not all knights were rich, so a dish of fried, eggy bread served with jam or honey would have fulfilled the requirements of etiquette without breaking the bank.

Who invented champagne?

Not the French.

It may come as a surprise—even an outrage—to them, but champagne is an English invention.

As anyone who has made their own ginger beer knows, fermentation naturally produces bubbles. The problem has always been controlling it.

The English developed a taste for fizzy wine in the sixteenth century, importing barrels of green, flat wine from Champagne and adding sugar and molasses to start it fermenting. They also developed the strong coal-fired glass bottles and corks to contain it.

As the records of the Royal Society show, what is now called *méthode champenoise* was first written down in England in 1662. The French added finesse and marketing flair but it wasn't until 1876 that they perfected the modern dry or *brut* style (and even then it was for export to England).

The United Kingdom is France's largest customer for champagne. In 2004 34 million bottles were consumed in Britain. This is almost a third of the entire export market—twice as much as the United States, three times as much as the Germans, and twenty times as much as the Spanish.

The Benedictine monk Dom Pérignon (1638–1715) did not invent champagne: in fact he spent most of his time trying to remove the bubbles.

His famous exclamation, "Come quickly, I am drinking the stars," was devised for an advertisement in the late nineteenth century. Pérignon's real legacy to champagne was in the skillful blending of grape varieties from different vineyards and the use of a wire or hempen cage for the cork.

A legal loophole uniquely allows Americans to call their sparkling wines champagne. The Treaty of Madrid (1891) decreed that only the Champagne region may use that name. This was reaffirmed by the Treaty of Versailles (1919) but the United States signed a separate peace agreement with Germany.

When prohibition was lifted, American wine merchants took advantage of this loophole, freely selling their own champagne, much to the annoyance of the French.

The saucerlike coupe from which champagne is sometimes drunk is *not* based on a mold of Marie Antoinette's breast. It was first manufactured in 1663 (in England), well before her reign. No alternative English topless model has yet been suggested.

Where was the guillotine invented?

Halifax, in Yorkshire.

The Halifax Gibbet consisted of two fifteen-foot-tall wooden uprights between which hung an iron axe mounted on a lead-filled crossbeam controlled by a rope and pulley. Official records show at least fifty-three people were executed using it between 1286 and 1650.

Medieval Halifax made its fortune from the cloth trade. Large quantities of expensive cloth were left outside the mills to dry on frames. Theft was a serious problem, and the town's merchants needed an efficient deterrent.

This, and a similar, later, Scottish device called the Maiden, may well have inspired the French to borrow the idea and come up with their own name.

Dr. Joseph Ignace Guillotin was a humane, mild-mannered doctor who disliked public executions. In 1789 he put to the National Assembly an ambitious plan to reform the French penal system and make it more humane. He proposed a standardized mechanical method of execution which didn't discriminate against the poor (who were messily hanged), as opposed to the rich (who were relatively cleanly beheaded).

Most of the proposals were rejected out of hand, but the

notion of an efficient killing engine stuck. Guillotin's recommendation was picked up and refined by Dr. Antoine Louis, the Secretary of the Academy of Surgeons. It was he, not Guillotin, who produced the first working device, with its characteristic diagonal blade, in 1792. It was even called, briefly, a *Louison* or *Louisette*, after its sponsor.

But somehow, Guillotin's name became attached to it and, despite the best efforts of his family, there it has stubbornly remained. Contrary to popular folklore, Guillotin was not killed by his eponymous machine; he died in 1814 from an infected carbuncle on his shoulder.

The guillotine became the first "democratic" method of execution and was adopted throughout France. In its first ten years, historians estimate fifteen thousand people were decapitated. Only Nazi Germany has used it to execute more, with an estimated forty thousand criminals being guillotined between 1938 and 1945.

The last French person to be guillotined was a Tunisian immigrant called Hamida Djandoubi, for the rape and murder of a young girl in 1977. The death penalty was finally abolished in France in 1981.

It is impossible to test accurately how long a severed head remains conscious, if at all. The best estimate is between five and thirteen seconds.

> THE MORE I SEE OF THE MONEYED CLASSES, THE MORE I UNDERSTAND THE GUILLOTINE.
>
> GEORGE BERNARD SHAW

How many prisoners were freed by the storming of the Bastille?

Seven.

In France, July 14, Bastille Day, is a national holiday and a glorious national symbol, equivalent to July 4 in the United States.

From the rousing paintings of the scene, you might think hundreds of proud revolutionaries flooded into the streets waving tricolors. In fact, only just over half a dozen people were being held at the time of the siege.

The Bastille was stormed on July 14, 1789. Shortly afterward ghoulish engravings of prisoners languishing in chains next to skeletons went on sale in the streets of Paris, forming the popular impression of the conditions there ever since.

The thirteenth-century fortress had been a jail for centuries; by the time of Louis XVI it mainly housed people arrested on the orders of the king or his ministers for offenses like conspiracy and subversion. Distinguished former inmates included Voltaire, who wrote *Oedipus* there in 1718.

The seven prisoners in residence that day were: four forgers, the Comte de Solanges (inside for a sexual misdemeanor) and two lunatics (one of whom was an English or Irish man named Major Whyte, who sported a waist-length beard and thought he was Julius Caesar).

One hundred lives were lost in the attack, including that of the governor, whose head was carried through Paris on a pike.

The prison guard were a contingent of *invalides*—soldiers invalided out of regular service—and conditions were fairly comfortable for most inmates, with relaxed visiting hours and furnished lodgings.

The painter Jean Fragonard's sketch of visiting day in 1785 shows fashionable ladies promenading around the courtyard with the prisoners, who were given a generous spending allowance, plenty of tobacco and alcohol, and were allowed to keep pets.

Jean François Marmontel, an inmate from 1759 to 1760, wrote: "The wine was not excellent, but was passable. No dessert: it was necessary to be deprived of something. On the whole I found that one dined very well in prison."

Louis XVI's diary for the day of the storming of the Bastille reads "*Rien*."

He was referring to the bag in that day's hunt.

Who said "Let them eat cake"?

Wrong again. It wasn't her.

You probably remember the history lesson as if it were yesterday. It's 1789, and the French Revolution is under way. The poor of Paris are rioting because they have no bread and the Queen, Marie Antoinette—callously indifferent, trying to be funny or just plain stupid—comes up with the fatuous suggestion that they eat cake instead.

The first problem is that it wasn't cake, it was brioche (the original French is *Qu'ils mangent de la brioche*). According to Alan Davidson's *Oxford Companion to Food*, "Eighteenth-century brioche was only lightly enriched (by modest quantities of butter and eggs) and not very far removed from a good white loaf of bread." So, the remark might have been an attempt at kindness: "If they want bread, give them some of the good stuff."

Except Marie Antoinette didn't say it. The line had been in use in print as an illustration of aristocratic decadence since at least 1760. Jean-Jacques Rousseau claimed he'd first heard it as early as 1740.

Lady Antonia Fraser, Marie Antoinette's most recent biographer, attributes the remark to the Queen Marie-Thérèse, wife of Louis XIV, the Sun King, but there is a host of other grand eighteenth-century ladies who might have said it. It's also entirely possible it was made up for propaganda purposes.

There is another story that suggests Marie Antoinette introduced croissants to France from her native Vienna. This seems highly unlikely, as the earliest French reference to a croissant isn't until 1853.

Interestingly, wandering Austrian pastry chefs did introduce the flaky pastry to Denmark at about this time, the eponymous "Danish" pastries being known there as *wienerbrød* (Vienna bread).

In Vienna, they are called *Kopenhagener*.

What does a St. Bernard carry around its neck?

St. Bernards have never, ever carried brandy barrels.

The dog's mission is entirely teetotal—apart from anything else, giving brandy to someone with hypothermia is a disastrous mistake—but tourists have always loved the idea, so they still pose wearing them.

Before they were trained as mountain rescue dogs, they were used by the monks at the hospice in the Great St. Bernard Pass—the Alpine route that links Switzerland to Italy—to carry food, as their large size and docile temperament made them good pack animals.

The brandy barrel was the idea of a young English artist named Sir Edwin Landseer (1802–73), who was much favored by Queen Victoria. He was a renowned painter of landscapes and animals, best known for his painting *The Monarch of the Glen* and for sculpting the lions around the base of Nelson's Column.

In 1831 he painted a scene called *Alpine Mastiffs Reanimating a Distressed Traveler* featuring two St. Bernards, one of them carrying a miniature brandy barrel around its neck, which he added "for interest." St. Bernards have been saddled with the association ever since. Landseer is also credited with popularizing the name St. Bernard (rather than Alpine Mastiff) for the breed.

Originally, St. Bernards were known as Barry hounds, a corruption of the German *Bären*, meaning "bears." One of the first lifesavers was known as "Barry the Great," who rescued forty people between 1800 and 1814 but was unfortunately killed by the forty-first, who mistook him for a wolf.

Barry was stuffed and now has pride of place in the Natural History Museum in Berne. In his honor, the best male pup from each litter at the St. Bernard's Hospice is named Barry.

Sometimes, the hospice's duty to provide food and shelter for all who ask can prove troublesome. One night in 1708 Canon Vincent Camos had to provide food for more than four hundred travelers. To save manpower, he had a device built like a large hamster wheel attached to a spit. Inside, a St. Bernard trotted along, turning the meat skewer.

It's estimated the dogs have made more than twenty-five thousand rescues since 1800, though none at all in the last fifty years. As a result, the monastery has decided to sell them off and replace them with helicopters.

What goes "hunk-hunk"?

An Albanian pig.

Albanian dogs go "ham ham."

In Catalan, dogs go "bup bup." The Chinese dogs say "wang wang," the Greek dogs go "gav gav," the Slovenians "hov hov," and the Ukrainians "haf haf." In Iceland, it's "voff," in Indonesia, it's "gong gong," and in Italian, it's "bau bau."

Interestingly, when there is less variety in an animal's noise, languages seem to agree more commonly on its interpretation. For example, nearly every language has a cow going "moo," a cat going "meow" and a cuckoo going "cuckoo."

Dogs even develop regional accents, according to researchers at the Canine Behaviour Centre in Cumbria. Scouse and Scots dogs have the most distinctive accents. The Liver-pudlians have higher-pitched voices, whereas the Scots have a "lighter tone."

To gather their data the Centre asked for owners and their dogs to leave messages on their answering machine; experts then compared the pitch, tone, volume, and length of the sounds made by humans and dogs.

They concluded that dogs imitate their owners in order to bond with them; the closer the bond, the closer the similarity in sound.

Dogs also mimic their owners' behavior. A terrier owned by a young family will tend to be lively and difficult to control. The same dog living with an old lady will end up quiet, inactive, and prone to long periods of sleep.

What noise does the largest frog in the world make?

None at all. Particularly not "RIBBIT."

The three-foot-long Goliath frog, from central Africa, is mute.

There are 4,360 known species of frog, but only one of them goes "ribbit." Each species has its own unique call. The reason everyone thinks all frogs go "ribbit" is that "ribbit" is the distinctive call of the Pacific tree frog (*Hyla regilla*). This is the frog that lives in Hollywood.

Recorded locally, it has been plastered all over the movies for decades to enhance the atmosphere of anywhere from the Everglades to Vietnamese jungles.

Frogs make a huge variety of noises. They croak, snore, grunt, trill, cluck, chirp, ring, whoop, whistle, and growl. They make noises like cattle, squirrels, and crickets. The barking tree frog yaps like a dog; the carpenter frog sounds like two carpenters hammering nails out of sync; and Fowler's toad makes a noise like a bleating sheep with a heavy cold. The South American paradoxical frog (*Pseudis paradoxa*) grunts like a pig (it's paradoxical because the tadpoles are three times larger than the frog).

Female frogs are mostly silent. The noise is made by male frogs advertising themselves to potential mates. The loudest frog is the tiny *coquí* of Puerto Rico, whose Latin name, *Eleutherodactylus coqui*, measures more than its body. Male coquís congregate in dense forest—one to every ten square yards—and compete to see who can call loudest. From three feet away, this has been recorded at ninety-five decibels, about the same as a pneumatic drill, and close to the human pain threshold.

Recent research has solved the riddle of how frogs avoid bursting their own eardrums: They use their lungs to hear. By absorbing the vibrations of their own calls, the lungs equalize the internal and external pressure on the surface of the eardrums, protecting the delicate inner ear.

Frog calls operate rather like radio stations: each species selects its own frequency. So what we hear—a forest or pond full of competing froggy racket—is much less distracting to the lady frogs, who only tune in to the calls of their own species.

Internationally, frogs are generally regarded as making a similar sound to ducks. But not everywhere. In Thailand, for example they go "ob ob," in Poland "kum kum," in Argentina, "berp;" Algerian frogs make a "gar gar" noise, similar to the Chinese "guo guo"; Bengali frogs go "gangor-gangor"; in Hindi frogs go "me:ko:me:k me:ko:me:k" (the colon indicates that the preceding vowel is long and nasalized); Japanese frogs produce a "kerokero" sound; and Korean frogs go "gae-gool-gae-gool."

Which owl says "Tu-whit, tu-who"?

William Shakespeare first used the phrase "tu-whit, tu-who" in his song "Winter" from *Love's Labour's Lost:*

> Then nightly sings the staring owl,
> Tu-who;
> Tu-whit, tu-who: a merry note.
> While greasy Joan doth keel the pot.

No single owl has ever gone "tu-whit, tu-who."

Barn owls screech. Short-eared owls are largely silent. A long-eared owl makes an extended low pitched "oo-oo-oo" noise.

The owl noise that most resembles "tu-whit, tu-who" is made by tawny owls. Two of them.

The male tawny—also known as a brown owl—calls with a hooting "hooo-hoo-hooo," and the female replies with a hoarser "kew-wick."

What did Darwin do to dead owls?

He ate them, although only once.

Charles Darwin was driven by gastronomic, as well as scientific, curiosity. While halfheartedly reading divinity at Cambridge University, he became a member of the "Glutton" or "Gourmet Club," which met once a week and actively sought to eat animals not normally found on menus.

Darwin's son, Francis, commenting on his father's letters, noted that the Gourmet Club enjoyed, among other things, hawk and bittern, but that "their zeal broke down over an old brown owl," which they found "indescribable."

Over the years, Darwin sharpened up considerably in the academic arena and lost his faith in God, but he never lost his taste for the allure of an interesting menu.

During the voyage of the *Beagle*, he ate armadillos, which, he said, "taste & look like duck," and a chocolate-colored rodent that was "the best meat I ever tasted"—probably an agouti, whose family name is *Dasyproctidae*, Greek for "hairy butt." In Patagonia, he tucked into a plate of puma (the mountain lion *Felis concolor*) and thought it tasted rather like veal. In fact, he originally thought it *was* veal.

Later, after exhaustively searching Patagonia for the lesser rhea, Darwin realized he had already eaten one for his Christmas dinner, while moored off Port Desire in 1833. The bird had been shot by Conrad Martens, the ship's artist.

Darwin assumed it was one of the common greater rheas, or "ostriches," as he called them, and only realized his mistake when the plates were being cleared: "It was cooked and eaten before my memory returned. Fortunately the head, neck, legs, wings, many of the larger feathers, and a large part of the skin, had been preserved." He sent the bits back to the Zoological Society in London and the *Rhea darwinii* was named after him.

In the Galápagos, Darwin lived on iguana (*Conolophus subcristatus*) and, on James Island, wolfed down a few helpings of giant tortoise. Not realizing the importance of giant tortoises to his later evolutionary theory, forty-eight specimens were loaded aboard the *Beagle*. Darwin and his shipmates proceeded to eat them, throwing the shells overboard as they finished.

A Phylum Feast is a shared meal using as many different species as possible, eaten by biologists on February 12 to celebrate Darwin's birthday.

Can barnacles fly?

No, although this is a relatively recent insight.

For hundreds of years people thought the feathery-legged shellfish were the embryos of geese. Because geese breed in the Arctic Circle, no one had seen them mate or lay eggs. When they flew south in the autumn, by complete coincidence, barnacle-laden driftwood also blew ashore. Some bright fellow spotted this and made the connection.

The Latin for Irish goose is *Anser hiberniculae*, *Hibernia* being Latin for Ireland. This was shortened to *bernacae* and by 1581, "barnacle" was used for both the geese and the shellfish. The confusion was widespread and persistent.

This caused problems for the Irish Church. Some dioceses allowed the eating of geese on fast days because they were a kind of fish, others because they came from a bird-bearing tree, and were "not born of the flesh," and therefore a kind of vegetable or nut. Others didn't, so papal intervention was required. Pope Innocent III finally banned goose eating on fast days in 1215.

Four hundred years later, the Royal Society still carried accounts of wood laden with "shells carrying the embryos of geese" and even Linnaeus gave some credence to the legend by naming two species of barnacle *Lepas anatifera* (duck-bearing shellfish) and *Lepas anserifera* (goose-bearing shellfish).

Abiogenesis, the idea that living creatures arise from nonliving matter, was one of the less useful legacies of Aristotle. Despite the work of seventeenth-century scientists like van Leeuwenhoek and Francesco Redi in showing that all living creatures, however small, reproduce, the theory persisted well into the nineteenth century. It wasn't until Pasteur showed that even bacteria reproduce that the idea of spontaneous generation could finally be thrown out.

How many senses does a human being have?

At least nine.

The five senses we all know about—sight, hearing, taste, smell, and touch—were first listed by Aristotle, who, while brilliant, often got things wrong. (For example, he taught that we thought with our hearts, that bees were created by the rotting carcasses of bulls, and that flies had only four legs.)

There are four more commonly agreed senses:

1. Thermoception, the sense of heat (or its absence) on our skin.
2. Equilibrioception—our sense of balance—which is determined by the fluid-containing cavities in the inner ear.
3. Nociception, the perception of pain from the skin, joints, and body organs. Oddly, this does not include the brain, which has no pain receptors at all. Headaches, regardless of the way it seems, don't come from inside the brain.
4. Proprioception, or "body awareness." This is the unconscious knowledge of where our body parts are

without being able to see or feel them. For example, close your eyes and waggle your foot in the air. You still know where it is in relation to the rest of you.

Every self-respecting neurologist has their own opinion about whether there are more than these nine. Some argue that there are up to twenty-one. What about hunger? Or thirst? The sense of depth, or the sense of meaning, or language? Or the endlessly intriguing subject of synaesthesia, where senses collide and combine so that music can be perceived in color?

And what about the sense of electricity, or even impending danger, when your hair stands on end?

There are also senses which some animals have but we don't. Sharks have keen electroception, which allows them to sense electric fields; magnetoception detects magnetic fields and is used in the navigation systems of birds and insects; echolocation and the lateral line are used by fish to sense pressure; and infrared vision is used by owls and deer to hunt or feed at night.

How many states of matter are there?

Three, that's easy. Solid, liquid, gas.

Actually, it's more like fifteen, although the list grows almost daily.

Here's our latest best effort: solid, amorphous solid, liquid, gas, plasma, superfluid, supersolid, degenerate matter, neutronium, strongly symmetric matter, weakly symmetric matter, quark-gluon plasma, fermionic condensate, Bose-Einstein condensate, and strange matter.

Without going into impenetrable (and, for most purposes, needless) detail, one of the most curious is Bose-Einstein condensate.

A Bose-Einstein condensate, or bec, occurs when you cool an

element down to a very low temperature (generally a tiny fraction of a degree above absolute zero, –273°C, the theoretical temperature at which everything stops moving).

When this happens, seriously peculiar things begin to happen. Behavior normally only seen at an atomic level occurs at scales large enough to observe. For example, if you put a bec in a beaker, making sure to keep it cold enough, it will actually climb the sides and de-beaker itself.

This, apparently, is a futile attempt to reduce its own energy (which is already at its lowest possible level).

Bose-Einstein condensate was predicted to exist by Einstein in 1925 after studying the work of Satyendra Nath Bose, but wasn't actually manufactured until 1995 in America—work that earned its creators the 2001 Nobel Prize in Physics. Einstein's manuscript itself was only rediscovered in 2005.

What is the normal state of glass?

It's a solid.

You may have heard it said that glass is a liquid which has cooled but not crystallized, and which just flows fantastically slowly. This is untrue—glass is a bona fide solid.

In support of the assertion that glass is a liquid, people often point to old church windows, where the glass is thicker at the bottom of the pane.

The reason for this is not that the glass has flowed over time, but that medieval glaziers sometimes couldn't cast perfectly uniform sheets of glass. When that happened, they preferred to stand the glass into the window with the thick edge at the bottom, for obvious reasons.

The confusion about whether glass is a liquid or solid stems from a misreading of the work of German physicist Gustav Tammann (1861–1938), who studied glass and described its behavior as it solidifies.

He observed that the molecular structure of glass is irregular and disordered, unlike the neat arrangement of molecules in, say, metals.

Reaching for an analogy, he compared it to "a frozen super-cooled liquid." But saying glass is like a liquid doesn't mean it *is* a liquid.

These days, solids are categorized as either crystalline or amorphous. Glass is an amorphous solid.

Which metal is liquid at room temperature?

In addition to mercury, gallium, caesium, and francium can all be liquids at room temperature. As these liquids are very dense (being metals), bricks, horseshoes, and cannon balls theoretically float in them.

Gallium (Ga) was discovered by French chemist Lecoq de Boisbaudran in 1875. Everyone assumed it was a patriotic name but *gallus* is Latin for "a Gaul" *and* "rooster"—as in Lecoq. It was the first new element to confirm Dmitri Medeleeyev's prediction of the periodic table. Gallium is used chiefly in microchips because of its strange electronic properties. Compact disc players also make use of it because when mixed with arsenic it transforms an electric current directly into laser light, which is used to read the data from the discs.

Caesium (Cs) is most notably used in atomic clocks—it is used to define the atomic second (see page 198). It also explodes extremely violently when it comes into contact with water. Caesium's name means "sky blue" because of the bright blue lines it produces as part of its spectrum. It was discovered in 1860 by Robert Bunsen using the spectroscope he had invented with Gustav Kirchoff, the man who had earlier discovered that signals travel down telegraph wires at the speed of light.

Francium (Fr) is one of the rarest elements: it has been calculated there are only ever thirty grams of it present on earth. This is because it is so radioactive it quickly decays into other, more stable elements. So it is a liquid metal, but not for very long—a few seconds at most. It was isolated in 1939 by Marguerite Perey at the Curie Institute in Paris. It was the last element to be found in nature.

These elements are liquid at unusually low temperatures for metals because the arrangement of electrons in their atoms makes it hard for them to get close enough to each other to form a crystalline lattice.

Each atom floats around freely, without being attracted to its neighbors, which is exactly what happens in other liquids.

Which metal is the best conductor?

Silver.

The best conductor of both heat and electricity is also the most reflective of all the elements. Its drawback is that it is expensive. The reason we use copper wire in our electrical equipment is because copper—the second most conductive element—is much cheaper.

As well as its decorative uses, silver is now mostly used in the photographic industry, for long-life batteries, and for solar panels.

Silver has the curious property of sterilizing water. Only tiny amounts are needed—just ten parts per billion. This remarkable fact has been known since the fifth century B.C., when Herodotus reported that the Persian king Cyrus the Great traveled with his own personal water supply taken from a special stream, boiled, and sealed in silver vessels.

Both the Romans and Greeks noticed that food and drink put in silver containers did not spoil as quickly. Silver's strong antibacterial qualities were made use of for many centuries before bacteria were discovered. This may also explain why silver coins are often found at the bottom of ancient wells.

A word of caution before you start filling your silver tankard.

First, while silver will certainly kill bacteria in the lab, whether or not it will do so in the body is controversial. Many of the supposed advantages are unproven: the U.S. Food and Drug Administration has forbidden companies from advertising its health benefits.

Second, there is a disease called argyria, which is linked to the intake of silver particles diluted in water, the most obvious symptom of which is a conspicuously blue skin.

On the other hand, silver salts in swimming pools are a safe substitute for chlorine and, in the United States, athletes' socks are impregnated with silver to stop their feet from smelling.

Water is an exceptionally poor conductor of electricity, especially pure water, which is actually used as an insulator. What conducts the electricity is not the H_2O molecules but the chemicals dissolved in it—salt, for example.

Seawater is a hundred times better at conducting electricity than fresh water, but it's a *million* times worse at conducting electricity than silver.

What's the densest element?

It's either osmium or iridium, depending on how you measure it.

The two metals are extremely close in density and have changed places several times over the years. The third-densest element is platinum, followed by rhenium, neptunium, plutonium, and gold. Lead is way, way down the list—it's only half as dense as either osmium or iridium.

Osmium (Os) is a very rare, very hard, silvery blue metal discovered (along with iridium) in 1803 by the English chemist Smithson Tennant (1761–1815).

Tennant was a vicar's son from Richmond who was also the first man to show that diamond is a form of pure carbon.

He named osmium from *osme*, Greek for "smell." It gives off highly toxic osmium tetroxide, which has a pungent, irritating odor and can damage the lungs, skin, and eyes and cause intense headaches. Osmium tetroxide has been used in fingerprinting because its vapor reacts with minute traces of oil left by the fingers to form black deposits.

Its extreme hardness and resistance to corrosion made osmium useful in the manufacture of long-life gramophone styluses, compass needles, and the nibs of quality fountain pens—hence the trade name Osmiroid.

Osmium also has an unusually high melting point of 3,054°C. In 1897 this inspired Karl Auer to create an osmium electric lightbulb filament to improve on the bamboo one used by Edison. Osmium was eventually replaced by tungsten, which melts at 3,407°C. The name Osram was registered by Auer in 1906. It derives from OSmium and WolfRAM, the German for "tungsten."

Less than 220 pounds of osmium are produced worldwide every year.

Iridium (Ir) is a yellowish white metal which, like osmium, is closely related to platinum. The name comes from *iris*, Greek for "rainbow," because of the many beautiful colors its compounds produce.

Iridium also has an extremely high melting point (2,446°C) and is mainly used to make crucibles for metal foundries and to harden platinum.

Iridium is one of the rarest elements on earth (eighty-fourth out of ninety-two) but improbably large amounts of it are found in the thin geological layer known as the KT boundary laid down about 65 million years ago.

Geologists have confirmed that this can only have come from space, and it adds support to the theory that an asteroid impact caused the extinction of the dinosaurs.

Where do diamonds come from?

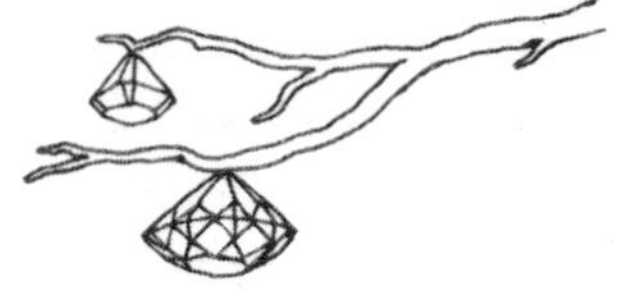

Volcanoes. All diamonds are formed under immense heat and pressure beneath the earth and are brought to the surface in volcanic eruptions.

They are formed 100 to 300 miles underground. Most are found inside a volcanic rock called kimberlite and mined in areas where volcanic activity is still common. Any other diamonds are found loose, having been washed out of their original kimberlite.

Twenty countries in the world produce diamonds. South Africa is now the fifth largest after Australia, the Democratic Republic of the Congo, Botswana, and Russia.

Diamonds are made of pure carbon. So is graphite, the stuff that the lead in pencils is made from, but with the carbon atoms arranged differently. A diamond is one of the hardest naturally occurring substances on earth with a score of ten on the Mohs Hardness scale, but graphite is one of the softest, with a score of one and a half, only just harder than talcum powder.

> THERE ARE THREE THINGS THAT ARE EXTREMELY HARD: STEEL, A DIAMOND, AND TO KNOW ONE'S SELF.
>
> BENJAMIN FRANKLIN

The largest known diamond is 2,500 miles across and measures ten billion trillion trillion carats. Found directly above Australia (eight light-years away) the diamond sits inside the star Lucy in the constellation Centaurus.

Lucy got its nickname from the Beatles' classic "Lucy in the Sky with Diamonds," but its technical name is white dwarf BPM 37093. The Beatles' song was named after a picture drawn by John Lennon's son Julian of his four-year-old friend Lucy Richardson.

Diamonds were once the world's hardest known material. However, in August 2005 scientists in Germany managed to create a harder one in a laboratory. Called aggregated carbon nanorods (ACNR), it was made by compressing and heating super-strong carbon molecules to 2,226°C.

Each of these molecules comprises sixty atoms that interweave in pentagonal or hexagonal shapes; they're said to resemble tiny footballs. ACNR is so tough it scratches diamonds effortlessly.

How do we measure earthquakes?

The MMS Scale.

In the last decade, the Richter scale has been superseded in seismological circles by the Moment Magnitude Scale, or MMS.

The MMS was devised in 1979 by seismologists Hiroo Kanamori and Tom Hanks (no relation) of the California Institute of Technology, who found the Richter scale unsatisfactory because it only measures the strength of the shock waves, which do not fully describe an earthquake's impact. On the Richter scale, large earthquakes may have the same score but cause wildly different degrees of devastation.

The Richter scale measures the seismic waves or vibration as experienced 373 miles away. It was devised in 1935 by Charles Richter, who was also, like Kanamori and Hanks, a Caltech seismologist. He developed it with Beno Gutenberg, the first man to measure accurately the radius of the earth's core. Gutenberg died of flu in 1960 without living to measure the Great Chilean Earthquake (the largest ever recorded, which took place four months later).

The MMS, by contrast, is an expression of the energy released by an earthquake. It multiplies the distance of the slip between the two parts of the fault by the total area affected. It was designed to give values that make sense when compared to their Richter equivalent.

Both scales are logarithmic: a two-point increase means 100 times more power. A hand grenade scores 0.5 on the Richter scale, the Nagasaki atom bomb 5.0. The MMS is only used for large earthquakes, above 3.5 on the Richter scale.

According to the U.S. Geological Survey, on the basis of the area of damage (231,660 square miles) and the area it was felt in (1,930,502 square miles), the largest known earthquakes in North America were the little-known Mississippi River valley earthquakes of 1811–12. They created new lakes and changed the whole course of the Mississippi. The area of strong shaking was ten times larger than that in San Francisco in 1906. Church bells rang spontaneously as far away as Massachusetts.

It is impossible to predict when an earthquake will happen. One expert claims that the best way is to count the number of missing cats and dogs in the local newspaper.

Britain has up to three hundred earthquakes a year but they are so small that the public notices only about 10 percent of them.

What's the most common material in the world?

a. Oxygen
b. Carbon
c. Nitrogen
d. Water

None of the above. The answer is perovskite, a mineral compound of magnesium, silicon, and oxygen.

Perovskite accounts for about half the total mass of the planet. It's what the earth's mantle is mostly made from. Or so scientists suppose: nobody has yet taken a sample to prove it.

Perovskites are a family of minerals named after the Russian mineralogist Count Lev Perovski in 1839. They may prove to be the Holy Grail of superconductor research—a material that can conduct electricity without resistance at normal temperatures.

This would make a world of "floating" trains and unimaginably fast computers a reality. At present, superconductors only function at unhelpfully low temperatures (the best so far recorded is –135°C).

Apart from perovskite, it is thought that the mantle is made from magnesio-wusstite (a form of magnesium oxide also found in meteorites), and a small amount of shistovite (named after Lev Shistov, a graduate student at Moscow University who synthesized a new high-pressure form of silicon oxide in his lab in 1959).

The earth's mantle sits between the crust and the core. It is generally assumed to be solid, but some scientists believe that it is actually a very slow-moving liquid.

How do we know any of this? Even the rocks spewed out of volcanoes have only come from the first 125 miles below the surface and it's more than 400 miles before the lower mantle starts.

By sending pulses of seismic waves downward and recording the resistance they encounter, both the density and the temperature of the earth's interior can be estimated.

This can then be matched to what we already know about the structure of minerals we do have samples of—from the crust and in meteorites—and what happens to these minerals under intense heat and high pressure.

But like much else in science, it's really only a highly educated guess.

What does the moon smell like?

Like gunpowder, apparently.

Only twelve people have walked on the moon, all of them American. Obviously, in their airtight space suits the astronauts could not actually smell the moon, but moondust is clingy stuff, and plenty of it was traipsed back into the cabin when they returned from the moon's surface.

They reported that moondust feels like snow, smells like gunpowder, and doesn't taste too bad. The dust is actually mostly made of silicon dioxide glass created by meteors slamming into the moon's surface. It also contains minerals like iron, calcium, and magnesium.

NASA employs a small team to sniff every single piece of equipment that goes onto its space flights. This is to ensure that no items that could change the delicate balance of the climate of the International Space Station make it onto shuttles.

The idea that the moon was made of cheese seems to date from the sixteenth century. The first citation, from John Heywood's *Proverbs* (1564), says "the moon is made of greene chees." It is thought that in this context, the word "greene" means "new," rather than having a green color, as young cheeses would often have a more mottled appearance; much like the cratered moon.

Does the earth go around the moon or the moon around the earth?

Both. They go around each other.

The two bodies orbit a common center of gravity located about 1,000 miles below the surface of the earth, so the earth makes three different rotations: around its own axis, around the sun, and around this point.

Confused? Even Newton claimed that thinking about the motion of the moon gave him a headache.

How many moons does the earth have?

At least seven.

Certainly *the* moon (or Luna, as astronomers call it) is the only celestial body to observe a strict orbit of the earth. But there are now six other "Near-Earth" Asteroids (NEAs) that do follow the earth around the sun, despite being invisible to the naked eye.

The first of these co-orbitals to be identified was Cruithne (pronounced *Cru-een-ya*, and named after Britain's earliest recorded Celtic tribe), a three-mile-wide satellite, discovered in 1997. It has an odd, horseshoe-shaped orbit.

Since then, six more have been identified: the snappily named 2000 PH_5, 2000 WN_{10}, 2002 AA_{29}, 2003 YN_{107}, and 2004 GU_9.

Are they really moons? Many astronomers would say no, but they are certainly more than just run-of-the-mill asteroids. Like earth they take roughly a year to orbit the sun (think of two cars going round a race track at the same speed but in different lanes) and do occasionally come close enough to exert a very slight gravitational influence.

So whether you call them pseudo-moons, quasi-satellites, or companion asteroids, they are worth watching, not least because some or all of them may one day settle down into a more regular orbital pattern.

How many planets are there in the solar system?

Eight. If you still think there are nine, you've obviously been living in a parallel solar system.

On August 24, 2006, the general assembly of the International Astronomers Union finally agreed its long overdue definition of a "planet." Planets must fulfill three criteria: they have to orbit the sun, have enough mass to be spherical, and to have "cleared the neighborhood" around their orbit. Pluto only managed the first two, so was demoted to the status of "dwarf planet."

It's not perfect—some astronomers argue that neither Earth, Jupiter, nor Neptune have cleared their orbits either—but it does resolve the anomalous position of Pluto.

Even the planet's discoverers in 1930 weren't fully convinced of its status, referring to it as a trans-Neptunian object, or TNO—something on the edge of the solar system, beyond Neptune.

Pluto is much smaller than all the other planets, a fifth the mass of the Moon and smaller than seven of the moons of other planets. It isn't much larger than its own main moon, Charon (two other, smaller Plutonian moons, Nix and Hydra, were discovered in 2005). Its orbit is eccentric and on a different plane to the other planets, and its composition is completely different.

The four innermost planets are medium-size and rocky; the next four are gas giants. Pluto is a tiny ball of ice—one of at least sixty thousand small, cometlike objects forming the Kuiper belt right on the edge of the solar system.

All these planetoid objects (including asteroids, TNOs, and a host of other subclassifications) are known collectively as minor planets. There are 371,670 of them already registered; 5,000 new ones are discovered each month and it is estimated that there may be almost two million such bodies with diameters greater than a kilometer. Most are much too small to be considered planets but twelve of them give Pluto a run for its money.

One of them, discovered in 2005 as 2003 UB_{313} and now named Eris, is actually larger than Pluto. Others such as Sedna, Orcus, and Quaoar aren't far off.

Now Pluto, Eris, and Ceres—the largest body in the asteroid belt between Mars and Jupiter—have been officially adopted as the first three dwarf planets.

This change isn't unprecedented. Ceres, like Pluto, was considered a planet from its discovery in 1801 until the 1850s when it was downgraded to an asteroid.

The American Dialect Society voted "pluto," meaning "to demote or devalue someone or something" their Word of the Year for 2006.

How would you fly through an asteroid belt?

Keep an eye open, but it's really unlikely you'll collide with anything.

Despite what you may have seen in sci-fi films, asteroid belts are typically quite desolate places. Busy when compared with the rest of space, but desolate nonetheless.

Generally, the gap between large asteroids (ones which could do significant damage to a spaceship) is nearly 1.25 million miles.

Although there are some clusters called "families," which have been recently formed from a larger body, it would not be too difficult to maneuver around an asteroid belt. In fact, if you picked a random course, you'd be lucky to see a single asteroid.

If you did, you might like to give it a name.

These days the International Astronomical Union has a fifteen-person Committee for Small-Body Nomenclature to control the naming of the ever-expanding roll call of minor planets. It's not an entirely serious business, as these recent examples show:

> (15887) Daveclark, (14965) Bonk, (18932) Robinhood, (69961) Millosevich, (2829) Bobhope, (7328) Seanconnery, (5762) Wanke, (453) Tea, (3904) Honda, (17627) Humpty-dumpty, (9941) Iguanodon, (9949) Brontosaurus, (9778) Isabelallende, (4479) Charlieparker, (9007) James Bond, (39415) Janeausten, (11548) Jerrylewis, (19367) Pink Floyd, (5878) Charlene, (6042) Cheshirecat, (4735) Gary, (3742) Sunshine, (17458) Dick, (1629) Pecker, and (821) Fanny.

Smith, Jones, Brown, and Robinson are all official names of asteroids; so are Bikki, Bus, Bok, Lick, Kwee, Hippo, MrSpock, Roddenberry, and Swissair.

Eccentricity in planet-naming isn't new. Pluto was named in 1930 by an eleven-year-old Oxford schoolgirl called Venetia

Burney, whose grandfather passed on her breakfast-time suggestion to his good friend Herbert Hall Turner, the Oxford professor of astronomy.

Perhaps 2003 UB_{313} will after all be named Rupert, Douglas Adams's name for the tenth planet in *The Hitchhiker's Guide to the Galaxy*. Stranger things have happened. The day before Adams suddenly died in 2001, the asteroid (18610) Arthurdent was first named. And now he has one of his very own: (25924) Douglasadams.

What's in an atom?

Mostly nothing. The vast majority of an atom is empty space.

To get it into perspective, imagine an atom the size of an international sports stadium. The electrons are right up at the top of the stands, each smaller than a pinhead. The nucleus of the atom is on the center spot of the field, and is about the size of a pea.

For many centuries, atoms, which were entirely theoretical, were thought to be the smallest possible units of matter, hence the word, which means "not cut" in Greek.

Then, in 1897, the electron was discovered, followed in 1911 by the nucleus. Then the atom was split, and the neutron was discovered in 1932.

NOTHING EXISTS EXCEPT ATOMS AND EMPTY SPACE; EVERYTHING ELSE IS OPINION.

DEMOCRITOS OF ABDERA

This was by no means the end of the matter. The positively charged protons and uncharged neutrons in the nucleus are made of still smaller elements.

These even tinier units, called quarks, are given names like "strangeness" and "charm" and come not in different shapes and sizes but "flavors."

The distant satellites of the nucleus, the negatively charged electrons, are so odd they are no longer even called that but "Probability Density Charges."

By the 1950s, so many new subatomic particles (more than 100) had been found that it was becoming an embarrassment. Whatever matter might be, no one seemed able to get to the bottom of it.

Enrico Fermi, the Italian-born physicist who won the Nobel Prize in Physics in 1938 for his work on atomic reactors, was quoted as saying: "If I could remember the names of all these particles, I'd be a botanist."

Since Fermi's time, scientists have settled on the number of subatomic particles inside an atom at twenty-four. This best guess is known as the Standard Model, giving the impression that we have a pretty good idea what's what.

The universe in general, as far as we can tell, is as underpopulated as the atom itself. Space, on average, contains just a couple of atoms per cubic meter.

Occasionally, gravity pulls them together into stars, planets, and giraffes, which seems equally extraordinary.

What's the main ingredient of air?

a. Oxygen
b. Carbon dioxide
c. Hydrogen
d. Nitrogen

Nitrogen. As every twelve-year-old knows, it accounts for 78 percent of the air.

Less than 21 percent of air is oxygen. Only three-hundredths of 1 percent of the air is carbon dioxide.

The high percentage of nitrogen in the air is a result of volcanic eruptions during the formation of the earth. Vast amounts of it were released into the atmosphere. Being heavier than hydrogen or helium, it has stayed closer to the surface of the planet.

A person weighing 168 pounds contains almost 2.25 pounds of nitrogen.

Niter is the old name for saltpeter, or potassium nitrate. A key ingredient in gunpowder, it is also used to cure meat, as a preservative in ice cream, and the anaesthetic in toothpaste for sensitive teeth.

For several hundred years, the richest source of saltpeter was the organic mulch that had seeped into the earth floor of human houses. In 1601, the unscrupulous activities of "Saltpeetermen" were raised in Parliament. They would break into houses and even churches, dig up the floors, and sell the earth for gunpowder.

The word *nitrogen* means "soda-forming" in Greek.

Beer cans with pressure-sensitive widgets contain nitrogen, not carbon dioxide. The smaller nitrogen bubbles make a smoother, creamier head.

The only other significant gas in air is argon (1 percent).

It was discovered by William John Strutt, Lord Rayleigh, who was also the first man to work out why the sky is blue.

Where would you go for a lungful of ozone?

Don't bother going to the seaside.

The nineteenth-century cult of healthy sea air was based on a fundamental misunderstanding. The bracing, salty tang has nothing to do with ozone, an unstable and dangerous gas.

Ozone was discovered in 1840 by the German chemist Christian Schönbein. Investigating the peculiar odor that lingers around electrical equipment, he traced it to a gas, O_3, which he named after the Greek for "to smell" (*ozein*).

Ozone, or "heavy air," found favor with medical scientists still in the grip of the miasma theory of disease, where ill health was thought to spring from bad smells. Ozone, they thought, was just the thing to clear the lungs of harmful effluvia, and the seaside was just the place to get it.

A whole industry grew up around ozone cures and ozone hotels (there are still some carrying the name in Australasia). As late as 1939, Blackpool was still boasting "the healthiest ozone in Britain."

Nowadays, we know that the seaside doesn't smell of ozone—it smells of rotting seaweed. There's no evidence this smell does you good or harm (it's mostly compounds of sulfur). It may simply trigger positive associations in your brain, linking back to happy childhood holidays.

As for ozone, the fumes from your car's exhaust (when combined with sunlight) create far more ozone than anything on the beach. If you really want a lungful, the best thing would be to clamp your mouth round an exhaust pipe. This is emphatically not recommended. Apart from doing irreparable damage to your lungs, you could burn your lips.

Ozone is used to make bleach and to kill bacteria in drinking water as a less noxious alternative to chlorine. It is also generated by high-voltage electrical equipment such as televisions and photocopiers.

Some trees, such as oaks and willows, release ozone, which can poison nearby vegetation.

The shrinking ozone layer, which protects the planet from dangerous ultraviolet radiation, would be fatal if inhaled. It is 15 miles above the earth's surface and smells faintly of geraniums.

What speed does light travel at?

That depends.

It's often said that the speed of light is constant, but it isn't. Only in a vacuum does light reach its maximum speed of nearly 186,282 miles per second.

In any other medium, the speed of light varies considerably, always being slower than the figure everyone knows. Through diamonds, for example, it goes less than half as fast: about 80,000 miles per second.

Until recently, the slowest recorded speed of light (through sodium at –272°C) was just over 38 mph: slower than a bicycle.

In 2000 the same team (at Harvard University) managed to bring light to a complete standstill by shining it into a bec (Bose-Einstein condensate) of the element rubidium.

Rubidium was discovered by Robert Bunsen (1811–99), who didn't invent the Bunsen burner—it's named after him.

Astoundingly, light is invisible.

You can't see the light itself, you can only see what it bumps into. A beam of light in a vacuum, shining at right angles to the observer, cannot be seen.

Although this is very odd, it's quite logical. If light itself was visible, it would form a kind of fog between your eyes and everything in front of you.

Darkness is equally strange. It's not there but you can't see through it.

Where is the highest mountain?

It's on Mars.

The giant volcano Mount Olympus—or Olympus Mons in Latin—is the highest mountain in the solar system and in the known universe.

At 14 miles high and 388 miles across, it is almost three times the height of Mount Everest and so wide that its base would cover Arizona, or the whole of the area of the British Isles. The crater on the top is around 45 miles wide and nearly 2 miles deep, easily big enough to swallow London.

Olympus Mons doesn't conform to most people's idea of a mountain. It is flat-topped, like a vast plateau in a sea drained of water, and its sides aren't even steep. Their slight incline of between one and three degrees means you wouldn't even break a sweat if you climbed it.

We traditionally measure mountains by their height. If we measured them by their size, it would be meaningless to isolate one mountain in a range from the rest. That being so, Mount Everest would dwarf Olympus Mons. It is part of the gigantic Himalaya–Karakoram–Hindu-Kush–Pamir range, which is nearly 1,500 miles long.

How many legs does a centipede have?

Not a hundred.

The word *centipede* is from the Latin for "a hundred feet," and though centipedes have been extensively studied for more than a hundred years, not one has ever been found that has exactly a hundred legs.

Some have more, some less. The one with the number of legs closest to one hundred was discovered in 1999. It has 96 legs, and is unique among centipedes in that it is the only known species with an even number of pairs of legs: 48.

All other centipedes have an odd number of pairs of legs ranging from 15 to 191 pairs.

How many toes has a two-toed sloth?

It's either six or eight.

For reasons known only to taxonomists, the sloths in question are called "two-toed" rather than "two-fingered." Both two-toed and three-toed sloths have three "toes" on each foot. Two-toed sloths are distinguished from three-toed sloths by the fact that they have two fingers on each hand, whereas three-toed sloths have three.

Despite their obvious similarities, three-toed sloths and two-toed sloths are not related to one another. Two-toed sloths are slightly faster. Three-toed sloths have nine bones in their necks; two-toed have six.

Three-toed sloths make good pets, but two-toed sloths are vicious. Three-toed sloths produce shrill whistles through their nostrils. Two-toed sloths will hiss if disturbed.

Sloths generally are the world's slowest mammals. Their top speed is slightly over a mile an hour, but they mostly inch along at less than six feet a minute.

They sleep for fourteen to nineteen hours a day and spend their entire lives hanging upside down in trees. They eat, sleep, mate, give birth, and die upside down. Some move so little that two species of algae take root on them, giving them a greenish tinge, which also acts as useful camouflage. Several species of moth and beetle also make their home in sloth fur.

> THE SPANISH FOR SLOTH IS *PEREZOSO*, "THE SLOTHFUL ONE," NOT TO BE CONFUSED WITH *PEREZOSA* WHICH MEANS "DECKCHAIR."

Their metabolism is slow, too. It takes then more than a month to digest their food, and they pass urine and feces only once a week. They do this at the base of the trees they live in, these unsavory piles being romantically known as "trysting places."

Like reptiles, they practice thermoregulation—basking in the sun to warm up, creeping into the shade to cool down.

This slows down their complex and lethargic digestive rate. During the rainy season, when they stay put under leaves to stay dry, some sloths perform the astonishing feat of starving to death on a full stomach.

How many eyes does a no-eyed, big-eyed wolf spider have?

a. No eyes
b. No eyes, but big ones
c. One big eye that doesn't work
d. 144 eyelike warts

It has no eyes.

The blind arachnid was first discovered in 1973 and the entire population lives in three pitch black caves on the volcanic island of Kauai, in Hawaii.

Like other cave-dwelling beasts, it evolved without needing to see but, as it's a member of the big-eyed wolf spider family, it gets to call itself big-eyed (i.e., if it did have any eyes left, they'd be big ones).

It's about the size of a quarter when fully grown. Its rooming buddy and main source of nourishment is the Kauai cave amphipod, a small crustacean that resembles a blind, semitransparent shrimp.

How many penises does a European earwig have?

a. Fourteen
b. None at all
c. Two (one for special occasions)
d. Mind your own business

The answer is *c.* The European or black earwig carries a spare one in case the first one snaps off, which happens quite frequently.

Both penises are very brittle and relatively long; at just under a half inch in length, they are often longer than the earwig itself. Two gentlemen at Tokyo Metropolitan University discovered this when one of them playfully pinched a male earwig's rear end during the act of sexual intercourse. Its penis snapped off inside the female, but miraculously it produced a backup.

Earwigs are named for the almost universal belief that they crawl into people's ears and burrow into their brain. The word *earwig* is Anglo-Saxon for "ear-creature." Their French name is *perce-oreille* (ear-piercer); in German it's *Ohrwurm* (ear-worm); in Turkish *kulagakacan* (ear-fugitive).

Earwigs don't crawl into ears any more than any other insect, but Pliny the Elder recommended that if one does do so, you spit in the person's ear until the earwig comes out again. They definitely do not burrow into brains.

An alternative suggestion for the name is that the pincers on the rear of an earwig resemble the tool once used for ear piercing.

This idea seems to have more appeal to Latins. The Spanish have two words for earwig: *contraplumas* (which also means "penknife"), and *tijereta* (which also means "scissor-kick"). In Italian, an earwig is *forbicina* (little scissors).

A giant species of earwig (3.3 inches long) lived on St. Helena, the South Atlantic island where Napoleon Bonaparte spent his final years in exile. They may still be living there, but the last one was sighted in 1967.

Nicknamed the "Dodo of the Dermaptera" (the order to which they belong, meaning "skin wing"), the slim hope that they may still exist was enough for environmentalists to prevent a new airport being built on the island in 2005.

Two species of Malayan earwig feed exclusively on the body oozings and dead skin of naked bats.

Which animals are the best-endowed of all?

Barnacles. These unassumingly modest beasts have the longest penis relative to their size of any creature. It can be seven times longer than their body.

Most of the 1,220 species of barnacles are hermaphrodites. When one barnacle decides to be "mother" it lays eggs inside its own shell and at the same time releases some alluring pheromones. A nearby barnacle will respond by playing "male" and fertilize the eggs by extending its massive penis, releasing sperm into the cavity of the "female."

Barnacles stand on their heads and eat with their feet. Using a very strong glue, they attach themselves headfirst to a rock or the hull of a ship. The opening we see as the top of the barnacle is actually the bottom; through it their long, feathery legs catch small plants and animals that float past.

Other well-endowed species are the nine-banded armadillo (its penis extends to two-thirds of its body length) and the blue whale, whose penis, despite a relatively modest proportion in comparison to size, is still the biggest physical organ of all, averaging 6 to 10 feet in length and around 18 inches in girth.

A blue whale's ejaculate is estimated to contain about 35 pints based on its testes, which weigh more than 150 pounds each.

Whale's penises were useful. In Herman Melville's *Moby-Dick* (1851), there is an account of how the outer skin can be transformed into a floor-length waterproof apron, ideal for protection when gutting the dead whale.

Like most other mammals, whales have a penis bone, the *baculum* or *os penis*. These, along with the *baculi* of walruses and polar bears, are used by Eskimo peoples as runners for their sleds or as clubs.

Other uses for mammalian *baculi* ("little rod" in Latin) are as tiepins, coffee stirrers, or love tokens. The bones are incredibly diverse in shape—they are probably the most varied of any bone—and are useful in working out the relationships between mammalian species. Humans and spider monkeys are the only primates without them.

Biblical Hebrew does not have a word for penis. This has led two scholars (Gilbert and Zevit in the *American Journal of Medical Genetics* in 2001) to suggest that Eve was made out of Adam's penis bone rather than his rib (Genesis 2:21–23). This would explain why males and females have the same number of ribs but the man has no penis bone.

The biblical account also states that afterward "the Lord God closed up the flesh," the suggestion being that this is the "scar" (known as the *raphe*) that runs down the underside of the penis and scrotum.

What is a rhino's horn made from?

A rhinoceros horn is not, as some people think, made out of hair.

It's made out of tightly packed strands of keratin fibers. Keratin is the protein found in human hair and fingernails as well as animal claws and hooves, birds' feathers, porcupine quills, and the shells of armadillos and tortoises.

Rhinos are the only animal to have a horn that is entirely made from keratin; unlike those of cattle, sheep, antelopes, and giraffes, they don't have any bone core. A dead rhino's skull shows no evidence that it ever had horns; in life they are anchored on a roughened bump on the skin, above the nasal bone.

A rhino's horn sometimes unravels if cut or damaged, but young rhinos can completely regrow them if that happens. No one knows what their function is, though females with their horns removed fail to look after their offspring properly.

Rhinoceroses are endangered animals largely due to the demand for their horns. Africa's rhinoceros horns have long been in demand for both medicines and traditional dagger handles in the Middle East, especially Yemen. Since 1970 nearly 150,000 pounds of rhinoceros horn have been imported into

Yemen. Based upon an average horn weight of 6.6 pounds, this volume represents the horns of 22,350 rhinoceroses.

A persistent misconception is that rhino horn is used as an aphrodisiac. Chinese herbalists say this is untrue; its effect is cooling rather than warming, and it is used in treating high blood pressure and fever.

Rhinoceros comes from the Greek words *rhino* (nose) and *keras* (horn). There are five living species of rhino: black, white, Indian, Javan, and Sumatran. Only sixty Javan rhinos survive, making it the world's fourth most endangered species after the Vancouver Island marmot, the Seychelles sheath-tailed bat, and the South China tiger.

White rhinos aren't white. It's a corruption of the Afrikaans *wyd*, meaning "white." This refers to the animal's mouth, rather than its girth—white rhinos lack the agile lip of the black species, which is used in grazing tree branches.

A rhinoceros has an excellent sense of smell and hearing but its eyesight is terrible. They are generally solitary animals, coming together only to mate.

When surprised, rhinos urinate and defecate prodigiously. To attack, Asian rhinos bite; African rhinos charge. A black rhino, despite its short legs, can reach speeds of about 35 mph.

Which African mammal kills more humans than any other?

The hippopotamus.

Unfortunately hippos like to hang out near slow-moving fresh water bordered by grass—the same habitat favored by humans.

Most accidents occur either because a submerged hippo has been inadvertently whacked on the head with a paddle and decides to overturn the boat or because people are out walking at night, just the time when hippos leave the water to graze. Being trampled by a startled hippo is not a dignified way to die.

Hippopotamuses, once believed to be members of the pig family, but now shown to be most closely related to whales, are divided into two species: common and pygmy. The common hippo is the third-largest land mammal after the African and Asian elephants.

Not many animals are stupid enough to attack a hippo. They are very irritable beasts, especially when they have young. They dispose of lions by plunging them into deep water and drowning them; crocodiles, by biting them in half; and sharks, by dragging them out of the water and trampling them to death. However, they are strict vegetarians, so their aggression is mostly to do with self-defense. Hippos mainly eat grass.

The skin of a hippopotamus weighs a ton. It is 1.5 inches thick—bulletproof as far as most guns are concerned—and accounts for 25 percent of the animal's weight. It exudes an oily red fluid that keeps it from drying out, which used to make people think that hippos sweat blood. Don't be fooled by their bulk. A fully grown hippo can easily outrun a man.

Hippos are the only mammal other than whales and dolphins to mate and give birth underwater. They can close their nostrils, flatten their ears, and stay completely submerged for up to five minutes at a time.

Hippos have appalling breath. When they appear to be yawning, they are in fact blasting everything around them with halitosis as a warning to stay clear. This is good advice: a hippo's tusks are sharp and a snap of the jaws can easily sever a limb.

Hippos have only four teeth, which are made of ivory. Part of George Washington's set of false teeth was made from hippopotamus ivory.

According to the *Oxford Companion to Food*, the best part of a hippopotamus to eat is their breasts, pot roasted with herbs and spices. Failing that, the back muscles, cooked in the same manner, are acceptable.

Where do most tigers live?

The United States.

A century ago, there were about 40,000 tigers in India. Now there are between 3,000 and 4,700. Some scientists estimate that there are only between 5,100 and 7,500 wild tigers left on the planet.

On the other hand, there are thought to be 4,000 tigers living in captivity in Texas alone. The American Zoo and Aquarium Association estimates that up to 12,000 tigers are being kept as private pets in the United States. Mike Tyson personally owns four of them.

Part of the reason for America's enormous tiger population relates to legislation. Only nineteen states have banned private ownership of tigers, fifteen require only a licence, and sixteen states have no regulations at all.

They're not particularly expensive, either. A tiger cub will set you back a mere $1,000 while $3,500 will buy you a pair of Bengal tigers; $15,000 is enough for a fashionable blue-eyed white tiger.

Ironically, it is the success of breeding programs at American zoos and circuses that has driven this. An overabundance of cubs in the 1980s and 1990s brought the prices right down. The Society for the Prevention of Cruelty to Animals estimates that there are now 500 lions, tigers, and other big cats in private ownership just in the Houston area.

Wild tiger populations were crippled during the twentieth century. Tigers were extinct around the Caspian Sea by the 1950s, and the tigers on the islands of Bali and Java disappeared between 1937 and 1972. The South China tiger is nearly extinct in the wild, with only thirty animals remaining.

Despite the efforts of conservationists, all species of tiger are expected to be extinct in the wild by the end of the current century.

A domestic cat is about 1 percent the size of a tiger.

Tigers cannot abide the smell of alcohol. They will savage anyone who has been drinking.

Tigers fade as they get older, and who can blame them.

What would you use to overpower a crocodile?

a. Paper clip
b. Crocodile clip
c. Paper bag
d. Handbag
e. Rubber band

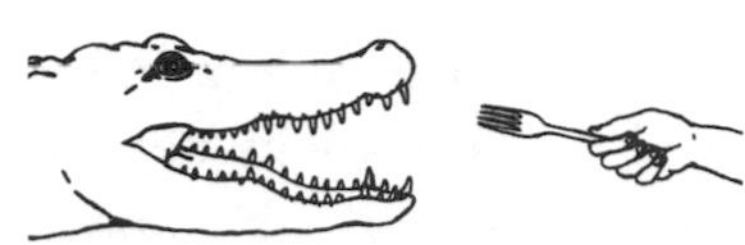

For crocodiles up to 6.5 feet long, an ordinary rubber band should be sufficient for you to make your escape.

The muscles that close the jaws of a crocodile or alligator are so strong that they have the same downward force of a truck falling off a cliff. But the muscles that open their jaws are weak enough for you to hold their mouths shut with one hand.

The technical difference between alligators and crocodiles is that crocs have a longer, narrower snout, eyes further forward, and their fourth tooth sticks out from the lower jaw rather than fitting neatly into the upper jaw. Also, some crocodiles live in salty water; alligators generally live in fresh water.

Crocodile means "lizard," from the Greek *krokodeilos.* This name was first recorded by Herodotus, who remarked on them basking on the pebbly banks of the Nile. *Alligator* is a corruption of the Spanish *el lagarto das Indias*, "the lizard of the Indies."

> NO CALL ALLIGATOR LONG MOUTH TILL YOU CROSS THE RIVER.
>
> JAMAICAN PROVERB

Neither animal cries as it savages you to death. Crocodile tears are a myth from medieval travelers' tales. Sir John Mandeville, writing in 1356, observed,

"In many places of Inde are many cokadrilles—that is, a manner of long serpent. These serpents slay men and eat them weeping."

Crocodiles do have tear ducts, but they discharge straight into the mouth, so no tears are visible externally. The origin of the legend may be in the proximity of the throat to the glands which lubricate the eye. These can cause the eye to water a little from the effort of swallowing something large or reluctant. They can't smile, either: crocodiles and alligators have no lips.

The digestive juices of crocodiles contain enough hydrochloric acid to dissolve iron and steel. On the other hand, there is no need to worry about alligators living in city sewers. They can't survive without the ultraviolet radiation from the sun that enables them to process calcium. This urban legend can be traced back to a *New York Times* article in 1935, which reported that some boys had dragged an alligator out of a sewer in Harlem and beat it to death with shovels. It probably swam up a storm conduit after falling from a boat.

What's the bravest species of animal?

The carrier pigeon, which has received more than half of all the Dickin Medals for Animal Bravery ever issued.

The medal was instituted by Mrs. Maria Dickin, founder of the People's Dispensary for Sick Animals (P.D.S.A.) in the United Kingdom in 1943. Between 1943 and 1949 the P.D.S.A. awarded fifty-four Dickin Medals to thirty-two pigeons, eighteen dogs, three horses, and one cat. Recently a few more awards have been given out, most notably to two guide dogs that led their owners to safety down more than seventy floors in the World Trade Center on September 11, 2001.

Messenger pigeons were used throughout World War II during communication blackouts and attacks. One of the first to win the D.M. was Winkie, who was on a plane when it crashed. Winkie broke free and found her way back to her owner in Scotland.

From her oily and bedraggled appearance, Winkie's owner could roughly estimate how long she had been flying. Using this information, along with the last known coordinates of the plane, the crew were saved.

A few years later, a pigeon named Gustav was issued to the war correspondent Montague Taylor, and braved a 150-mile trip to deliver the first account of the Normandy landings. Gustav came to a sticky end after the war when someone cleaning out his loft accidentally sat on him.

In 1942 behavioral scientist B. F. Skinner came up with the idea of using trained pigeons to guide weapons. The system worked by training pigeons to earn a food reward by pecking at the image of a ship. Three of them were then placed in the nose of a missile. Once launched, the pigeons would see the ship in their window and peck at it, triggering a corrective mechanism linked to the missile's guidance system.

The closer the ship got, the bigger it appeared in the screen, and the more the pigeons pecked, so that just before they hit the target and were obliterated, they were being showered with grain.

The system worked well in simulations but the navy eventually balked at putting it into practice.

The pigeon guidance technology work wasn't entirely wasted—for a while, the United States Coast Guard used pigeons to guide rescue helicopters. They were trained to peck at orange dots, which meant they could be used in searches for orange life jackets in open seas, their eyesight being ten times sharper than that of the pilots.

What's three times as dangerous as war?

Work is a bigger killer than alcohol, drugs, or war.

Around two million people die every year from work-related accidents and diseases, as opposed to a mere 650,000 who are killed in wars.

Worldwide, the most dangerous jobs are in agriculture, mining, and construction. According to the U.S. Bureau of Labor Statistics, in the year 2000, 5,915 people died at work—including those who had a heart attack at their desks.

Lumberjacks had the most dangerous job, with 122 deaths per 100,000 employed. The second most dangerous job was fishing, and third was airplane pilots—with a death rate of 101 per 100,000. Nearly all of the pilots, you'll be reassured to hear, died in small-plane crashes, not passenger jets.

Structural metalworkers and people in mining and drilling came fourth and fifth, though the death rate for both was less than half that of timber cutters.

The third most common cause of death on the job in all occupations was murder, which claimed 677 workers. Fifty policemen were murdered. But so were 205 salespeople.

Falls were the second most common cause of death, accounting for 12 percent of the total. Roofers and structural metalworkers were the main victims.

The most common cause of death on the job was the car accident, accounting for 23 percent of the total. Even police officers were slightly more likely to die behind the wheel than by homicide.

The single most dangerous specific job is said to be that of Alaskan crab fishermen working in the Bering Sea.

The risk of death can be calculated using the Duckworth scale, devised by Dr. Frank Duckworth, editor of the Royal Statistical Society magazine. It measures the likelihood of dying as a result of any given activity. The safest kind of activity scores 0 and 8 will result in certain death.

One game of Russian Roulette carries a risk of 7.2. Twenty years of rock climbing weighs in at 6.3. The chances of a man being murdered are 4.6. A 100-mile car journey by a sober middle-aged driver scores 1.9: slightly more risky than a destructive asteroid impact (1.6).

On the Duckworth scale, 5.5 is particularly perilous. It's the risk of death by car crash or an accidental fall for men, as well as the chance of either sex dying while vacuuming, washing up, or walking down the street.

What killed most sailors in an eighteenth-century sea battle?

A nasty splinter.

Cannon balls fired from men o' war didn't actually explode (no matter what Hollywood thinks), they just tore through the hull of the ship, causing huge splinters of wood to fly around the decks at high speed, lacerating anyone within range.

British naval ships of the period were often rotten and unseaworthy. Many of the officers had no idea how to sail, fight, or control their men. Hernias caused by manhandling acres of wet canvas were so common that the navy was forced to issue trusses. To cap it all there wasn't a single pay raise for a century.

At close range, a 32-pound ball was capable of penetrating wood to a depth of two feet. The best way to stop splinters (other than by building a metal ship) was to use a type of wood found in the southeastern United States that resisted splintering.

As well as being one of the hardest of all woods, the live oak (*Quercus virginiana*) is the state tree of Georgia and a symbol of strength and resistance for the Southern states. It is the tree draped with long garlands of moss in films like *Gone With the Wind.*

What's the word for Napoleon's most humiliating defeat?

Rabbits.

While Waterloo was no doubt Napoleon's most crushing defeat, it was not his most embarrassing.

In 1807 Napoleon was in high spirits, having signed the Peace of Tilsit, a landmark treaty between France, Russia, and Prussia. To celebrate, he suggested that the Imperial Court should enjoy an afternoon's rabbit shooting.

It was organized by his trusted chief of staff, Alexandre Berthier, who was so keen to impress Napoleon that he bought thousands of rabbits to ensure that the Imperial Court had plenty of game to keep them occupied.

The party arrived, the shoot commenced, and the gamekeepers released the quarry. But disaster struck. Berthier had bought tame, not wild, rabbits, who mistakenly thought they were about to be fed rather than killed.

Rather than fleeing for their life, they spotted a tiny little man in a big hat and mistook him for their keeper bringing them food. The hungry rabbits stormed toward Napoleon at their top speed of 35 mph.

The shooting party—now in shambolic disarray—could do nothing to stop them. Napoleon was left with no other option but to run, beating the starving animals off with his bare hands. But the rabbits did not relent and drove the emperor back to his carriage while his underlings thrashed vainly at them with horsewhips.

According to contemporary accounts of the fiasco, the Emperor of France sped off in his coach, comprehensively beaten and covered in shame.

I SUPPOSE NOBODY HAS EVER BEEN STRUCK A DIRECT BLOW BY A RABBIT. AT LEAST, NOT DELIBERATELY.

SIR WILLIAM CONNOR

Who blew the nose off the Sphinx?

The Sphinx, which means "strangler" in Greek, was a mythical beast with the head of a woman, the body of a lion, and the wings of a bird. As you may have noticed, its giant 6,500-year-old statue beside the pyramids has no nose.

Over the centuries, many armies and individuals—British, German, and Arab—have been accused of deliberately blowing it off for various reasons, but Napoleon generally gets the blame.

Almost none of these accusations is true. In fact, the only person that we can definitely say damaged it at all was an Islamic cleric named Sa'im al-dahr, who was lynched for vandalism in 1378.

The British and the German armies in either of the two World Wars are not guilty: there are photographs of the Sphinx without its nose dating from 1886.

As for Napoleon, there are sketches in existence of a noseless Sphinx done in 1737, thirty-two years before he was even born. When he first clapped eyes on it as a twenty-nine-year-old general, it had probably been missing for hundreds of years.

Napoleon went to Egypt with a view to disrupting British communications with India. He fought two battles there: the battle of the Pyramids (which wasn't, as it happens, at the Pyramids), and the battle of the Nile (which wasn't at the Nile). As well as 55,000 troops, Napoleon brought with him 155 civilian experts known as *savants*. It was the first professional archaeological expedition to the country.

When he returned to France after Nelson sank his fleet, the emperor left behind his army and the savants, whose work continued. They produced the *Description de l'Egypte*, the first accurate picture of the country to reach Europe.

Despite all this, Egyptian guides at the Pyramids today still tell tourists that the Sphinx's nose was "stolen by Napoleon" and taken back to the Louvre in Paris.

The most likely reason for the missing organ is the action of six thousand years of wind and weather on the soft limestone.

What did Nero do while Rome burned?

He certainly didn't play the fiddle, which wasn't invented until the fifteenth century.

The other charge was that Nero sang a song about the burning of Troy while Rome burned in A.D. 64 implying that he had set fire to the city himself in order to do so.

In fact, when the fire broke out, he was more than 35 miles away at his seaside holiday home. When told the news, he raced back to Rome and took personal charge of the firefighting efforts.

The suspicion that he wanted to burn down Rome may have arisen from his stated ambition to redevelop the city. He eventually managed to shift the blame onto the Christians.

As to what Nero actually did: he was a transvestite who loved acting in women's clothes, singing, playing music, and having orgies, and he had his mother killed. He was very proud of his musical abilities; his dying words are reported to have been "What an artist the world is losing in me!"

According to some, he generally accompanied himself on the kithara (related to the lyre) but he also played the bagpipes.

Dio Chrysostom, a Greek writing around A.D. 100, noted: "They say that he can write, carve statues, play the *aulos* both with his mouth, and also with the armpit, a bag being thrown under it."

Early in the sixth century, Procopius, a Greek historian, mentions that the bagpipes were the instrument of choice of the Roman infantry while the trumpet was used in the cavalry.

Nero also invented ice cream (runners brought mountain snow flavored with fruit juice) and his personal poisoner, Locusta, was history's first documented serial killer.

Locusta means "lobster" or "locust": Latin uses the same word for both.

What's more likely: being killed by lightning or by an asteroid?

Absurd as it may seem, death by asteroid is more likely.

It is estimated that a large asteroid

(nowadays known as a Near Earth Object, or NEO) hits the earth once every million years. Statistically, this event is now well overdue.

A "dangerous" NEO is one more than 1.2 miles in diameter. The shock of the impact would be equivalent to one million megatons of TNT. If it happened, the death toll would be in excess of two billion, so the chances of you personally dying in any given year are one in three million.

The chance of being killed by lightning in the U.S. in any given year is about one in four million, roughly the same as dying in an air crash.

Lightning is a giant electrical spark, with a brightness equivalent to a 100 million lightbulbs going on and off. Some strokes reach a peak current of 100,000 amps and 200 million volts, creating a temperature of 30,000°C, five times hotter than the surface of the sun. A bolt of lightning travels at speeds up to 100 million feet per second, or more than 70 million mph.

Each flash is really composed of several strokes, each lasting less than a millionth of a second. Because they are so short, the energy value of lightning is limited—a single stroke would only generate enough energy to run an average household for a day. Lightning strikes the earth more than eight million times every day, or about fifty times a second.

Strikes are most common in coastal areas, occurring at a rate of about one per square mile per year. They don't seem to do much damage: the electricity dissipates rapidly across the surface of the sea, and whales have been observed to sing quite happily through ferocious electrical storms.

> BEFORE THE CURSE OF STATISTICS FELL UPON MANKIND WE LIVED A HAPPY, INNOCENT LIFE, FULL OF MERRIMENT AND GO AND INFORMED BY FAIRLY GOOD JUDGMENT.
>
> HILAIRE BELLOC

Human beings, on the other hand, are struck by lightning ten times more frequently than they ought to be under the laws of chance.

Men are struck by lightning six times more often than women.

Between three and six Britons and a hundred Americans are killed by lightning every year, many of them because they are carrying portable lightning conductors about their person—golf clubs, carbon-fiber fishing rods, and underwire bras.

If caught in a thunderstorm in the open, the safest position is well away from any trees, crouching down, with your bottom sticking up in the air.

How did Roman emperors order the death of a gladiator?

Thumbs up.

Neither Roman spectators calling for the death of a gladiator, nor Roman emperors authorizing one, ever gave a thumbs down. In fact, the Romans didn't use a thumbs-down sign at all.

If death was desired, the thumb was stuck up—like a drawn sword. For a loser's life to be spared, the thumb was tucked away inside the closed fist—as with a sheathed weapon. This is expressed in Latin as *pollice compresso favor iudicabatur*, (goodwill is decided by the thumb being kept in).

Before Ridley Scott agreed to direct *Gladiator*, Hollywood executives showed him the painting *Pollice Verso* by the nineteenth-century artist Jean-Léon Gérôme. In the painting, a Roman gladiator waits while the emperor stretches his thumb down to give the death sentence. Scott was captivated by the image, and decided on the spot that he must direct the film.

Little did Scott know that the source of his inspiration was utterly wrong. The painting is single-handedly responsible for one of the greatest fallacies of the last two centuries, namely that thumbs down indicated death.

Historians agree that Gérôme wrongly assumed that the Latin *pollice verso*—"turned thumb"—meant "turned down" when in fact it meant "turned up."

If further proof were needed, in 1997 a Roman medallion of the second or third century A.D. was discovered in southern France. It shows two gladiators at the end of a battle and a referee pressing his thumb against a closed fist. The inscription reads: "Those standing should be released."

The use of thumb signs can still be dangerously ambiguous in the modern world. In the Middle East, South America, and Russia, a "thumbs up" is considered to be a very rude insult, comparable to the Western V-sign. This has been problematic in Iraq, where American soldiers are unsure whether locals are welcoming them or about to blow them up.

Desmond Morris, author of *The Naked Ape*, traces the positive connotations of the "thumbs up" in Britain to the Middle Ages, where it was used to close business deals. It found a new lease on life in World War II when U.S. Air Force pilots adopted it as a signal to ground crews before takeoff.

Ridley Scott was eventually told about the "thumbs down" fallacy but felt obliged to have Commodus give the "thumbs up" when sparing Maximus, in order "not to confuse the audience."

What's interesting about the birth of Julius Caesar?

Almost nothing is known about the birth of Julius Caesar, except that, contrary to the assertion in the *Oxford English Dictionary* and countless other reference books, it did not take place by Caesarean section.

Such operations did occur at the time, but they always involved the death of the mother, and Caesar's mother, Aurelia, is known to have survived into his adulthood. The suggestion that he was born by C-section does not appear in any of the contemporary sources, and is first mentioned in medieval times. It was not used in a medical context in English before 1615.

The confusion probably started with Pliny the Elder who, in his *Natural History* (circa 77 A.D.) claims that the first Caesar was "cut from his mother's womb." This may well have been true, but it wasn't the Caesar we know as Gaius Julius Caesar.

The Roman three-part naming convention meant that Gaius was his given name and he was part of the Caesar branch of the Julian clan, so no one knows how many Caesars there had been previously. Nor do we know exactly what *Caesar* means—and none of the meanings are particularly apt to our man. There is Pliny's "cut" from *caedere*. Or *caeseries*, meaning "hairy" (but he was balding); or *caesius*, "gray" (but his eyes were black) or even "elephant" (from the Phoenician and perhaps applied to a Julian ancestor who had killed one).

The Roman's pronounced "Caesar" as *kaiser* (which is still the German word for "king" and, like the Russian *czar*, ultimately derived from *Caesar*). All the Roman emperors after Julius, until Hadrian, were called "Caesar."

Caesar salad is no relation, however. It was invented by Cesar Cardin in an Italian restaurant in Tijuana, Mexico, in 1923.

What's a *vomitorium* for?

Vomitorium, despite being derived from the Latin *vomere*, meaning "to spew forth," isn't the place where the Romans threw up after their meals. It was the name for the entrance or exit from an amphitheater, and is still used in that sense today in some sports stadiums.

The *vomitoria* of the Colosseum in Rome were so well designed that it's said the venue, which seated at least 50,000, could fill in fifteen minutes. (There were eighty entrances at ground level, seventy-six for ordinary spectators and four for the imperial family.)

The confusion of the exit with a specialized vomit chamber appears to be a recent error. The earliest citation in the *Oxford English Dictionary* finds Aldous Huxley using the term incorrectly in his 1923 comic novel, *Antic Hay*, with the stern comment "erron." Lewis Mumford in *The City in History* (1961) compounded the confusion by saying the exits were named after the chambers where gluttons threw up "in order to return to their couches empty enough to enjoy the pleasures of still more food."

The problem with this theory is that no Roman writer ever refers to them, nor have any purpose-built rooms that fit the bill been found. Romans certainly threw up on purpose. Indeed, in ancient times vomiting seems to have been a standard part of the fine-dining experience. The orator Cicero, in *Pro Rege Deiotaro* (45 B.C.), says that Julius Caesar "expressed a desire to vomit after dinner" and elsewhere suggests that the dictator took emetics for this purpose.

But where did they do it, if there was no special room? Some sources suggest the street or garden; others are adamant it was at the table. In his *Moral Epistles* the Roman philosopher Seneca writes: "When we recline at a banquet, one slave wipes up the spittle; another, situated beneath the table, collects the leavings of the drunks."

In another passage, in a letter to his mother, Helvia, he links this to the decadent pursuit of the new and the exotic: "They vomit that they may eat, they eat that they may vomit, and they do not deign even to digest the feasts for which they ransack the whole world."

What is the Number of the Beast?

616.

For 2,000 years, 666 has been the symbol of the dreaded Anti-Christ, who will come to rule the world before the Last

Judgment. For many, it's an unlucky number: even the European Parliament leaves seat number 666 vacant.

The number is from Revelation, the last and strangest book in the Bible: "Let him that hath understanding count the number of the beast: for it is the number of a man; and his number is Six hundred threescore *and* six."

But it's a wrong number. In 2005, a new translation of the earliest known copy of the Book of Revelation clearly shows it to be 616 not 666. The seventeen-hundred-year-old papyrus was recovered from the rubbish dumps of the city of Oxyrhynchus in Egypt and deciphered by a paleographical research team from the University of Birmingham led by Professor David Parker.

If the new number is correct, it will not amuse those who have just spent a small fortune avoiding the old one. In 2003, U.S. Highway 666—known as "The Highway of the Beast—was renamed Highway 491. The Moscow Transport Department will be even less amused. In 1999 they picked a new number for the jinxed 666 bus route. It was 616.

The controversy has been around since the second century AD. A version of the Bible citing the Number of the Beast as 616 was castigated by Saint Iranaeus of Lyon (ca. 130–200) as "erroneous and spurious." Karl Marx's friend Friedrich Engels analyzed the Bible in his book *On Religion* (1883). He too calculated the number as 616, not 666.

Revelation was the first book of the New Testament to be written, and it is full of number puzzles. Each of the twenty-two letters of the Hebrew alphabet has a corresponding number, so that any number can also be read as a word.

Both Parker and Engels argue that the Book of Revelation is a political, anti-Roman tract, numerologically coded to disguise its message. The Number of the Beast (whatever that may be) refers to either Caligula or Nero, the hated oppressors of the early Christians, not to some imaginary bogeyman.

The fear of the number 666 is known as *Hexakosioihexekonta-*

hexaphobia. The fear of the number 616 (you read it here first) is *Hexakosioidekahexaphobia.*

The numbers on a roulette wheel added together come to 666.

Where does the word *assassin* come from?

Not from hashish.

The earliest authority for the medieval sect called the Assassins taking hashish in order to witness the pleasures awaiting them after death is the notoriously unreliable Marco Polo. Most Islamic scholars now favor the more convincing etymology of *assassiyun*, meaning people who are faithful to the *assass*, the foundation of the faith. They were, literally, fundamentalists.

This makes sense when you look at their core activities. The Al-Hashishin, or Nizaris as they called themselves, were active for two hundred years. They were Shi'ite Muslims, dedicated to the overthrow of the Sunni caliph (a kind of Islamic king). The Assassins considered the Baghdad court decadent and little more than a puppet regime of the Turks. Sound familiar?

The sect was founded in 1090 by Hassan-i Saban, a mystic philosopher who was fond of poetry and science. They made their base at Alamut, an unassailable fortress in the mountains south of the Caspian Sea. It housed an important library and beautiful gardens, but it was Hasan's political strategy that made the sect famous. He decided they could wield huge influence by using a simple weapon: terror.

Dressed as merchants and holy men they selected and murdered their victims in public, usually at Friday prayers, *in* the mosque. They weren't explicitly suicide missions, but the assassins were almost always killed in the course of their work.

They were incredibly successful, systematically wiping out all the major leaders of the Muslim world and effectively destroying any chance of a unified Islamic defense against the Western crusaders.

What finally defeated them was, ironically, exactly what defeated their opponents. In 1256 Hulagu Khan assembled the largest Mongol army ever known. They marched westward, destroying the assassins' power base in Alamut before sacking Baghdad in 1258.

Baghdad was then the world's most beautiful and civilized city. A million citizens perished, and so many books were thrown into the Tigris River it ran black with ink. The city remained a ruin for hundreds of years afterward.

Hulagu destroyed the caliphs and the assassins. He drove Islam into Egypt and then returned home only to perish, in true Mongol style, in a civil war.

What are chastity belts for?

The idea of a crusader clapping his wife in a chastity belt and galloping off to war with the key round his neck is a nineteenth-century fantasy designed to titillate readers.

There is very little evidence for the use of chastity belts in the Middle Ages at all. The first known drawing of one occurs in the fifteenth century. Konrad Kyeser's *Bellifortis* was a book on contemporary military equipment written long after the crusades had finished. It includes an illustration of the "hard iron breeches" worn by Florentine women.

In the diagram, the key is clearly visible—which suggests that it was the lady and not the knight who controlled access to the device, to protect herself against the unwanted attentions of Florentine bucks.

In museum collections, most "medieval" chastity belts have now been shown to be of dubious authenticity and removed from display. As with "medieval" torture equipment, it appears that most of it was manufactured in Germany in the nineteenth century to satisfy the curiosity of "specialist" collectors.

The nineteenth century also witnessed an upturn in sales of new chastity belts—but these were not for women.

Victorian medical theory was of the opinion that masturbation was harmful to health. Boys who could not be trusted to keep their hands to themselves were forced to wear these improving steel underpants.

But the real boom in sales has come in the last fifty years, as adult shops take advantage of the thriving bondage market.

There are more chastity belts around today than there ever were in the Middle Ages. Paradoxically, they exist to stimulate sex, not to prevent it.

What was Tutankhamun's curse?

There wasn't one. It was made up by the papers.

The story of the "pharaoh's curse" striking down all those who entered Tutankhamun's tomb when it was discovered by Howard Carter in 1922, was the work of the Cairo correspondent of the *Daily Express* (later repeated by the *Daily Mail* and the *New York Times*).

The article reported an inscription that stated: "They who enter this sacred tomb shall swiftly be visited by wings of death."

There is no such inscription. The nearest equivalent appears over a shrine dedicated to the god Anubis and reads: "It is I who hinder the sand from choking the secret chamber. I am for the protection of the deceased."

In the run-up to Carter's expedition, Sir Arthur Conan Doyle—who also famously believed in fairies—had already planted the seeds of "a terrible curse" in the minds of the press. When Carter's patron, Lord Caernavon, died from a septic mosquito bite a few weeks after the tomb was opened, Marie Corelli, writer of sensational best sellers and the Dan Brown of her day, claimed she had warned him what would happen if he broke the seal.

In fact, both were echoing a superstition that was less than a hundred years old, established by a young English novelist named Jane Loudon Webb. Her hugely popular novel *The Mummy* (1828) single-handedly invented the idea of a cursed tomb with a mummy returning to life to avenge its desecrators.

This theme found its way into all sorts of subsequent tales—even Louisa May Alcott, author of *Little Women*, wrote a mummy story—but its big break came with the advent of "Tutankhamun fever."

No curse has ever been found in an ancient Egyptian tomb. Of the alleged twenty-six deaths caused by Tutankhamun's "curse," thorough research published in the *British Medical Journal* in 2002 has shown that only six died within the first decade of its opening, and Howard Carter, surely the number one target, lived for another seventeen years.

But the story just won't go away. As late as the 1970s, when the exhibition of artifacts from the tomb toured the West, a policeman guarding it in San Francisco complained of a mild stroke brought on by the "mummy's curse."

In 2005 a CAT scan of Tutankhamun's mummy showed that the nineteen-year-old was 5 feet 6 inches tall and skinny, with a goofy overbite. Rather than being murdered by his brother, it seems he died from an infected knee.

What did feminists do with their bras?

No, they didn't.

Arguably the most influential feminist protest in history occurred at the 1968 Miss America beauty pageant in Atlantic City, New Jersey.

A small group of protesters picketed the pageant with provocative slogans such as "Let's judge ourselves as people" and "Ain't she sweet; making profits off her meat."

They produced a live sheep, which they crowned Miss America, and then proceeded to toss their high-heeled shoes, bras, curlers, and tweezers into a "Freedom Trash Can."

What they didn't do was burn their bras. They wanted to, but the police advised that it would be dangerous while standing on a wooden boardwalk.

The myth of the bra-burning began with an article by a young *New York Post* journalist named Lindsay Van Gelder.

In 1992 she told *Ms.* magazine: "I mentioned high in the story that the protesters were planning to burn bras, girdles, and other items in a freedom trash can . . . The headline writer took it a step further and called them 'bra-burners.' "

The headline was enough. Journalists across America seized on it without bothering to even read the story. Van Gelder had created a media frenzy.

Even scrupulous publications such as the *Washington Post* were caught out.

They identified members of the National Women's Liberation Group as the same women who "burned undergarments during a demonstration at the Miss America contest in Atlantic City recently."

The incident is now used as a textbook case in the study of how contemporary myths originate.

What color is the universe?

a. Black with silvery bits
b. Silver with black bits
c. Pale green
d. Beige

It's officially beige.

In 2002, after analyzing the light from 200,000 galaxies collected by the Australian Galaxy Redshift Survey, American scientists from Johns Hopkins University concluded that the universe was pale green. Not black with silvery bits, as it appears. Taking the Dulux paint range as a standard, it was somewhere between Mexican Mint, Jade Cluster, and Shangri-La Silk.

A few weeks after the announcement to the American Astronomical Society, however, they had to admit they'd made a mistake in their calculations, and that the universe was, in fact, more a sort of dreary shade of taupe.

Since the seventeenth century, some of the greatest and most curious minds have wondered why it is that the night sky is black. If the universe is infinite and contains an infinite number of uniformly distributed stars, there should be a star everywhere we look, and the night sky should be as bright as day.

This is known as Olbers' Paradox, after the German astronomer Heinrich Olbers, who described the problem (not for the first time) in 1826.

Nobody has yet come up with a really good answer to the problem. Maybe there is a finite number of stars, maybe the light from the furthest ones hasn't reached us yet. Olbers' solution was that, at some time in the past, not all the stars had been shining and that something had switched them on.

It was Edgar Allan Poe, in his prophetic prose poem *Eureka* (1848), who first suggested that the light from the most distant stars is still on its way.

In 2003 the Ultra Deep Field Camera of the Hubble Space Telescope was pointed at what appeared to be the emptiest piece of the night sky and the film exposed for a million seconds (about eleven days).

The resulting picture showed tens of thousands of hitherto unknown galaxies, each consisting of hundreds of millions of stars, stretching away into the dim edges of the universe.

What color is Mars?

Butterscotch.

Or brown. Or orange. Maybe khaki with pale pink patches.

One of the most familiar features of the planet Mars is its red appearance in the night sky. This redness, however, is due to the dust in the planet's atmosphere. The surface of Mars tells a different story.

The first pictures from Mars were sent back from *Viking I*, seven years to the day after Neil Armstrong's famous moon landing. They showed a desolate red land strewn with dark rocks, exactly what we had expected.

This made the conspiracy theorists suspicious: they claimed that NASA had deliberately doctored the pictures to make them seem more familiar.

The cameras on the two *Viking* rovers that reached Mars in 1976 didn't take color pictures. The digital images were captured in gray-scale (the technical term for black-and-white) and then passed through three color filters.

Adjusting these filters to give a "true" color image is extremely tricky and as much an art as a science. Since no one has ever been to Mars, we have no idea what its true color is.

In 2004 the *New York Times* stated that the early color pictures from Mars were published slightly "overpinked," but that later adjustments showed the surface to be more like the color of butterscotch.

NASA's *Spirit* rover has been operating on Mars for the past two years. The latest published pictures show a green-brown, mud-colored landscape with gray-blue rocks and patches of salmon-colored sand.

We probably won't know the "real" color of Mars until someone goes there.

In 1887 the Italian astronomer Giovanni Schiaparelli reported seeing long straight lines on Mars which he called *canali*, or channels. This was mistranslated as "canals," starting rumors of a lost civilization on Mars.

Water is thought to exist on Mars in the form of vapor, and as ice in the polar ice caps, but since more powerful telescopes have been developed, no evidence of Schiaparelli's "canals" has ever been found.

Cairo, or *al-Qāhirah*, is Arabic for Mars.

What color is water?

The usual answer is that it isn't any color; it's clear or transparent and the sea only appears blue because of the reflection of the sky.

Wrong. Water really is blue. It's an incredibly faint shade, but it is blue. You can see this in nature when you look into a deep hole in the snow, or through the thick ice of a frozen waterfall. If you took a very large, very deep white pool, filled it with water, and looked straight down through it, the water would be blue.

This faint blue tinge doesn't explain why water sometimes takes on a strikingly blue appearance when we look *at* it rather than *through* it. Reflected color from the sky obviously plays an important part. The sea doesn't look particularly blue on an overcast day.

But not all the light we see is reflected from the surface of the water; some of it is coming from under the surface. The more impure the water, the more color it will reflect.

In large bodies of water like seas and lakes the water will usually contain a high concentration of microscopic plants and algae. Rivers and ponds will have a high concentration of soil and other solids in suspension.

All these particles reflect and scatter the light as it returns to the surface, creating huge variation in the colors we see. It explains why you sometimes see a brilliant green Mediterranean sea under a bright blue sky.

What color was the sky in ancient Greece?

Bronze. There is no word for "blue" in ancient Greek.

The nearest words—*glaukos* and *kyanos*—are more like expressions of the relative intensity of light and darkness than attempts to describe the color.

The ancient Greek poet Homer mentions only four actual colors in the whole of the *Iliad* and the *Odyssey*, roughly translated as black, white, greenish yellow (applied to honey, sap and blood), and purply red.

When Homer calls the sky "bronze," he means that it is dazzlingly bright, like the sheen of a shield, rather than bronze-colored. In a similar spirit, he regarded wine, the sea, and sheep as all being the same color—purply red.

Aristotle identified seven shades of color, all of which he thought derived from black and white, but these were really grades of brightness, not color.

It's interesting that an ancient Greek from almost twenty-five hundred years ago and NASA's Mars rovers of 2006 both approach color in the same way.

In the wake of Darwin, the theory was advanced that the early Greeks' retinas had not evolved the ability to perceive colors, but it is now thought they grouped objects in terms of qualities other than color, so that a word which seems to indicate yellow or light green really meant fluid, fresh, and living, and so was appropriately used to describe blood, the human sap.

This is not as rare as you might expect. There are more languages in Papua New Guinea than anywhere else in the world but, apart from distinguishing between light and dark, many of them have no other words for color at all.

Classical Welsh has no words for brown, gray, blue or green. The color spectrum is divided in a completely different way. One word (*glas*) covered part of green; another the rest of green, the whole of blue and part of gray; a third dealt with the rest of gray and most, or part, of brown.

Modern Welsh uses the word *glas* to mean blue, but Russian has no single word for blue. It has two—*goluboi* and *sinii*—usually translated as "light blue" and "dark blue," but, to Russians, they are distinct, different colors, not different shades of the same color.

All languages develop their color terms in the same way. After black and white, the third color to be named is always red, the fourth and fifth are green and yellow (in either order), the sixth is blue, and the seventh brown. Welsh still doesn't have a word for brown.

How much of the earth is water?

Seven-tenths of the earth's surface area may be covered in water, but water accounts for less than a fiftieth of one percent of the planet's mass.

> HOW INAPPROPRIATE TO CALL THIS PLANET EARTH WHEN CLEARLY IT IS OCEAN.
>
> ARTHUR C. CLARKE

The earth is big—it weighs about 6 million, billion, billion kilograms. Half of this is contained in the lower mantle, the massive semimolten layer that begins 410 miles below the crust. Even on the apparently watery crust, the mass of the land is forty times greater than that of the oceans.

A Japanese experiment reported in *Science* in 2002 suggests that there may be five times as much water dissolved in the lower mantle than sloshing around on the earth's surface.

Using pressures of 200,000 kg per cm and temperatures of 1,600°C, the researchers created four mineral compounds similar to those found in the lower mantle. They then added water and measured how much of it was absorbed.

If the Japanese are right, the proportion of the world that is water will have to be revised upwards—to 0.1 percent.

Which way does the bathwater go down the drain?

a. Clockwise
b. Counterclockwise
c. Straight down
d. It depends

It depends. The widely held belief that it is the Coriolis force, created by the earth's spin, that drives bathwater into a spiral is untrue.

Although it does influence large, long-lasting weather patterns such as hurricanes and ocean currents, it is by orders of magnitude too weak to have an effect on domestic plumbing. The direction of drainage is determined by the shape of the basin, the direction from which it was filled, and the vortices introduced into it by washing or when the plug is removed.

If a perfectly symmetrical pan, with a tiny drainhole and a plug which could be removed without disturbing the water, were filled and left for a week or so, so that all the motion settled completely, then it might in principle be possible to detect a small Coriolis effect, which would be counterclockwise in the Northern Hemisphere and clockwise in the South.

This myth was lent some credence by inclusion in Michael Palin's *Pole-to-Pole* series. They showed film of a showman in Nanyuki, Kenya, who purports to demonstrate the effect on either side of the equator, but even supposing the effect existed, this particular demonstration got the direction of circulation the wrong way around.

What do camels store in their humps?

Fat.

Camels' humps don't store water, but fat, which is used as an energy reserve. Water is stored throughout their bodies, particularly in the bloodstream, which makes them very good at avoiding dehydration.

Camels can lose 40 percent of their body weight before they are affected by it, and can go up to seven days without drinking. When they do drink, they really go for it—up to fifty gallons at a time.

Here are a few quite interesting facts about camels, which have nothing to do with their humps.

Before elephants acquired their reputation for long memories, the ancient Greeks believed it was camels that didn't forget.

Persian hunting hounds—Salukis—hunted on camels. They lay on the camel's neck watching for deer, and then leapt off in pursuit when they saw one. A Saluki can jump up to twenty feet from a standing start.

In 1977 in *Zoo Vet*, David Taylor observed that "camels may build up a pressure cooker of resentment toward human beings until the lid suddenly blows off and they go berserk." The camel handler calms it down by handing the beast his coat. "The camel gives the garment hell—jumping on it, biting it, tearing it to pieces. When the camel feels it has blown its top enough, man and animal can live together in harmony again."

Camel racing in the United Arab Emirates has started to use robot riders in place of the traditional child jockeys. The remotely operated riders were developed following a ban on the use of jockeys under sixteen years of age, imposed by the UAE Camel Racing Association in March 2004.

These laws are regularly flouted and there is a brisk child slave trade, with children as young as four being kidnapped in Pakistan and kept in Arab camel camps. The only qualifications needed to become a jockey are not to weigh much and be able to scream in terror (this encourages the camels).

The famous line from the Gospels of Matthew, Mark, and Luke, "it is easier for a camel to pass through the eye of a needle than for a rich man to enter the kingdom of God," is possibly a mistranslation, where the original Aramaic word *gamta*, "sturdy rope," was confused with *gamla*, "camel."

This makes more sense, and is a comforting thought for the well-off.

Where do camels come from?

North America.

The icons of the African and Arabian deserts are American in origin.

Like horses and dogs, camels evolved in the grasslands of America, twenty million years ago. In those days they were more like giraffes or gazelles than the humped beasts of burden we know and love. It wasn't until four million years ago that they crossed the Bering land bridge into Asia.

They became extinct in North America during the last Ice Age and, unlike horses and dogs, haven't made it back.

It is not clear why the North American camel species died out. Climate change is the obvious culprit. More specifically it may have been due to a change in the silica content of grass. As the North American climate got cooler and drier, silica levels in grass tripled. This new super-tough grass wore out the teeth of even the longest-toothed grazers and the horses and camels gradually died of starvation, as a result of being unable to chew.

There is also some evidence that these already weakened species, their escape route to Asia blocked by the disappearance of the Bering land bridge ten thousand years ago, were finished off by human hunters.

Who is America named after?

Not the Italian merchant and cartographer Amerigo Vespucci, but Richard Ameryk, a Welshman and wealthy Bristol merchant.

Ameryk was the chief investor in the second transatlantic voyage of John Cabot—the English name of the Italian navigator Giovanni Caboto, whose voyages in 1497 and 1498 laid the groundwork for the later British claim to Canada. He moved to London from Genoa in 1484 and was authorized by King Henry VII to search for unknown lands to the west.

On his little ship *Matthew*, Cabot reached Labrador in May 1497 and became the first recorded European to set foot on American soil, predating Vespucci by two years.

Cabot mapped the North American coastline from Nova Scotia to Newfoundland. As the chief patron of the voyage, Richard Ameryk would have expected discoveries to be named after him. There is a record in the Bristol calendar for that year: ". . . on Saint John the Baptist's day [June 24], the land of America was found by the merchants of Bristowe, in a ship of Bristowe called the *Mathew*," which clearly suggests this is what happened.

Although the original manuscript of this calendar has not survived, there are a number of references to it in other contemporary documents. This is the first use of the term *America* to refer to the new continent.

The earliest surviving map to use the name is Martin Waldseemüller's great map of the world of 1507, but it only applied to

South America. In his notes Waldseemüller makes the assumption that the name is derived from a Latin version of Amerigo Vespucci's first name, because Vespucci had discovered and mapped the South American coast from 1500 to 1502.

This suggests he didn't know for sure and was trying to account for a name he had seen on other maps, possibly Cabot's. The only place where the name "America" was known and used was Bristol—not somewhere the France-based Waldseemüller was likely to visit. Significantly, he replaced "America" with "Terra Incognita" in his world map of 1513.

Vespucci never reached North America. All the early maps and trade were British. Nor did he ever use the name of America for his discovery.

There's a good reason for this. New countries or continents were never named after a person's first name, but always after the second (as in Tasmania, Van Diemen's Land, or the Cook Islands).

America would have become Vespucci Land (or Vespuccia) if the Italian explorer had consciously given his name to it.

How many states are there in the United States?

Technically, there are only forty-six.

Virginia, Kentucky, Pennsylvania, and Massachusetts are all officially commonwealths.

This grants them no special constitutional powers. They simply chose this word to describe themselves at the end of the War of Independence. It made clear they were no longer royal colonies answering to the king, but states governed by the "common consent of the people."

Virginia (named after the "Virgin" Queen Elizabeth I) was one of the thirteen original states (hence the thirteen stripes on the American flag) and the first of the states to declare itself a commonwealth in 1776.

Pennsylvania and Massachusetts followed suit shortly afterward, and Kentucky, which was originally a county of Virginia, became a commonwealth in 1792.

There are also two American commonwealths overseas. In July 1952 the Caribbean island of Puerto Rico drew up its own constitution, which declared itself a commonwealth of the United States. The Northern Mariana Islands in the Pacific Ocean did the same in 1975. Neither are U.S. states.

Who was the first American president?

Peyton Randolph.

He was the first of fourteen pre-Washington presidents of the Continental Congress, or the United States in Congress Assembled.

The Continental Congress was the debating body formed by the thirteen colonies to formulate their complaints to the British Crown. In its second meeting, under Randolph, it resolved that Britain had declared war on the colonies, and, in response, created the Continental Army, appointing George Washington as its commander in chief.

Randolph's successor, John Hancock, presided over the declaration of independence from Great Britain, where the Congress asserted its right to govern the thirteen colonies.

Randolph was followed by thirteen other presidents until, on April 30, 1789, the triumphant George Washington was sworn in as the president of the independent United States of America.

> DEMOCRACY IS TWO WOLVES AND A LAMB VOTING ON WHAT TO HAVE FOR LUNCH. LIBERTY IS A WELL-ARMED LAMB CONTESTING THE VOTE.
>
> BENJAMIN FRANKLIN

What were George Washington's false teeth made from?

Mostly hippopotamus.

Washington was a martyr to his teeth. According to John Adams he lost them because he used them to crack Brazil nuts, although modern historians suggest it was probably the mercury oxide he was given to treat illnesses such as smallpox and malaria.

He lost his first tooth when he was twenty-two and had only one left by the time he became president. He had several sets of false teeth made, four of them by a dentist called John Greenwood.

Contrary to traditional wisdom, none of these sets was made of wood. The set made when he became president was carved from hippopotamus and elephant ivory, held together with gold springs. The hippo ivory was used for the plate, into which real human teeth and also bits of horses' and donkeys' teeth were inserted.

Dental problems left Washington in constant discomfort, for which he took laudanum, and this distress is apparent in many of the portraits of him painted while he was in office—including the one still used on the $1 bill.

The awkward look of a man with a mouth full of hippopotamus teeth is thought to have been deliberately exaggerated by the portraitist Gilbert Stuart, who didn't get on with the president.

Until the invention of modern synthetic materials, the false tooth of choice was another human tooth, but these were hard to come by. In addition, they could fall out if they were rotten, or if their previous owner had syphilis.

The best source for decent false teeth was dead (but otherwise healthy) young people, and the best place to find them was a battlefield.

One such was Waterloo; fifty thousand men died in the battle and their teeth were plundered wholesale for the denture market. For years afterward dentures were known as "Waterloo teeth," even when they came from other sources.

Real human teeth continued to be used in dentures until the 1860s, when the American Civil War provided a plentiful supply.

Artificial false teeth came in at the end of the nineteenth century. Celluloid was one of the first materials to be tried, though not with conspicuous success.

Celluloid teeth tasted of Ping-Pong balls and melted if you drank hot tea (see page 128).

Whose official motto is *e pluribus unum*?

E pluribus unum (out of the many, one) is the motto of the Portuguese football club Sport Lisboa e Benfica—usually abbreviated to Benfica.

E pluribus unum used to be the national motto of the United States, referring to the integration of the thirteen founding states (it has thirteen letters), but it was replaced by "In God we trust" (a line from "The Star-Spangled Banner") as the official national motto in 1956. The confusion arises because *e pluribus unum* is still used in the Great Seal, on the ribbon streaming from the eagle's mouth, which appears on the reverse of the dollar bill and on all U.S. coins.

The phrase was originally used to describe an herby cheese spread. In a Latin recipe poem called *Moretum*, once attributed to Virgil, the poet describes the lunch of a simple farmer in which he grinds cheese, garlic, and herbs together into a ball (*color est e pluribus unus*).

By the eighteenth century it had become a well-worn phrase meaning "unity" or "friendship."

Benfica was created as a merger of two clubs in 1908. It is Portugal's most popular soccer club, but also fields teams in a range of other sports as well.

Why do deaf Americans feel at home in Paris?

American Sign Language bears a striking similarity to the old French sign language system.

This is because a deaf Frenchman, Laurent Clerc, was one of the first teachers of sign language in the United States in the nineteenth century.

American Sign Language (ASL) is a complex visual-spatial language used by the deaf in the United States and parts of English-speaking Canada. It is a linguistically complete language, spoken as the native tonguue of many deaf people as well as some hearing children of deaf families. Though American universities such as Yale do not offer courses in ASL because "it is not an academic language," ASL is one of the most common languages used in the United States today, easily in the top dozen.

Not only is American Sign Language totally different from British Sign Language (BSL), it is so different in grammatical structure to American English that ASL has more in common with spoken Japanese than it does with spoken English. Deaf Americans will find it much easier to make themselves understood in France than in Britain.

Sign languages are not feeble, mimed versions of spoken or written speech but languages in their own right, with grammatical structures and syntax that do not correspond to their spoken or written forms. They are not universally intelligible. They differ from country to country even more than normal speech, and it is not uncommon for sign languages to differ from city to city in the same country.

From 1692 to 1910, nearly everyone on Martha's Vineyard, an island off the coast of Massachusetts, was bilingual in Martha's Vineyard Sign Language (MVSL). The first deaf person arrived there in 1692 and, as a result of the remote nature of the island and of intermarriage between people with the deafness gene, there was a very high rate of hereditary deafness in the area. In some villages, as many as one in four were deaf.

Deafness on the island was so common that many people believed it to be contagious, but it was never considered a handicap.

In 1817 the school now known as the American School for the Deaf opened on the mainland in Hartford, Connecticut, and most of the deaf children were sent there to be educated. Many settled and married nearby, and the hereditary deaf gene on Martha's Vineyard fizzled out. The last deaf native died in 1950, and MVSL is now extinct, although modern ASL still retains some of its features.

How do the Cherokee pronounce "Cherokee"?

They don't. Cherokee speech has no *ch* or *r* sound.

The correct spelling (and pronounciation) is *Tsalagi. Cherokee* is a Creek Indian word meaning "people with another language." The preferred Cherokee word for themselves is *Aniyounwiya*, which means "the principal people."

There are about 350,000 Cherokee alive today, of whom about 22,000 speak the language. Their written alphabet was devised by Sequoyah, a Cherokee Indian also known as George Guess. He is the only known example in history of an illiterate person inventing a written language.

Sequoyah (1776–1843) was the son of a Cherokee mother and Nathaniel Guess, a German-born fur trader. He was either born handicapped or injured while young, hence his name Sik-wo-yi, which means "pig's foot" in Cherokee.

He first became interested in creating a Cherokee alphabet in 1809. An accomplished silversmith and—despite his handicap—a brave soldier, Sequoyah fought for the United States in the Cherokee Regiment under Andrew Jackson against the British and the Creek Indians at the Battle of Horseshoe Bend in 1814. A wealthy Georgian farmer named Charles Hicks showed him how to write his own name so he could sign his work as a silversmith. During his military service, Sequoyah became convinced of the need for an alphabet because he saw that—unlike the white soldiers—the Tsalagi were unable to write to or receive letters from home, and all battle orders had to be committed to memory.

It took him twelve years to work out the alphabet. He called the eighty-five letters his "talking leaves." On showing it to the Tsalagi chiefs in 1821, it was accepted immediately, and was so simple that, within a year, almost the whole tribe became literate.

Seven years after its adoption, the first Tsalagi-language newspaper, *The Cherokee Phoenix*, was printed in 1828.

Jimi Hendrix, Dolly Parton, and Cher have all claimed Cherokee descent.

What did Buffalo Bill do to buffaloes?

Nothing. There are no buffaloes in North America. However, he did kill a lot of *bison*—4,280 of them in fewer than eighteen months.

The word *buffalo* is frequently misapplied to bison. The North American Plains Bison (*Bison bison*) is related to neither genus of true buffalo—the water buffalo *Bubalus* and the African buffalo *Synceros*. Their most recent common ancestor died out six million years ago.

The bison population fell from sixty million in the seventeenth century to just a few hundred by the late nineteenth. There are about fifty thousand bison roaming the range today. Bison/cattle crosses are bred for meat, called "cattalo" or "beefalo." They have cattle fathers and bison mothers. Off spring of a male bison and female cattle are too broad-shouldered for the cow to deliver safely.

William Frederick "Buffalo Bill" Cody, hunter, Indian fighter, and showman, joined the Pony Express—the West's legendary mail service—at the age of fourteen, in response to an ad which ran: "WANTED young skinny wiry fellows not over eighteen. Must be expert riders willing to risk death daily. Orphans preferred. Wages $25 a week."

The Pony Express only lasted nineteen months and was superseded by the railroad. In 1867 Cody was hired to hunt bison to feed the construction crews of the Kansas Pacific Railroad, which is where he notched up his astounding total.

He ran his Wild West Show from 1883 to 1916. The show was hugely popular; its European tour was attended by Queen Victoria. On his death in 1917—and despite the fact there was a war going on—Cody received tributes from the king of England, the German Kaiser, and President Woodrow Wilson.

Although he had specified in his will that he should be buried near the town of Cody, Wyoming (which he had founded), his wife stated that he had converted to Catholicism on his deathbed and asked for him to be buried on Lookout Mountain, near Denver.

In 1948 the Cody branch of the American Legion offered a $10,000 reward for the "return" of the body, so the Denver branch mounted a guard over the grave until a deeper shaft could be blasted into the rock.

Hatchets weren't buried until 1968, when there was an exchange of smoke signals between Lookout Mountain (Denver) and Cedar Mountain (Cody), while the spirit of Buffalo Bill was transported symbolically from one mountain to the other on a riderless white horse.

Where was baseball invented?

England.

Baseball (originally base ball) was invented in England and first named and described in 1744 in *A Little Pretty Pocket Book*. The book was very popular in England and was reprinted in America in 1762.

Baseball is not based on rounders, the first description of which didn't appear in print until 1828, in the second edition of *The Boy's Own Book*. The first mention of rounders in the United States is in 1834 in *The Book of Sports* by Robin Carver. He credited *The Boy's Own Book* as his source, but called the game "base ball" or "goal ball."

In the first chapter of *Northanger Abbey*, written in 1796, the young heroine Catherine Morland is described as preferring "cricket, baseball, riding on horseback, and running about the country to books."

The baseball authorities were so paranoid about the non-American origin of the game that in 1907 they carried out a shameless fraud. In a report into the game's origins commissioned by the Major League's executive board, they advanced the story that the game was invented by the Civil War general and hero Abner Doubleday in Cooperstown, New York, in 1839.

A legend was born. Despite the evidence of numerous bat-and-ball games being played all over early Puritan America, and the fact that Doubleday never visited Cooperstown, or ever mentioned baseball in his diaries, it stuck firm in the American psyche. As one wag put it, "Abner Doubleday didn't invent baseball, baseball invented Abner Doubleday."

If any one person should be credited with inventing the

modern U.S. game, it is Alexander Cartwright, a Manhattan bookseller. He had been a volunteer fireman and in 1842 founded the Knickerbocker Baseball Club (after the Knickerbocker Fire Engine Company).

He and other firemen played on a field at Forty-seventh and Twenty-seventh Streets. The rules of the modern game are based on their by-laws and Cartwight was the first to draw a diagram of the diamond-shaped field.

He was finally inducted into the Baseball Hall of Fame in 1938.

What's the only sport invented entirely in the United States?

Basketball.

And although it was invented in the United States, it was actually devised by a Canadian, James Naismith, in 1891—the same year as ping-pong was invented.

Naismith was a P.E. instructor at Springfield College (then the Y.M.C.A. training school) in Springfield, Massachusetts, from 1890 to 1895. He was asked to create a sport that could be played indoors without special new equipment. He is supposed to have thought of the idea as he screwed up sketch after sketch of ideas for games and aimed the balls of paper at his wastepaper basket across the room.

> THE ONLY DIFFERENCE BETWEEN A GOOD SHOT AND A BAD SHOT IS WHETHER IT GOES IN OR NOT.
>
> CHARLES BARKLEY

Initially, players dribbled a soccer ball up and down any old indoor space. Points were earned by landing the ball in a peach basket nailed to a balcony or high on a wall. It was twenty-one years before anyone got around to putting a hole in the bottom of the basket. Until 1912, after every score, someone had to climb a ladder up to the basket or poke the ball out with a long pole.

In 1959, twenty years after his death, James Naismith was inducted into the Basketball Hall of Fame (now called the Naismith Memorial Hall of Fame).

One of the apocryphal reasons given for the success of VHS in becoming the world standard videocassette is that the original Sony Betamax was slightly too short to record an entire basketball game.

What do you call someone from the United States?

Not American, that really irritates the Canadians.

In fact there is no agreed upon right answer. In the United Kingdom, the use of "U.S." as an adjective is common in media and government house styles. In Spanish, *americano* tends to refer to any resident of the Americas; English spoken in Latin America often makes this distinction as well. In the North American Free Trade Agreement (1994), the Canadian French word for an American is given as *étatsunien;* in Spanish it is *estadounidense.* This is clumsy in English. U.S.-American is better, and that's what the Germans tend to use (*US-Amerikaner*).

Some (not all serious) suggestions for a specific English word meaning "citizen of the U.S." have included: Americanite; Colonican; Columbard; Columbian; Fredonian; Statesider; Uessian; United Statesian; United Statesman; USen; Vespuccino; Washingtonian. And Merkin—from the way Americans pronounce "American."

The likely source for *Yankee* is the Dutch name *Janke*, meaning "little Jan" or "little John," dating from the 1680s when the Dutch ran New York. During the Civil War, *yankee* referred only to those loyal to the Union. Now the term carries less emotion—except, of course, for baseball fans. The word *gringo* is widely used in Latin America to mean a U.S. citizen, particularly in

Mexico, though not necessarily in a pejorative way. It's thought to come from the Spanish *griego* (Greek)—hence any foreigner (as in the English "it's all Greek to me").

What was Billy the Kid's real name?

a. William H. Bonney
b. Kid Antrim
c. Henry McCarty
d. Brushy Bill Roberts

Billy the Kid was born Henry McCarty in New York City. William H. Bonney was just one of his aliases, the one he was using when he was sentenced to death.

Born in New York City, his mother, Catherine, was a widow who resettled with Henry and his brother, Joe, in Wichita, Kansas, in 1870. It was a wild place, the center of the cattle trade. "In Wichita," according to a contemporary newspaper, "pistols are as thick as blackberries."

> YOU CAN GET MUCH FURTHER WITH A KIND WORD AND A GUN THAN YOU CAN WITH A KIND WORD ALONE.
>
> AL CAPONE

By November 1870, the town had 175 buildings and a population of nearly 800. Mrs. McCarty was well-known in town for the hand laundry she ran on North Main Street. The family later moved to Santa Fe, New Mexico, where Billy's mother was married to William Antrim, a homesteader.

It was in the deserts of New Mexico that Billy began to rustle cattle and make a name for himself as a gunslinger. By 1879, with perhaps seventeen deaths to his name, he was offered an amnesty by the governor of New Mexico, Lew Wallace, best remembered today as the author of *Ben Hur*, the bestselling American novel of the nineteenth century.

Billy turned himself in, then had second thoughts and broke jail. He was pursued and finally killed by Pat Garrett in 1881, but not before he had sent a series of letters imploring Wallace to honor his promise of an amnesty. They went unacknowledged.

Despite the official death warrant, there were persistent stories that the Kid had survived. In 1903 Wallace's successor as governor of New Mexico had the case reopened to establish whether he had really died and whether he deserved to be pardoned. The investigation was never concluded.

In 1950 a member of Buffalo Bill the bison-killer's Wild West Show known as Brushy Bill Roberts died claiming that he was in fact Billy the Kid.

Billy the Kid is said to be the real-life person who has been most depicted in films; he's portrayed in at least forty-six movies.

Carty/Antrim/Bonney didn't become known as Billy the Kid until the end of the last full year of his life. Until then, he was known, simply, as "the Kid."

What do we have Thomas Crapper to thank for?

a. The manhole cover
b. The bathroom showroom
c. The ballcock
d. The flush toilet

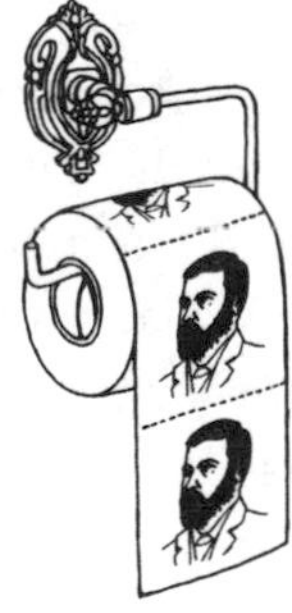

All of them except the last one.

Thomas Crapper (1836–1910) was a London plumber who held nine patents: for manhole covers, drains, pipe joints, and, most notably, the ballcock.

His innovative Chelsea showroom was a big hit, though ladies were said to faint at the sight of the unmentionables on display. Crapper's, on the King's Road, started by his nephew George, only closed in 1966.

Crapper & Co. held four royal warrants. When the Prince of Wales (later Edward VII) bought Sandringham in 1880, they did all the plumbing.

In *Flushed with Pride* (1969), the author Wallace Reyburn claimed Crapper invented the flush toilet, and was knighted and cited in the *Encyclopaedia Britannica*. As any plumber will tell you, none of these things is true.

Though Crapper's "Silent Valveless Waste Water Preventer" was a flush toilet, the patent was not his: it was filed by a Mr. Alfred Giblin in 1819.

The first flush toilet was discovered in China in 2000 in the palace of a king of the Han Dynasty (206 B.C.–A.D. 220). It is a stone latrine with a seat, armrest, and a system of pipes for flushing the pan. Arguably, the first modern WC was invented in 1592 by Sir John Harington, a godson of Queen Elizabeth I.

As for Crapper's surname being the origin of the slang for a lavatory, this is just possible. The word doesn't appear in print until the 1930s. *Crap* dates from 1440, but it meant "chaff" and had fallen out of use by 1600. Victorians would not have understood the word *crapper*, let alone found it funny.

The story goes that English settlers took the word with them to America, where it was vulgarized to its present meaning. When American G.I.s came to Britain during World War I, they found the name Crapper engraved on all the lavatories hilarious, and the name stuck.

Wallace Reyburn went on to publish *Bust-Up: The Uplifting Tale of Otto Titzling* (1971), a ludicrous fiction about the supposed inventor of the bra.

What was Mozart's middle name?

Wolfgang.

His full name was Johann Chrysostomus Wolfgangus Theophilus Mozart. He usually called himself Wolfgang Amade (not Amadeus) or Wolfgang Gottlieb. *Amadeus* is Latin for *Gottlieb* and means "God's love."

Other memorable middle names include Richard Tiffany Gere, Rupert Chawney Brooke, William Cuthbert Faulkner and Harry S. Truman, where the S stands for nothing, despite the period.

Apparently Truman's parents couldn't agree whether he should be named after Anderson *Shipp* Truman or *Solomon* Young, his grandfathers.

For punctuation fiends, we draw your attention to the *Chicago Manual of Style:* "all initials given with a name should for convenience and consistency be followed by a period even if they are not abbreviations of names."

How did Mark Twain get his name?

He stole it.

The usual explanation is that he took the name from the call of the leadsman on a Mississippi paddle boat steamer. "Mark Twain" was the second mark on the leadline used to calculate the river's depth. It indicated a depth of two fathoms (twelve feet), which was "safe water."

This isn't wrong, it's just that someone else had got there first. The name was already being used by Captain Isaiah Sellers (1802–1863), the river news correspondent for the *New Orleans Picayune.*

The young Samuel Longhorn Clemens (1835–1910) cut his teeth writing parodies of Sellers under the pen name Sergeant Fathom. According to Clemens, Sellers was "not of a literary turn or capacity" but was "a fine man, a high-minded man, and greatly respected both ashore and on land." The Sergeant Fathom burlesques mortified him. Clemens later wrote: "He had never been held up to ridicule before; he was sensitive, and he never got over the hurt which I had wantonly and stupidly inflicted upon his dignity."

This didn't stop him from stealing Sellers's pen name, as Twain (Mark II) explained in a letter to a reader:

> *Dear Sir,*
>
> *"Mark Twain" was the* nom de plume *of one Capt. Isaiah Sellers, who used to write river news over it for the* New Orleans Picayune. *He died in 1863, and as he could no longer need that signature, I laid violent hands upon it without asking permission of the proprietor's remains. That is the history of the* nom de plume *I bear.*
>
> *Yours truly,*
> *Samuel L. Clemens*

How did Nome, Alaska, get its name?

a. By mistake
b. To attract good luck: "Nomes" are a type of Alaskan pixie
c. After Sir Horace Nome (1814–72), Scottish explorer
d. After an Inuit greeting: *Nome nome* ("Here you belong")

It was a spelling mistake.

In the 1850s a British ship noted the existence of a prominent but unnamed point of land in Alaska. A ship's officer scribbled "Name?" next to the point on a manuscript map. When the map was being copied at the Admiralty, a cartographer misread the scribble, and wrote in the new point's name as Cape Nome.

In 1899 the burghers of Nome tried to change the name of their town to Anvil City, but the U.S. Postal Service objected on the grounds that it risked confusion with the nearby settlement of Anvik, so the name stuck.

As the city's community website www.nomealaska.org reminds us: "There's no place like Nome."

What is the name of the capital city of Thailand?

Grung Tape.

The city's day-to-day name, which means "City of Angels" (the same as Los Angeles), is an abbreviation for the official name, which is the longest place name in the world.

Only ignorant foreigners call it Bangkok, which hasn't been used in Thailand for more than two hundred years. For Europeans (and every single one of their encyclopedias) to go on calling the capital of Thailand Bangkok is a bit like Thais insisting that the capital of Britain is called Billingsgate or Winchester.

Grung Tape (the rough pronunciation) is usually spelled Krung Thep.

Bangkok was the name of the small fishing port that used to exist before King Rama I moved his capital there in 1782, built a city on the site, and renamed it.

The full official name of Krung Thep is Krungthep Mahanakhon Amorn Rattanakosin Mahintara Yudthaya Mahadilok Pohp Noparat Rajathanee Bureerom Udomrajniwes Mahasatarn Amorn Pimarn Avaltarnsatit Sakatattiya Visanukram Prasit.

In Thai, this is written as a single word of 152 letters or 64 syllables.

It translates roughly as "Great City of Angels, the supreme repository of divine jewels, the great land unconquerable, the grand and prominent realm, the royal and delightful capital city full of nine noble gems, the highest royal dwelling and grand palace, the divine shelter and living place of the reincarnated spirits."

The front part of the name Bangkok is the common Thai word *bang* meaning village. The second part is supposed to have come from an old Thai word *makok*, which means some kind of fruit (either olives or plums or some sort of mixture of the two). So it could be "Village of Olives" or "Village of Plums." Nobody seems to be quite sure which—or to care.

Krung Thep (or Bangkok if you insist) is the only city in Thailand. It is almost forty times bigger than the next largest town.

What's the world's largest city?

a. Mexico City
b. São Paolo
c. Mumbai
d. Honolulu
e. Tokyo

Honolulu, although it's a bit of a trick question.

Under a Hawaiian state law established in 1907, the City and County of Honolulu are one and the same. The county not only includes the rest of the main island of Oahu but also the rest of the northwestern Hawaiian islands, which stretch 1,500 miles into the Pacific.

This means that Honolulu covers the largest area of any city—2,127 square miles—despite only having a population of 876,156. Seventy-two percent of the city is covered in seawater.

The world's most populous city is Mumbai (formerly Bombay), with 12.8 million people living in 170 square miles: an astonishing 75,294 people per square mile. If the whole metropolitan area is included, the most populous city is Tokyo, with 35.2 million living in 5,200 square miles.

Honolulu is the state capital of Hawaii, but it is not on the island of Hawaii. It is on Oahu, which is much smaller but much more densely populated. Hawaii is the most isolated major population center on earth.

The islands of the Hawaiian Archipelago are the projecting tips of the world's biggest mountain range. Hawaii is the only U.S. state that grows coffee. More than a third of the world's pineapples come from Hawaii, and Hawaiians are the world's largest per capita consumers of SPAM, getting through seven million cans a year.

SPAM's popularity is mysterious but is probably due to the heavy U.S. military presence since World War II and the fact that tinned meat is handy during a hurricane. SPAM fried rice is a Hawaiian classic.

Captain Cook discovered the Hawaiian islands in 1778 and renamed them the Sandwich Islands in memory of his patron, the Earl of Sandwich. Cook was murdered on Hawaii in 1779.

By the early nineteenth century the islands were known as the Kingdom of Hawaii. Although it became an American territory in 1900, and the fiftieth state in 1959, Hawaii is the only U.S. state that still uses the Union Jack on their flag.

What's the largest lake in Canada?

Great Bear Lake. None of the five Great Lakes are entirely in Canada.

While both Huron and Superior are larger than Great Bear Lake, neither are wholly inside Canada; Erie and Ontario are neither wholly inside Canada nor bigger than Great Bear Lake; and Lake Michigan, though larger than Great Bear Lake, isn't in Canada at all.

> VERY LITTLE IS KNOWN OF THE CANADIAN COUNTRY SINCE IT IS RARELY VISITED BY ANYONE BUT THE QUEEN AND ILLITERATE SPORTFISHERMEN.
>
> P. J. O'ROURKE

Great Bear Lake, up in the Northwest Territories, is on the same parallel as the Bering Strait and lays partly inside the Arctic Circle. It has a total area of 19,166 square miles, larger than the Canadian portions of Lake Superior, Lake Erie, and Lake Ontario. Despite its relatively low profile, it is the fourth-largest lake in the Americas.

It is also larger than more than seventy of the world's countries, including Albania, Belgium, Israel, Lesotho, and Haiti.

There are somewhere in the region of two million lakes in Canada—no one knows exactly how many—covering about 7.6 percent of the Canadian landmass.

The second-largest lake wholly inside Canada is Great Slave Lake (17,751 square miles), which is also the deepest lake in Canada (2,014 feet).

There are 31,752 lakes with an area of at least one square mile and an uncounted number of smaller ones. One square mile is about 640 acres, which is a pretty big lake: almost seven times the area of Vatican City.

There are so many lakes in the country that naming them seems to have been a bit of a problem. There are 204 Long Lakes and 182 Mud Lakes. Other popular choices are: Lac Long (152), Long Pond (144), Lac Rond (132), Lac à la Truite (109), Round Lake (107), Otter Lake (103), Little Lake (101), Lac Perdu (101), and Moose Lake (100).

What's the single largest man-made structure on earth?

Wrong answers include the Great Pyramid, the Great Wall of China, and (for clever Dicks) Mubarak al-Kabir Tower, Kuwait.

> THERE IS ALWAYS SOMETHING LARGER OR SMALLER.
>
> ANAXAGORAS

Our answer is Fresh Kills, the rubbish dump on Staten Island, New York, though we quite like Jimmy Carr's alternative suggestion—Holland.

Opened in 1948, the Fresh Kills landfill site (named after the Dutch word *kil*, meaning "small river") soon became one of the largest projects in human history, eventually trumping (by volume) the Great Wall of China as the world's largest man-made structure.

The site is 4.6 square miles in area and, when operational, twenty barges, each carrying 650 tons of rubbish, were shipped in every day. Had Fresh Kills continued to stay open as planned, it would have grown to be the highest point on the Eastern Seaboard. At its peak the dump was already more than 80 feet higher than the Statue of Liberty.

Under local pressure, the landfill closed in March 2001, only to be opened again to cope with the enormous amount of debris created by the destruction of the World Trade Center.

It is now completely shut down, and new restrictions mean it can't reopen (no landfill is allowed within New York City limits). The site is currently being flattened and landscaped into parkland and a wildlife facility. Nice.

Arguably, there are structures which are spread across more space—the U.S. Interstate System, perhaps? The Internet? The GPS satellite network?—but the Fresh Kills landfill is the largest single cohesive structure.

Where's the coolest place in the universe?

It's in Finland.

In 2000 a team from Helsinki University of Technology cooled a piece of rhodium to a tenth of a billionth of a degree above absolute zero (–273°C).

Rhodium is a rare metal whose main use is in catalytic converters for cars.

The next coldest spot is in the Massachusetts Institute of Technology. In 2003 a team led by Wolfgang Ketterle produced extremely cool sodium gas.

Ketterle won the Nobel Prize in Physics in 2001 for his work on Bose-Einstein condensate, a new state of matter that only exists close to absolute zero. As a child, his interest in science was sparked by playing with LEGO blocks.

These extremely cold temperatures produced in laboratories are remarkable. Even in deep space, the temperature rarely falls below –245°C.

The only known exception to this is the Boomerang Nebula, identified by Australian astronomers in 1979. It looks like a boomerang (or possibly a bow tie). At its core is a dying star, three times heavier than our own sun.

The Boomerang Nebula has been spraying out gas at a speed of more than 300,000 mph for the last fifteen hundred years. Just as our breath cools when we force it through the narrow hole of our mouths, the gas squeezed out of the nebula is two degrees lower than the space it is expanding into. It reaches –271°C, the lowest natural temperature so far recorded.

The coldest temperature in the solar system, –235°C, measured in 1989 by *Voyager II* on the surface of Triton, one of Neptune's moons, is barely chilly by comparison; and the coldest temperature ever recorded on earth, –89.2°C in Antarctica in 1983, is positively tropical.

Low temperature research is important in the study of superconductors, materials which have zero electrical resistance but which so far have only been found to work at very low temperatures.

If superconductors can be harnessed, they will totally transform the world.

They will massively increase the power of computers while hugely reducing the cost of electricity and the emission of greenhouse gases. They will provide fuel-free transport, an alternative way of seeing inside the human body without the use of dangerous X-rays, and the E-bomb—a weapon which destroys the enemy's electronics without the need to kill anyone.

When did the most recent Ice Age end?

We're still in it.

Geographers define an ice age as a period in the earth's history when there are polar ice caps. Our current climate is an interglacial period. This doesn't mean "between ice ages." It is used to describe the period within an ice age when the ice retreats because of warmer temperatures.

Our interglacial started ten thousand years ago, in what we think is the Fourth Ice Age.

When it will end is anyone's guess; ideas about the duration of the interglacial period range from twelve thousand to fifty thousand years (without allowing for man-made influences).

The causes of the fluctuations are not well understood. Possible factors include the position that the landmasses happen to be in, the composition of the atmosphere, changes in the earth's orbit around the sun and possibly even the sun's own orbit around the galaxy.

The Little Ice Age, which began in 1500 and lasted for three hundred years, saw the average temperature in northern Europe drop by 1°C. It also coincided with a period of extremely low sunspot activity, though whether the two were linked is still being argued over.

During this period, the Arctic ice sheet extended so far south that Eskimos are recorded as reaching Scotland in kayaks on six different occasions, and the inhabitants of Orkney had to fight off a disoriented polar bear.

Recent research at Utrecht University has linked the Little Ice Age with the Black Death.

The catastrophic decline in population across Europe meant that abandoned farmland was gradually covered by millions of trees. This would have led to a significant absorption of carbon dioxide from the atmosphere, forcing the average temperature down in an anti-greenhouse effect.

Who lives in igloos?

Probably no one anymore.

The word *igloo* (or *iglu*) means "house" in Inuit. Most igloos are made of stone or hide.

Snow-block igloos were part of the lifestyle of the Thule, the precursors of the Inuit, and were used until fairly recent history in central and eastern Canada.

But only Canadian Eskimos build igloos from snow. They are completely unknown in Alaska and, according to a 1920s census of fourteen thousand Eskimos living in Greenland, only three hundred had ever seen one. Few remain anywhere today.

The first igloos seen by Europeans were encountered by Martin Frobisher on Baffin Island in 1576 during his search for the Northwest Passage. He was shot in the bottom by an Eskimo. In return, Frobisher's men killed a few Inuit, captured one of them, and took him to London, where he was exhibited like an animal.

In the 1920s, a newspaper in Denver, Colorado, erected a snow igloo at the municipal buildings near where some reindeer were kept, and hired an Alaskan Eskimo to explain to visitors that he and the other reindeer herders of Alaska lived in that type of house when they were at home. In fact, he had never seen one before except in the movies.

In Thule, in northeastern Greenland, by contrast, the locals were such expert igloo builders that they built vast halls of ice for dancing, singing, and wrestling competitions during the long, dark winters.

The community was so remote that, until the start of the nineteenth century, they believed themselves to be the only people in the world. . . .

Would you call someone an Eskimo?

The term *Eskimo* covers a range of distinct groups and is not necessarily (as is sometimes asserted) insulting.

Eskimo describes those who live in the high Arctic regions of Canada, Alaska, and Greenland. Bestowed by Cree and Algonquin Indians, the name has several possible meanings, including "one who speaks another language," "one who is from another country," or "one who eats raw meat."

In Canada (where the politically correct term is *Inuit*), it is regarded as rude to describe someone as an Eskimo but Alaskan Eskimos are perfectly happy about it. In fact, many prefer Eskimo because they are emphatically *not* Inuit, a people who live mainly in northern Canada and parts of Greenland.

To call the Kalaallit in Greenland, the Inuvialuit in Canada, and the Inupiat, Yupiget, Yuplit, and Alutiit in Alaska "Inuit" is like calling all black people "Nigerians," or all white people "German." The Yupik of southwestern Alaska and Siberia don't even know what the word *Inuit* means. As it happens, *Inuit* means "the people"; *Yupik* goes one better: it means "real person."

The languages of the Eskimo-Aleut family are related to one another but to no other languages on earth.

Inuit, which is thriving, is spoken in northern Alaska and Canada as well as in Greenland, where it is now the official language and the one used in schools. Also known as Inupiaq or Inuktitut, it has only three vowels and no adjectives. The Inuit language was banned in the United States for seventy years.

Eskimos buy refrigerators to stop their food from getting too cold and if they need to count to more than twelve, they have to do it in Danish.

They do not rub noses when greeting one another. Most get annoyed at this suggestion. The *kunik* is a sort of affectionate (rather than sexual) snuffling, mostly practiced between mothers and infants but also between spouses.

In some Eskimo languages the words for "kiss" and "smell" are the same.

In 1999 Canadian Eskimos were given one-fifth of the land of Canada (the second largest country in the world) as their own territory. Nunavut is one of the world's newest nation states: it means "our land" in Inuit.

At five to a car, all the Eskimos in the world could park at Los

Angeles International Airport. More people use computers in Iqualuit, capital of Nunavut, than in any other town in Canada. It also has the highest suicide rate of any town in North America.

The average Eskimo is 5 feet 4 inches tall with a life expectancy of thirty-nine years.

How many words do Eskimos have for snow?

No more than four.

It's often said that Eskimos have fifty, one hundred, or even four hundred words for snow, compared to English's one, but this is not so. In the first place, there is more than one English word for snow in various states (ice, slush, crust, sleet, hail, snowflakes, powder, etc.).

Second, most Eskimo groups will admit to only two words equivalent to snow. It seems that out of all of the languages of Eskimo groups, there are no more than four root words for snow altogether.

Eskimo-Aleut tongues are agglutinative languages, in which the word *word* itself is virtually meaningless. Adjectival and verbal bits are added in strings onto basic stems, so that many word clumps are more like our equivalent of sentences. In Inupiaq, *tikit-qaag-mina-it-ni-ga-a* means "he (A) said that he (B) would not be able to arrive first" (literally "to arrive first be able would not said him he").

The number of basic word stems is relatively small but the number of ways of qualifying them is virtually unlimited. Inuit has more than four hundred affixes (bits added at the end or in the middle of stems) but only one prefix. Thus, it has many "derived words" as in the English "anti-dis-establish-ment-arian-ism."

Sometimes these appear to be unnecessarily complicated renderings of what is a simple concept in English. *Nalunaar-asuar-ta-at* ("that by which one communicates habitually in a hurry") is an 1880s Greenlandic coinage for "telegraph."

If you were looking beyond the words for snow for something that really sets Eskimo-Aleut languages apart, it is demonstrative pronouns.

English has only four (*this, that, these,* and *those*). Eskimo-Aleut languages—notably Inupiaq, Yupik, and Aleut—have more than thirty such words. Each of the words for "this" and "that" can take eight different cases, and there is a wealth of ways of expressing distance, direction, height, visibility, and context in a single such demonstrative pronoun.

For example, in Aleut, *bakan* means "that one high up there" (as in a bird in the air), *qakun* is "that one in there" (as in another room), and *uman* means "this one unseen" (i.e., smelled, heard, felt).

What did human beings evolve from?

Not apes. And certainly not monkeys.

Homo sapiens sapiens and apes both evolved from a common ancestor, though this elusive chap has not been found yet. He lived in the Pliocene era, more than five million years ago.

This creature descended from squirrel-like tree-shrews, which in turn evolved from hedgehogs, and before that, starfish.

The latest comparison of genomes of humans and our closest relative, the chimpanzee, shows that we split much later than was previously assumed. This means we quite possibly interbred to produce unrecorded and now extinct hybrid species before the final separation 5.4 million years ago.

Stephen Jay Gould once remarked that *Homo sapiens sapiens* is a recent African twig on the bushy tree of human evolution. While none of the evidence completely rules out the evolution of humans in other locations, the spread of humans from Africa remains the most plausible theory.

Genetic evidence suggests that one of the first populations outside Africa were the Andaman islanders, off the coast of

India. They have been isolated for sixty thousand years—longer even than the Australian aborigines.

> THE MISSING LINK BETWEEN ANIMALS AND THE REAL HUMAN BEING IS MOST LIKELY OURSELVES.
>
> KONRAD LORENZ

There are fewer than four hundred Andamanese left. Half of these belong to two tribes: the Jarawa and the Sentinelese, who have almost no contact with the outside world. So isolated are the one hundred or so Sentinelese that no one has ever studied their language. The other Andamanese languages have no known relatives. They have five numbers: one, two, one more, some more, and all. On the other hand, they have twelve words to describe the different stages of ripeness of fruit, two of which are impossible to translate into English.

The Andamanese are one of only two tribal groups in the world who are not able to make fire (the other are the Ake pygmies of central Africa). Instead they have elaborate procedures for keeping and transporting embers and smouldering logs in clay containers. These have been kept alight for millennia, probably having originated in lightning strikes.

Though this seems strange to us, they have a rather familiar idea of God. Their supreme deity, Puluga, is invisible, eternal, immortal, all-knowing, the creator of everything except evil; he is angered by sin and offers comfort to those in distress. To punish men for their wrongdoing he sent a great flood.

The tsunami of 2004 hit the Andamans with its full force but, as far as we are able to tell, it left its ancient tribes unharmed.

Who coined the phrase "the survival of the fittest"?

Herbert Spencer.

Spencer was an engineer, philosopher, and psychologist, who in his day was as famous as Darwin.

He first coined the phrase "survival of the fittest" in his *Principles of Biology* (1864), having been inspired by Darwin's theory of natural selection.

Darwin paid him the compliment of using it himself in the fifth edition of *The Origin of Species* in 1869, commenting: "I have called this principle, by which each slight variation, if useful, is preserved, by the term *natural selection*, in order to mark its relation to man's power of selection. But the expression often used by Mr. Herbert Spencer, of the Survival of the Fittest, is more accurate, and is sometimes equally convenient."

Herbert Spencer (1820–1903) was the eldest of nine children, all the rest of whom died in infancy. Trained as a civil engineer, he became a philosopher, psychologist, sociologist, economist, and inventor. He sold more than a million books in his lifetime and was the first to apply evolutionary theory to psychology, philosophy, and the study of society.

He also invented the paper clip. The device was called Spencer's Binding Pin and was produced on a modified hook-and-eye machine by a manufacturer called Ackermann whose offices were on the Strand in London.

It did well in its first year, making Spencer £70, but demand dried up, Ackermann shot himself, and the invention had entirely disappeared by 1899 when the Norwegian engineer Johann Vaaler filed his patent for the modern paper clip in Germany.

During World War II, paper clips were an emotive symbol of Norwegian resistance to the German occupation, worn on the lapel in place of the forbidden badges of the exiled King Haakon VII. A giant paper clip was later erected in Oslo in Johann Vaaler's memory.

Today, more than 11 billion paper clips are sold annually, but a recent survey claimed that of every 100,000 sold, only five are actually used to hold papers together. Most are adapted as poker chips, pipe cleaners, safety pins, and toothpicks. The rest are dropped and lost, or bent out of shape during dull or awkward phone calls.

Who invented the ballpoint pen?

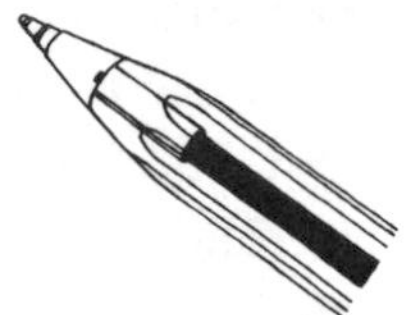

a. Mr. Biro
b. Mr. Bich
c. Mr. Quiet
d. Mr. Loud

Writing was a hazardous activity before the advent of the ballpoint pen. Fountain pens had to be regularly dipped into an ink pot and were prone to leakages, and Indian ink (invented in China) was slow to dry on the page.

These problems were first recognized in a patent registered on October 30, 1888, by a leather tanner named John J. Loud. He created a pen with a small rotating ball for a nib that was constantly fed by an ink reservoir. Although the pen still leaked, it was much more effective for writing on leather than a fountain pen. Loud failed to exploit his patent. If he had, we might be talking about disposable "louds" instead of "biros."

The Hungarian László Biró (1899–1985) originally trained as a doctor but never graduated. He had brief stints as a hypnotist and a racing driver before taking up journalism.

Puzzled by the difference in drying times between newspaper ink and the slow-drying substance in his fountain pen, Biró and his chemist brother, György, fitted a pen with a small ball-bearing which successfully drew down the printing ink as it rotated. The biro was born.

The pair patented the pen in Hungary in 1938 and emigrated to Argentina in 1940 to avoid the Nazis, repatenting it there in 1943. An early customer was the RAF, encouraged by the pen's performance at high altitude. This ensured the name *biro* became synonymous with the ballpoint in Britain.

The first biros sold to the public were manufactured in 1945. At the same time, Biró licensed his pen to Frenchman Marcel Bich.

Bich called his company BiC and, by modifying Biró's design, set up a mass-production process that meant the pens could be sold incredibly cheaply.

BiC remains the world's ballpoint market leader with annual sales of $1.85 billion. In 2005 they sold their 100 billionth pen. The bestselling BiC Cristal sells 14 million units a day.

As a mark of respect to Biró, the Argentines—who call the pens *birome*—celebrate Argentinian Inventors Day on September 29, his birthday.

What do we use to write on a blackboard?

Gypsum.

School chalk is not chalk. Chalk is made of calcium carbonate—as is coral, limestone, marble, the skeletons of humans and fish, the lenses of eyes, the limescale in kettles, and the indigestion pills Rennies, Setlers, and Tums.

Gypsum is made of calcium sulphate. You may think it's a picky distinction but though the two *look* similar they are in fact quite different and are not even made of the same chemical elements.

Many substances that *appear* to be radically different are actually made of exactly the *same* chemical elements. Take carbon, hydrogen, and oxygen. Combined in different proportions, they make stuff as wildly different as testosterone, vanilla, aspirin, cholesterol, glucose, vinegar, and alcohol.

Technically known as hydrated calcium sulphate, gypsum is one of the most widely available minerals in the world. It has been mined for at least four thousand years—the plasterwork inside the Pyramids is made of gypsum—and it is used today in a huge range of industrial processes, the most common of which is ordinary building plaster.

About 75 percent of all gypsum is used for plaster and products such as plasterboard, tiles, and plaster of Paris. Gypsum is a key ingredient of cement and is used in the manufacture of fertilizer, paper, and textiles. A typical new American home contains more than seven tons of gypsum.

Plaster of Paris is so called because there are large deposits of gypsum in the clay soil in and around Paris, especially in Montmartre.

Gypsum also occurs naturally in the form of alabaster, a snow white, translucent material used to make statues, busts, and vases.

Alabaster can be artificially dyed any color and, if heated, can be made to resemble marble. Powdered alabaster made into a salve was traditionally believed to be a cure for bad legs. It was common for people to chip pieces off church statues to make the ointment.

Ironically, the word gypsum comes from the Greek *gypsos*, meaning "chalk."

Where does the equal sign come from?

Wales.

This essential constituent of mathematics wasn't a product of the Greeks, the Babylonians, or the Arabs, but the small coastal town of Tenby, in South Wales. There, in 1510, the astronomer and mathematician Robert Recorde was born. Recorde was a child prodigy who rose to prominence as Royal physician to Edward VI and Queen Mary, and later as controller of the Royal Mint.

He was also a prolific author, writing a sequence of popular math textbooks, of which *The Whetstone of Witte* (1557) is the most famous. Not only did it introduce algebra to an English audience for the first time, but it also introduced the equal sign (=).

Recorde's reason for adopting two parallel lines is refreshingly to the point: "bicause noe 2 thynges, can be moare equalle." It took a while to catch on: "||" and *ae* (from *aequalis*) were used well into the seventeenth century.

One Recorde invention that didn't stick was his word describing numbers to the eighth power, e.g., 2^8=256. *Zenzizenzizenzic* was based on the German *zenzic*, a version of the Italian *censo*, meaning "squared" (so, it means "x squared, squared, and squared again"). It does, however, comfortably hold the record for the number of *z*s in a single word.

Despite his facility with numbers, Recorde was less good with his personal finances. Poor political judgment meant he got on the wrong side of the Earl of Pembroke, who called in a debt for the then astronomical sum of £1,000. This broke Recorde, and he died in the King's Bench debtor's prison in Southwark, aged forty-eight.

What did Robert Bunsen invent?

Many things, but not the Bunsen burner.

Robert Wilhelm Bunsen (1811–99) was an influential German chemist and teacher who devised or improved the design of a number of pieces of laboratory equipment still in use today. However, the item he is most famous for was actually invented by the English chemist Michael Faraday and then improved by Peter Desaga, Bunsen's technician at the University of Heidelberg.

Bunsen first became renowned in the scientific community for his work on arsenic. He eventually discovered the only known antidote to the poison, but not before losing his sight in one eye and almost dying of arsenic poisoning.

He went on to produce a galvanic battery that used a carbon element instead of the much more expensive platinum. Using this he was able to isolate pure chromium, magnesium, aluminum, and other metals. At the same time, he also solved the riddle of how geysers worked by building a working model in his lab.

The need for a new style of burner grew out of his work with a young physicist named Gustav Kirchoff. Together they pioneered the technique that became known as spectroscopy. By filtering light through a prism, they discovered that every element had its own signature spectrum. In order to produce this light by heating different materials, they needed a flame that was very hot but not very bright.

Bunsen developed this new heat source using Faraday's burner as his starting point. In the earlier model, the oxygen was added at the point of combustion, which led to a smoky, flickery flame. Bunsen conceived a burner where oxygen was mixed with gas *before* combustion in order to make a very hot, blue flame. He took his ideas to Desaga, who built the prototype in 1855.

Within five years, Bunsen and Kirchoff had used the combination of their new burner and sceptroscope to identify the elements caesium and rubidium. Their lab became famous, and Bunsen's modesty and eccentricity (he never washed) brought him international renown. Mendeleyev, the Russian inventor of the periodic table, was one of his many devoted pupils.

Although he didn't get to give his name to the burner he built, Desaga did get the rights to sell it, which his family did very successfully (and profitably) for several generations.

Despite its iconic status, the Bunsen burner has now largely been replaced in chemistry labs by the cleaner and safer electric hot plate.

What's made of celluloid?

Ping-Pong balls and collar stiffeners.

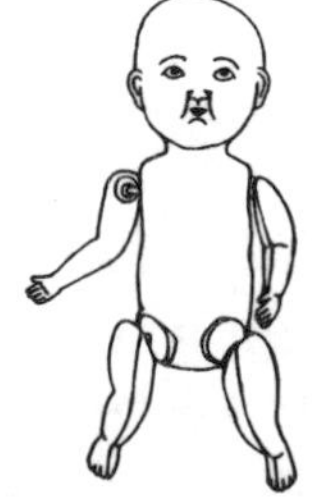

Film isn't made of celluloid anymore. The main ingredient of celluloid is cellulose nitrate; modern film is made from cellulose acetate.

Celluloid is generally regarded as the first plastic. In technical terms, it is a thermoplastic, which means it can be molded each time it is reheated.

It is made from cellulose nitrate and camphor. Cellulose occurs naturally in the cell walls of plants. Camphor comes from the camphor tree and smells distinctively of the mothballs into which it is also made.

Celluloid was first manufactured in Birmingham, England, by Alexander Parkes, who patented it for use in waterproofing clothing in 1856. Another early use was as a cheap ivory substitute: for billiard balls and false teeth.

Celluloid made the movies possible because of its flexibility: Rigid glass plates don't run through projectors. But it is both highly flammable and quick to decompose, so it is difficult to store and is now rarely used.

It has largely been replaced by more stable plastics such as cellulose acetate (made from wood pulp) and polyethylene (a by-product of petroleum).

Cellulose nitrate (or nitrocellulose) was invented by accident in 1846 by Christian Schönbein, the man who, six years earlier, had discovered ozone.

Experimenting in his kitchen with nitric and sulphuric acid, he broke a bottle, wiped up the mess with his wife's cotton apron, and put it on the stove to dry. It immediately burst into flames: Schönbein had discovered the first new explosive since gunpowder was invented by the ancient Chinese.

The new explosive was called *guncotton.* It was smokeless and four times as powerful as gunpowder. Schönbein patented it at once and sold the exclusive manufacturing rights to John Hall and Sons. The next year, it blew up their factory in Faversham, Kent, killing twenty-one people.

Lethal explosions followed in France, Russia, and Germany. It was forty years before a stable use was found for cellulose nitrate, when James Dewar and Frederick Abel created cordite in 1889.

Seven years earlier, Dewar had invented the Thermos flask.

Who invented rubber boots?

a. Amazonian Indians
b. The Duke of Wellington
c. Charles Goodyear
d. Charles Macintosh

Amazonian Indians have been making instant gumboots since time immemorial by standing knee-deep in liquid latex until it dries.

The boots designed for, and named after, the Duke of Wellington in 1817 were made of leather. The first rubber boots didn't appear until 1851, the year before the duke died.

> THE GREATEST OF ALL INVENTORS IS ACCIDENT.
>
> MARK TWAIN

Rubber was a disastrous failure for clothing when first tried, because it either melted all over you in hot weather or set as hard as granite in winter. The breakthrough came in 1839, when Charles Goodyear heated rubber mixed with sulfur and accidentally spilled some on the family stove.

Goodyear's story is inspiring and tragic by turns. He struggled in desperate poverty all his life—six of his twelve children died of malnutrition—but rubber was his obsession, and he never gave up trying to improve the qualities of what he called "vegetable leather."

The process he had inadvertently discovered solved the rubber problem by giving it a stable consistency. In his excitement Goodyear shared his samples with Thomas Hancock and Charles Macintosh, who became successful British rubber merchants.

After analyzing them, they were able to reproduce the process and patented it in 1843, calling it vulcanization, after the Roman god of fire. Goodyear sued unsuccessfully, and not for the first time was forced to spend time in a debtor's prison—or his "hotel" as he liked to call it.

He died, still deep in debt, although widely acclaimed for his vision and perseverance. He once wrote: "Life should not be estimated exclusively by the standard of dollars and cents. I am not disposed to complain that I have planted and others have gathered the fruits. A man has cause for regret only when he sows and no one reaps."

Forty years after he died, his immortality was assured when the founders of the Goodyear Tire Rubber Company, now the world's largest, named their business in his honor. Their 2005 revenues were $19.7 billion.

What Edison invention do English speakers use every day?

The word *hello*.

The first written use of *hello* spelled with an *e* is in a letter of Edison's in August 1877 suggesting that the best way of starting a conversation by telephone was to say "hello" because it "can be heard ten to twenty feet away."

Edison discovered this while testing Alexander Graham Bell's prototype telephone. Bell himself preferred the rather nautical "Ahoy, hoy!"

Edison used to shout "hello!" into telephone receivers at Menlo Park Labs while he was working on improvements to Bell's design. His habit spread to the rest of his coworkers and then to telephone exchanges until it became common usage. Before "hello" was used, telephone operators used to say, "Are you there?" or "Who are you?" or "Are you ready to talk?"

Once "hello" became standard the operators were called "hello girls."

"Hullo" was used at the time purely to express surprise. Charles Dickens used the word in this way in *Oliver Twist* (1839) when the Artful Dodger first notices Oliver with a "Hullo, my covey! What's the row?"

"Halloo" was used to call hounds and ferrymen and was also a favorite word of Edison's. When he first discovered how to record sound (July 18, 1877) the word he shouted into the machine (the strip phonograph) was "Halloo": "I tried the experiment, first on a strip of telegraph paper, and found that the point made an alphabet. I shouted the word 'Halloo! Halloo!' into the mouthpiece, ran the paper back over the steel point and heard a faint 'Halloo! Halloo!' in return! I determined to make a machine that would work accurately, and gave my assistants instructions, telling them what I had discovered."

The earliest recorded use of delegate badges saying "Hello, my name is . . ." was at the first telephone operators' convention in Niagara Falls in 1880.

Was the first computer bug a real insect?

Yes and no.

First, the "yes." In 1947, at Harvard University, the U.S. Navy's Mark II computer, housed in a large unair-conditioned room, was brought to a standstill by a moth getting itself jammed in a relay switch. The operators removed the battered corpse of the insect and taped it next to the entry in the log book before restarting the machine.

The mechanical nature of this computer made it particularly vulnerable to insect interference. Most of the early computers, like ENIAC (Electronic Numerical Integrator and Computer) at the University of Pennsylvania were electronic and used moth-proof vacuum tubes.

But was this the origin of the term *bug*? No. Used to mean an error or fault in a piece of machinery, the word *bug* dates from the nineteenth century. The *OED* cites a newspaper report from 1889, in which Thomas Edison "had been up the two previous nights searching for a bug in his phonograph." Webster's dictionary also gives the modern meaning of *bug* in its 1934 edition.

And regardless of what numerous books and websites say, *de-bugging* was also being used before the moth brought things to a standstill at Harvard.

This is a rather satisfying example of life imitating language: a metaphor that literally came to life.

What is the most likely survivor of a nuclear war?

Cockroaches is the wrong answer.

Quite why so many of us persist in the belief that cockroaches are indestructible is an interesting subject in its own right.

They have been around a lot longer than we have (about 280 million years) and are almost universally hated as hard-to-control carriers of disease. Plus, they can live for a week without their heads. But they aren't invincible and, since the groundbreaking research of Drs. Wharton and Wharton in 1959, we have known they would be one of the *first* insects to die in a nuclear war.

The two scientists exposed a range of insects to varying degrees of radiation (measured in rads). Whereas a human will die at exposure to 1,000 rads, the Whartons concluded that the cockroach dies at a dose of 20,000 rads, a fruit fly dies at a dose of 64,000 rads, while a parasitic wasp dies at a dose of 180,000 rads.

The king of radiation resistance is the bacterium *Deinococcus radiodurans*, which can tolerate a whopping 1.5 million rads, except when frozen, when its tolerance doubles.

The bacterium—fondly known by its students as "Conan the Bacterium"—is pink and smells of rotten cabbage. It was discovered happily growing in a can of irradiated meat.

Since then it's been found to occur naturally in elephant and llama dung, irradiated fish and duck meat, and even in granite from Antarctica.

Conan the Bacterium's resistance to radiation and cold, and its ability to preserve its DNA intact under these extreme conditions, have led NASA scientists to believe it might hold the clue to finding life on Mars.

Which is the hottest part of a chili?

A generation of television chefs have had us believe that the hottest bit of the chili pepper is its seeds. Not so.

It is the central membrane to which the seeds are attached. The membrane contains the highest levels of capsaicin, the colorless, odorless compound that gives chilies their distinctive heat.

Chili heat is measured using the Scoville Scale, created by American pharmacist Wilbur L. Scoville in 1912. In his early tests, Scoville mixed a range of chili extracts dissolved in alcohol and diluted in sugar water. He asked a panel of testers to consume a range of concentrations of various chilies until they ceased to taste hot. A numerical scale was then devised according to the heat of the chilies.

A jalapeño pepper, for example, is said to have 4,500 Scoville Heat Units (SHU), because it has to be diluted 4,500-fold before it loses its heat.

The hottest chili in the world is from Dorset, on the southwest coast of England. Michael and Joy Michaud's Dorset Naga—*naga* is Sanskrit for "serpent"—was grown on a plant from Bangladesh.

It was tested by two American laboratories in 2005, and came in at a palate-torching 923,000 SHU. Even half a small Naga would render a curry inedible, and consuming a whole one would mean a trip to the hospital. Despite this, 250,000 Nagas were sold last year.

To put it in perspective, pure capsaicin powder delivers

15 to 16 million SHU. It is so hot that pharmacists who experiment with it must work in a filtered "tox room" wearing a full protective bodysuit with a closed hood to prevent inhalation.

There are an estimated 3,510 varieties of chili.

Where do tulips come from?

Whether from Amsterdam or elsewhere, tulips are as famous a symbol of Holland as windmills and clogs, but they are not native to the Netherlands.

The natural habitat of the tulip is mountainous terrain.

It was only in 1554 that the first tulips were imported from Constantinople (now Istanbul) into the Netherlands. Wild tulips can be found in southern Europe, North Africa, and parts of Asia up to northeast China. The tulip is the national flower of both Turkey and Iran.

The name of the flower comes from the word *tülbent*, which is the Turkish pronunciation of the Persian word *dulband*, meaning "turban." This is because of what etymologists call a "fancied resemblance" of the shape of the flower when not in full blossom to a turban (or perhaps because the Turks traditionally wore the bloom in their headwear).

Tulips did become exceedingly popular in the Netherlands (as it should be called: "Holland" only describes two of the country's twelve provinces) but the stories of the great "tulipomania" bubble of the early seventeenth century now look rather overcooked.

According to Professor Peter Garber, head of Global Strategy at Deutsche Bank, the most lurid tales of people being ruined by the collapse of tulip prices stem mainly from a single book—*Extraordinary Popular Delusions & the Madness of Crowds*, by Charles Mackay, published in 1852—and were the result of a moralistic campaign by the Dutch government to spread scare stories to discourage tulip speculation.

It's true that the price of tulips was inflated (and that one bulb of the most valuable plants could cost as much as a house) but there are many instances of even higher values being achieved in other countries for other plants, for example, orchids in nineteenth-century England.

At its wildest, Garber says that the Dutch speculation "was a phenomenon lasting one month in the dreary Dutch winter of 1637 . . . and was of no real economic consequence."

Today, the Netherlands produces about three billion tulip bulbs a year, of which two billion are exported.

How many crocuses does it take to make a kilo of saffron?

Between 85,000 and 140,000. Which is why, even today, top-grade Spanish *mancha* saffron can retail at $7,000 per pound.

There are frescoes in Minoan Crete dated to 1600 B.C. showing saffron being gathered. Alexander the Great washed his hair in saffron to keep it a lovely shiny orange color. It was a seriously upmarket shampoo: at that time saffron was as rare as diamonds, and more expensive than gold.

In fifteenth-century Nuremberg and during the reign of Henry VIII in England, adulterating saffron by mixing it with something else was a capital offense. Culprits were burned at the stake or buried alive with their illegal wares.

The town of Saffron Walden in Essex takes its name from the spice: it was the center of the English saffron trade. Legend has it that this dates from the fourteenth century, when a pilgrim from the Middle East arrived with a stolen bulb of a saffron crocus hidden in his stick. Until then, the town was simply called Walden.

Only the arrival of tea, coffee, vanilla, and chocolate saw its cultivation decline, although it remained an important crop in Italy, Spain, and France.

The word saffron comes from the Arabic *asfar*, meaning "yellow."

What drives human sperm wild?

The smell of lily of the valley.

It appears sperm have "noses" which they use to navigate toward a woman's egg. Researchers experimented with a range of floral fragrances and lily of the valley came out on top, getting the random sperm wriggling in the same direction at twice the normal speed.

The research was carried out at Ruhr University in Germany in 2003. They discovered a new sperm protein, hOR17-4, which acted as a receptor for sperm in exactly the same way as protein sensors in the nose detect smells. They then tested their new sperm "nose" on hundreds of synthetic compounds, many of them used to mimic floral scents in commercial perfumes.

One of these, bourgeonal, is used to create the lily of the valley fragrance. It had two dramatic effects on the behavior of sperm: doubling its speed and changing undirected swimming behavior to direct movement. The "foot-to-the-floor" effect seems to derive from hOR17-4 making the sperm wag their "tails" harder.

Bourgeonal is now being used in fertility treatment to pick out the Mark Spitzes of the sperm world.

How many nostrils have you got?

Four. Two you can see; two you can't.

This discovery came from observing how fish breathe. Fish get their oxygen from water. Most of them have two pairs of nostrils, a forward-facing set for letting water in and a pair of "exhaust pipes" for letting it out again.

The question is, if humans evolved from fishes, where did the other pair of nostrils go?

The answer is that they migrated back inside the head to become internal nostrils called *choannae*—Greek for "funnels." These connect to the throat and are what allow us to breathe through our noses.

To do this they somehow had to work their way back through the teeth. This sounds unlikely but scientists in China and Sweden have recently found a fish called *Kenichthys campbelli*—a 395-million-year-old fossil—that shows this process at its halfway stage. The fish has two nostril-like holes between its front teeth.

> TO SEE WHAT IS IN FRONT OF ONE'S NOSE REQUIRES CONSTANT STRUGGLE.
>
> GEORGE ORWELL

Kenichthys campbelli is a direct ancestor of land animals, able to breathe in both air and water. One set of nostrils allowed it to lie in the shallows and eat while the other poked out of the water, a bit like a crocodile's.

Similar gaps between the teeth can also be seen at an early stage of the human embryo. When they fail to join up, the result is a cleft palate. So one ancient fish explains two ancient human mysteries.

The most recent research on noses, incidentally, shows that we use each of our two external nostrils to detect different smells, breathing different amounts of air into each to create a kind of nasal stereo.

What was the first invention to break the sound barrier?

The whip.

Whips were invented in China seven thousand years ago but it wasn't until the invention of high-speed photography in 1927 that the crack of the whip was seen to be a mini sonic boom and not the leather hitting the handle.

The whip's crack is caused by a loop that forms in the whip as you flick it. The loop travels along the length of the whip and, because the leather tapers to a fine tip, the loop speeds up as it travels, reaching more than ten times its original speed. The "crack" is when the loop breaks the sound barrier at about 742 mph.

> LIGHT TRAVELS FASTER THAN SOUND—ISN'T THAT WHY SOME PEOPLE APPEAR BRIGHT UNTIL YOU HEAR THEM SPEAK?
>
> STEVEN WRIGHT

The Bell X1 was the first aircraft to break the sound barrier, piloted by Chuck Yeager in 1947. In 1948 it reached 957 mph at 71,850 feet.

The record for the fastest manned flight is still held by the X-15A, which reached Mach 6.7 (4,520 mph) in 1967. The record altitude was reached in 1963 at 354,200 feet (67 miles).

The fastest any human has ever traveled was on the reentry of *Apollo X* in 1969. This was recorded at 24,791 mph.

What kind of music charms snakes most?

They don't care, it's all the same to them.

Cobras in snake-charming acts are responding to the *sight* of the flute, not its sound.

Snakes don't really "hear" music though they are certainly not deaf. They have no external ears or eardrums, but can sense vibrations transmitted up from the ground into their jaw and the belly muscles. They also seem to be able to detect airborne sounds via an inner ear.

It used to be thought that snakes could not hear at all because they don't respond to loud noises, but research at Princeton has shown that they have acute hearing.

The key discovery was how the snake's inner ear functions.

Snakes were wired to voltmeters and the effect of airborne sound on their brains measured. It appears that their hearing is "tuned" to the frequency range of noises and vibrations made by the movement of larger animals, so music would be meaningless to them.

"Charmed" cobras stand upright if threatened and sway in response to the movement of the instrument. If they strike at the flute, they hurt themselves, so they don't do it again.

Most cobras have had their fangs removed but, even so, they can only strike at a distance within their own length, rather as if you put your elbow on a table and strike downward with your hand.

The cobra's natural attitude is defensive, not aggressive.

What are violin strings made from?

Violin strings are *not* made of catgut, and never have been.

This is a myth started by medieval Italian violin makers who had discovered that sheep intestines made good strings for their instruments. Killing a cat brought terribly bad luck, so they protected their invention by telling everyone else their strings were made from the intestines of cats.

The legend was that a saddle maker called Erasmo, in the Abruzzi mountain village of Salle, near Pescara, heard the wind blowing through the strands of drying sheeps' guts one day and thought that they might make a good string for the early violin known as the renaissance fiddle.

Salle became the center of violin string production for six hundred years and Erasmo was canonized as the patron saint of string makers.

Bad earthquakes in 1905 and 1933 brought an end to the

industry in Salle itself, but two of the world's leading string makers—D'Addario and Mari—are still run by Sallese families.

Until 1750 all violins used sheep's-gut strings. The gut must be removed from the animal when warm, stripped of fat and waste, and soaked in cold water. The best sections are then cut into ribbons and twisted and scraped until a string of the required thickness is made.

Today a combination of gut, nylon, and steel are used, although most aficionados still believe that gut produces the warmest tone.

Richard Wagner circulated a terrible story to discredit Brahms, whom he loathed. He claimed Brahms had received a gift from Czech composer Antonín Dvořák of a "Bohemian sparrow-slaying bow." With this he allegedly took potshots at passing cats from his Viennese apartment window.

Wagner went on: "After spearing the poor brutes, he reeled them into his room after the manner of a trout fisher. Then he eagerly listened to the expiring groans of his victims and carefully jotted down in his notebook their *ante mortem* remarks."

Wagner had never visited Brahms nor seen his apartment; there seems to be no record of such a "sparrow bow" existing, let alone being sent by Dvořák.

Cats tend to die, like most other species, in silence.

Despite this, the rumors of felicide have stuck to Brahms and the claim has been reproduced as fact in several biographies.

What's the best floor of a building to throw a cat from?

Any of them above the seventh floor.

Higher than the seventh floor, it doesn't really matter how far the cat falls, as long as its oxygen holds out.

Like many small animals, cats have a nonfatal terminal

velocity—in cats this is about 60 mph. Once they relax, they orient themselves, spread out, and parachute to earth like a squirrel.

Terminal velocity is the point at which a body's weight equalizes against the resistance of the air and it stops accelerating—in humans it's about 120 mph, reached in free fall at about 1,800 feet.

> CATS ARE INTENDED TO TEACH US THAT NOT EVERYTHING IN NATURE HAS A FUNCTION.
>
> GARRISON KEILLOR

There are cats on record that have fallen thirty stories or more without ill effects. One cat is known to have survived a forty-six-story fall, and there is even evidence of a cat deliberately thrown out of a Cessna aircraft at 800 feet that survived.

A 1987 paper in the *Journal of the American Veterinary Medical Association* studied 132 cases of cats that had fallen out of high-rise windows in New York. On average they fell 5.5 stories. Ninety percent survived, though many suffered serious injuries. The data showed that injuries rose proportionally to the number of stories fallen—up to seven stories. Above seven stories, the number of injuries per cat sharply declined. In other words, the further the cat fell, the better its chances.

The most famous human free falls are Vesna Vulović, who fell 34,777 feet when a terrorist bomb destroyed her Yugoslavian Airlines DC-10 in 1972, and Flight Sergeant Nicholas Alkemade, an RAF tailgunner who leaped from his burning Lancaster in 1944, falling 19,000 feet.

Vulović, broke both legs and suffered some spinal damage, but was saved by the fact that her seat and the toilet booth it was attached to took the impact.

Alkemade's fall was broken by a pine tree and then a snowdrift. He escaped unharmed and remained sitting in the snow, quietly smoking a cigarette.

Why did the dodo die out?

a. Hunted for food
b. Hunted for sport
c. Loss of habitat
d. Competition with other species

The dodo (*Raphus cucullatus*) has the unenviable double distinction as a byword for being both dead and stupid.

A flightless native of Mauritius, it evolved in an environment free of ground-based predators and was wiped out in less than a hundred years by the destruction of its forest habitat and the introduction of pigs, rats, and dogs to the island.

Improbably enough, the dodo was a species of pigeon, but, unlike the other famous extinct fowl, the passenger pigeon, it was not hunted for food, as it was barely edible—the Dutch called it *walgvogel*, the disgusting bird.

The Portugese name *dodo* is also unkind; it means "simpleton" (as in "durrr-durrr"), a reference to the fact that it had no fear of humans so didn't run away, making it of limited value as a sporting bird. It was extinct by 1700.

In 1755 the director of the Ashmolean Museum in Oxford decided that their specimen was too moth-eaten to keep and threw it on a bonfire. It was the only preserved dodo in existence. A passing employee tried to rescue it, but could only save its head and part of one limb.

For a long time, all that was known about the dodo derived from these remains, a handful of descriptions, three or four oil paintings, and a few bones. We knew more about some dinosaurs. In December 2005 a large cache of bones was found on Mauritius which has allowed for a much more accurate reconstruction.

From the time of its extinction until the publication of *Alice in Wonderland* in 1865 the dodo was pretty thoroughly forgotten.

Charles Dodgson (better known as Lewis Carroll) was an Oxford math lecturer who must have seen it in the Ashmolean.

The dodo appears in *Alice in Wonderland* in the Caucus Race, a "race" with no precise start or end, in which everyone gets a prize. Each of the birds corresponds to a member of the boating party present when Dodgson first told the story and the dodo is said to be based on himself.

Sir John Tenniel's illustrations in the book quickly made the bird famous. The phrase "dead as a dodo" also dates from this period.

What buries its head in the sand?

Wrong.

No ostrich has ever been observed to bury its head in the sand. It would suffocate if it did. When danger threatens, ostriches run away like any other sensible animal.

The myth about ostriches may have arisen because they sometimes lie down in their nest (which is a shallow hole in the ground) with their necks stretched out flat and scan the horizon for trouble. If the predator gets too close they get up and leg it. They can run at speeds up to 40 mph for thirty minutes.

The ostrich is the largest bird in the world: a male can reach 9 feet tall, but their brains are the size of a walnut, smaller than their eyeballs.

The ostrich was classified by Linnaeus as *Struthio camelus* or "sparrow camel," presumably because they live in the desert and have long, camel-like necks. The Greek for ostrich was *ho megas strouthos*, "the big sparrow."

The head-burying myth was first reported by the Roman historian Pliny the Elder, who also thought ostriches could hatch their eggs by looking at them aggressively.

He didn't mention their ability to swallow odd things.

As well as the stones they use to aid digestion, ostriches will eat iron, copper, brick, or glass. One ostrich in the London Zoo was found to have eaten a meter-long piece of rope, a spool of film, an alarm clock, a cycle valve, a pencil, a comb, three gloves, a handkerchief, pieces of a gold necklace, a watch, and a number of coins.

Ostriches in Namibia have been known to eat diamonds.

Where do gorillas sleep?

In nests.

These large, muscular primates build new nests every evening (and sometimes after a heavy lunch) either on the ground or in the lower branches of trees.

Aside from the very young, it's strictly one gorilla, one nest.

They aren't works of art—bent branches woven together, with softer foliage as a mattress—and usually take ten minutes to make. Females and young animals prefer to sleep in trees; males, or silverbacks, sleep on the ground.

According to some accounts, lowland gorillas are hygienic and houseproud, whereas mountain gorillas regularly foul their nests and sleep on a mound of their own dung.

Gorillas cannot swim. They have forty-eight chromosomes, two more than people.

More gorillas are eaten by people in the form of bushmeat every year than there are in all the zoos in the world.

What's the most common bird in the world?

The chicken, by miles.

There are about 52 billion chickens in the world: that's almost nine for every human. Seventy-five percent of them will be eaten but, for almost three thousand years, they were farmed primarily for their eggs. Until the Romans came to Britain it had never occurred to anyone to eat the bird itself.

All the chickens in the world are descended from a kind of pheasant called the Red Jungle Fowl (*Gallus gallus gallus*), native to Thailand. Its nearest modern relative is the gamecock used in cockfighting.

Mass production of chickens and eggs started in about 1800. Eating chicken began as a by-product of egg production. Only chickens too old to produce enough eggs were killed and sold for meat. In 1963 chicken meat was still a luxury. It wasn't until the 1970s that it became the meat of choice for most families. Today it accounts for almost half of all meat eaten in the United Kingdom.

As a result of selective breeding and hormone treatment, it now takes less than forty days to grow a chicken to maturity, which is twice as fast as allowing nature to take its course.

Ninety-eight percent of all chickens raised anywhere in the world—even organic ones—come from breeds developed by three American companies. Over half the world's broilers (eating chickens) are Cobb 500s, developed in the 1970s by the Cobb Breeding Co.

There were no chickens at all in the Americas before 1500. They were introduced by the Spanish.

More than a third of all U.K. chicken is produced by one Scottish company, the Grampian Country Foods Group. They supply all the major supermarket chains, and are a major donor to the Conservative Party. They process 3.8 million chickens a week through their eight vast integrated chicken units, one of which is in Thailand. Their motto is "Traditional Goodness."

A HEN IS ONLY AN EGG'S WAY OF MAKING ANOTHER EGG.

SAMUEL BUTLER

Most chickens sold for eating are female. Male ones for eating are castrated cocks and are called capons. Nowadays castration is done chemically with hormones that cause the testicles to atrophy.

The industry term for chicken feet is *paws*. Most of America's paws get exported to China even though three billion chickens already live there.

Danish chickens go "gok-gok"; German chickens go "gak gak"; Thai chickens go "gook gook"; Dutch chickens go "tok tok"; Finnish and Hungarian chickens go "kot kot." The rather superior French hen goes "cotcotcodet."

What animal are the Canary Islands named after?

Dogs. Canary birds are named after the islands (where they are indigenous), not the other way around.

The archipelago gets its name from the Latin name for the largest of the islands, which the Romans named *Insula Canaria* (Isle of Dogs) after the large numbers of dogs there, both wild and domesticated.

The volcano on La Palma in the Canaries is said to have the potential to cause a catastrophic collapse of the western half of the island, creating a tsunami that could cross the Atlantic and hit the Eastern Seaboard of the United States of America eight hours later with a wave as high as ninety-eight feet.

In Canarian Wrestling, participants confront each other in a sand circle called a *terrero;* the aim is to make your opponent touch the sand with any part of his body other than the feet. No hitting is permitted. The sport originated with the Guanches, the islands' pre-Spanish indigenous people.

The *Silbo Gomero* (Gomeran Whistle) is a whistled language used in the Canary island of La Gomera to communicate across its deep valleys. Its speakers are called "silbadors." Although it was originally a Guanche language, it has been adapted so that modern silbadors are, effectively, whistling in Spanish. It's a compulsory subject for Gomeran schoolchildren.

Canaries are a kind of finch. For centuries, British mining regulations required the keeping of a small bird for gas detection. They were used in this way until 1986, and the wording wasn't removed from the regulations until 1995. The idea was that toxic gases like carbon monoxide and methane killed the birds before they injured the miners. Canaries were favored because they sing a lot, so it's noticeable when they go quiet and fall over.

Only the male canaries sing; they can also mimic telephones and other household devices. "Tweety" in the Warner Bros. cartoons is a canary.

Canaries were originally a mottled green-brown, but four hundred years of crossbreeding by human beings produced their familiar yellow color. No one has ever bred a red canary, but a diet of red peppers turns them orange.

London's Isle of Dogs was first so-called on a map dated 1588: perhaps because it was home to the royal kennels, though it may simply have been a term of abuse. It's an odd coincidence that Canary Wharf is located there.

What's the smallest dog in the world?

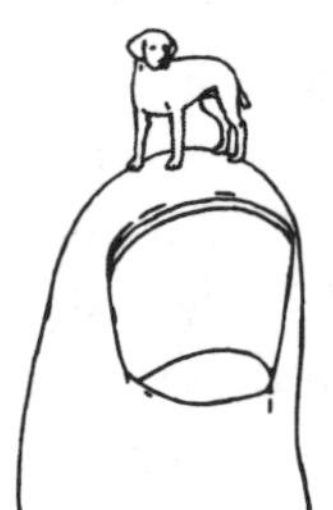

The smallest dog on record was a Yorkshire terrier owned by Arthur Marples of Blackburn. It was 2.5 inches high at the shoulder, 3.75 inches long from the tip of its nose to the root of its tail, weighed 4 ounces, and died in 1945.

The world's smallest breed of dog is usually said to be the chihuahua. Nonetheless, according to the *Guinness Book of World Records*, the record for today's smallest living dog is not necessarily held by one.

It depends what you mean by "smallest." The current record is shared by a chihuahua (shortest in length) and a Yorkshire terrier (shortest in height).

Whitney, the Yorkshire terrier, lives in Shoeburyness, Essex, and is 3 inches tall at the shoulder. The chihuahua, called Danka Kordak Slovakia, is 7.4 inches long and lives in Slovakia.

There are more than four hundred breeds of dog and all are members of the same species. Any dog can breed with any other. No other creature in the world comes in such a wide range of shapes and sizes. No one know why this is.

The unique variety among dogs owes a lot to human intervention, but the puzzle is that all dog breeds are originally descended from gray wolves.

Doberman pinschers were created from German pinschers, Rottweilers, Manchester terriers, and possibly pointers, in just thirty-five years, apparently flying in the face of the Darwinian evolution of species, a process thought to operate over thousands or even millions of years.

For some unknown reason, when dogs are crossbred, instead of getting an average between the two types you quite often get something totally unexpected. This new "breed" also retains the ability to interbreed.

The chihuahua is named after a state in Mexico, because it was believed (on the basis of Toltec and Aztec art) that the breed was indigenous there. However, there are no archaeological remains to support this belief; and it is now thought that the animal depicted is most probably a variety of rodent.

It is much more likely that the ancestors of the breed were brought by Spanish merchants from China, where the practice of dwarfing both plants and animals has had a long history.

Chihuahua cheese is popular in Mexico but it comes from the state, not from the dog.

How do dogs mate?

Dogs mate back to back, not doggy style.

When you see a dog doing the mount-and-pump it's actually performing a dominance gesture. Ejaculation is very rare.

That is why your next-door neighbor's dog seems to choose

children's legs to hump. It isn't primarily sexual: it's establishing its position in the pack and chooses the smallest first.

Dogs actually mate by going in from behind but then getting a leg over so that they end up rear-to-rear. Once this happens the tip of the male dog's penis (called the *bulbus glandis*) engorges with blood, making withdrawal impossible.

This is called "knotting" (as in the expression "get knotted!"). It is designed to minimize semen leakage: a classic example of sperm competition, or keeping other dogs' genetic material out. There's a period of jostling until ejaculation occurs and the penis eventually shrinks so the dogs can separate.

First-timers do sometimes react badly to finding themselves knotted. In these cases the jostling and its accompanying yelps sound much more like fighting than romance.

I WONDER IF OTHER DOGS THINK POODLES ARE MEMBERS OF A WEIRD RELIGIOUS CULT.

RITA RUDNER

How did Catherine the Great die?

Catherine the Great, Empress of all the Russias, died of a stroke, in bed, in 1796, aged sixty-seven.

It's true that when she collapsed from the stroke she was at her *toilette*, but she was cared for thereafter in bed, where she died.

She wasn't crushed by a well-hung stallion being lifted onto her, or through injuries sustained by crushing her chamber pot under her enormous derriere. Nor is there any evidence that she had an especial fondness for horses as a younger woman, except as creatures to ride on.

It isn't clear where these stories come from. It may be a spectacularly successful piece of black propaganda invented by her resentful son, Paul I, whose court was notoriously gossipy. Or it may be the dastardly French, who were at war with a coalition of nations, including Russia, in the years after the Revolution (the stories about Marie Antoinette were even worse).

Wherever it started, it is certainly true that Catherine's behavior created an erotic frisson. She did take many lovers, and it seems some of them were road-tested on her ladies-in-waiting. If they passed, they were given an honorary position and installed at Court.

One of her procurors was a former lover himself—Potemkin, of battleship fame, who died at the age of fifty-two "in consequence of eating a whole goose while in a high state of fever."

Whether her extramarital relationships number just eleven (confirmed by her correspondence) or the 289 cited by scandalmongers, Catherine's more important legacy is in her political and cultural achievements.

She built more of St. Petersburg than Peter the Great himself; sorted out the complexity of Russian law; commissioned magnificent gardens; filled Russian galleries with great European art; introduced smallpox inoculation; and became a patron of writers and philosophers across Europe, including Diderot and Voltaire, who called her "the Star of the North."

Her genetic legacy was less impressive. Her son Czar Paul I (1754–1801) once court-martialed and executed a rat for knocking over his toy soldiers. Later, he had his horse court-martialed and sentenced to fifty lashes. In due course, he was murdered by his own nobles (without trial) and replaced by his son.

How long do your fingernails and hair grow after death?

"For three days after death, hair and fingernails continue to grow but phone calls taper off" was one of the late, great Johnny Carson's best lines.

But hair and fingernails don't grow at all after death. This is a complete myth. When we die, our bodies dehydrate and our skin tightens, creating an illusion of hair and nail growth.

The idea owes a great deal to Erich Maria Remarque's classic novel *All Quiet on the Western Front*, in which the narrator, Paul Bäumer, reflects on the death of his friend Kemmerich: "It strikes me that these nails will continue to grow like lean fantastic cellar-plants long after Kemmerich breathes no more. I see the picture before me. They twist themselves into corkscrews and grow and grow, and with them the hair on the decaying skull, just like grass in a good soil, just like grass. . . ."

Despite this, there is plenty of action after death: your body will positively thrive with life. Bacteria, beetles, mites, and worms will enjoy a feeding frenzy, contributing enormously to the decomposition process.

One of your body's most enthusiastic customers is the hump-backed *phorid*, or "coffin fly." The fly, also known as the scuttle fly because of its awkward flight, is able to live its entire life underground in a corpse.

Scuttle flies are particularly greedy when it comes to human flesh, and it's not uncommon for them to dig nearly 3 feet down through the soil to reach a buried coffin.

One type of phorid, from the genus *Apocephalus*, has recently been deployed in an attempt to control the rampant fire ant populations in the American southeast which were introduced via a Brazilian cargo ship in the 1930s. The flies lay their eggs in the head of the ant. The larvae feed on the contents of the fire ant's head and emerge several days later.

What did Atlas carry on his shoulders?

Not the world but the heavens.

Atlas was condemned to support the sky by Zeus after the Titans revolted against the Olympians. However, he is often shown holding up something that looks like the globe, most famously on the cover of a collection of maps by the Flemish geographer Mercator.

Closer inspection reveals that this globe was, in fact, the heavens, not the earth. Furthermore, Mercator had actually named his volume, not after the Titan, but the mythical philosopher King Atlas of Mauretania (after whom the mountains are named) who was supposed to have produced the first such celestial (as opposed to terrestrial) globe.

The volume became known as *Mercator's Atlas* and the name was applied to any collection of maps thereafter.

Gerard Mercator, the son of a cobbler, was born Gerard Kremer, in 1512. His surname meant "market" in Flemish, so he latinized this to Mercator, meaning "marketeer."

Mercator was the father of modern cartography and arguably the most influential Belgian of all time.

His famous projection of 1569—the first attempt to portray the world accurately with straight lines of latitude and longitude—remains the most persuasive vision of the world for most people. More important, it enabled accurate navigation for the first time, giving the Age of Discovery its scientific basis.

Because of its distortions, Mercator's projection is now rarely used in maps and atlases: in 1989 the leading U.S. cartographic associations asked for it to be eliminated altogether.

Oddly, that hasn't stopped NASA from using it to map Mars.

How high is cloud nine?

According to the International Cloud Atlas scale, cloud zero is the highest type of cloud, known as cirrus, the wispy streaks that can be as high as 40,000 feet.

Cloud nine is the cumulonimbus, the massive, brooding thunder cloud. It's at the bottom of the scale because a single cloud can cover the whole range from as low as a few hundred feet to the very edge of the stratosphere (nearly 50,00 feet).

As with the origins of most phrases, it's unlikely that "cloud nine" can be tied to one specific source. Clouds seven, eight, and thirty-nine have all been recorded, so it seems likely that people settled on nine because it's regarded as a lucky number ("dressed up to the nines" and "the whole nine yards" have equally obscure origins). And the idea of being carried along on a big billowy cloud is undeniably attractive.

The International Cloud Atlas was published in 1896 as a result of the International Meteorological Conference establishing a Cloud Committee to agree an international system for the naming and identification of clouds.

The ten categories were themselves based on the pioneering work of Luke Howard (1772–1864), an English chemist, who published his *Essay on the Modification of Clouds* in 1802.

Howard's work was influenced by his experience of freak weather conditions as a child, when volcanic eruptions in Japan and Iceland in 1783 created a "Great Fogg" which covered much of Europe.

His work inspired the landscape paintings of John Constable, J.M.W. Turner, and Caspar David Friedrich. Goethe wrote four poems in Howard's honor and considered this modest English Quaker to be the "Godfather of Clouds."

Clouds are collections of tiny water droplets or ice crystals held in suspension in the atmosphere. The droplets or crystals are formed by the condensation of water vapor around even smaller particles of things like smoke or salt. These are called condensation nuclei.

Cirrus clouds are the only clouds in the sky made entirely of ice. They are much more common in the atmosphere than was once thought and help to regulate the earth's temperature. They are often triggered by the condensation trails of high-flying jets.

When air traffic was stopped after September 11, 2001, daily temperature variation across the United States grew by up to 3°C over the following forty-eight hours as the cirrus protection shrank: letting more heat out by night and more sunlight in by day.

What makes champagne fizz?

It's not carbon dioxide, it's dirt.

In a perfectly smooth, clean glass, carbon dioxide molecules would evaporate invisibly, so for a long time it was assumed that it was slight imperfections in the glass that enabled the bubbles to form.

However, new photographic techniques have shown that these nicks and grooves are much too small for bubbles to latch on to: it's the microscopic particles of dust and bits of fluff in the glass that enable them to form.

Technically speaking, the dirt/dust/lint in the glass act as condensation nuclei for the dissolved carbon dioxide.

According to Moët et Chandon, there are 250 million bubbles in the average bottle of champagne.

Chekhov's last words were "I haven't had champagne for a long time."

German medical etiquette of the time demanded that when there was no hope, the doctor would offer the patient a glass of champagne.

MY ONLY REGRET IN LIFE IS THAT I DID NOT DRINK MORE CHAMPAGNE.

JOHN MAYNARD KEYNES

What shape is a raindrop?

Raindrops are spherical, not teardrop-shaped.

Ball-bearing and lead-shot makers exploit this property of falling liquids in their manufacturing process: molten lead is dropped through a sieve from a great height into a cooling liquid, and comes out spherical.

Shot-drop towers used to be built for the purpose—until the Festival of Britain in 1951 there was one next to Waterloo Bridge in London.

At just over 234 feet Phoenix Shot Tower in Baltimore (still standing) was the tallest building in America until the Washington Monument surpassed it after the Civil War.

What produces most of the earth's oxygen?

Algae.

They release oxygen as a waste product of photosynthesis. Their net oxygen output is higher than that produced by all the trees and other land-based plants put together.

Ancient algae are also the main constituent of oil and gas. Blue-green algae or cyanobacteria (from Greek *kyanos*–"dark green-blue") is earth's earliest known life form, with fossils that date back 3.6 billion years.

While some algae are included with the plants in the Eukaryote domain (*eu,* "true," and *karyon,* "nut," referring to their cell's having true nuclei, which bacteria don't), the cyanobacteria are now firmly in the Bacteria kingdom with their own phylum.

One form of cyanobacteria, spirulina, yields twenty times more protein per acre than soya beans. It consists of 70 percent protein (compared with beef's 22 percent), 5 percent fat, no cholesterol, and an impressive array of vitamins and minerals. Hence the increasing popularity of the spirulina smoothie.

It also boosts the immune system, particularly the production of protein interferons, the body's front-line defense against viruses and tumour cells.

The nutritional and health benefits of spirulina were recognized centuries ago by the Aztecs, sub-Saharan Africans, and flamingos.

Its significance for the future may be that algae can be grown on land that isn't fertile, using (and recycling) brackish water. It's a crop that doesn't cause soil erosion, requires no fertilizers or pesticides, and refreshes the atmosphere more than anything else that grows.

What were World War I German uniforms made from?

Nettles.

During World War I, both Germany and Austria ran short on supplies of cotton.

In search of a suitable replacement, scientists chanced upon an ingenious solution: mixing very small quantities of cotton with nettles—specifically, the hardy fibers of the stinging nettle (*Urtica dioica*).

Without any form of systematic production, the Germans cultivated 1,413 tons of this material in 1915, and a further 2,976 tons the following year.

After a brief struggle, the British captured two German overalls in 1917, and their construction was analyzed with some surprise.

Nettles have many advantages over cotton for agriculture—cotton needs a lot of watering, it only grows in a warm climate, and requires a lot of pesticide treatment if it is to be grown economically.

There's no danger of being stung by a "full nettle jacket" either, as the stinging hairs—little hypodermic syringes made of silica and filled with poison—are not used in production. The long fibers in the stems are all that are useful.

The Germans were by no means the first to stumble across this plant's many uses. Archaeological remains from around Europe reveal that it's been used for tens of thousands of years for fishing nets, twine, and cloth.

The Bottle Inn, a pub in Marshwood, Dorset, England, holds an annual World Stinging Nettle Eating Championship. Rules are strict: no gloves, no mouth-numbing drugs (other than beer), and no regurgitation.

The trick appears to be to fold the top of the nettle leaf toward you and push it past your lips before swigging it down with ale. A dry mouth, they say, is a sore mouth. The winner is the one who has the longest set of bare stalks at the end of an hour.

The current record is 48 feet for men, and about 26 feet for women.

Who discovered penicillin?

Sir Alexander Fleming is a long way down the list.

Bedouin tribesmen in North Africa have made a healing ointment from the mold on donkey harnesses for more than a thousand years.

In 1897 a young French army doctor called Ernest Duchesne rediscovered this by observing how Arab stable boys used the mold from damp saddles to treat saddle sores.

He conducted thorough research identifying the mold as *Penicillium glaucum*, used it to cure typhoid in guinea pigs, and noted its destructive effect on *E. coli* bacteria. It was the first clinically tested use of what came to be called penicillin.

He sent in the research as his doctoral thesis, urging further study, but the Institut Pasteur didn't even acknowledge receipt of his work, perhaps because he was only twenty-three and a completely unknown student.

Army duties intervened, and he died in obscurity in 1912 of tuberculosis—a disease his own discovery would later help to cure.

Duchesne was posthumously honored in 1949, five years after Sir Alexander Fleming had received a Nobel Prize for his re-rediscovery of the antibiotic effect of penicillin.

> ONE SOMETIMES FINDS WHAT ONE IS NOT LOOKING FOR.
>
> ALEXANDER FLEMING

Fleming coined the word *penicillin* in 1929. He accidentally noticed the antibiotic properties of a mold which he identified as *Penicillium rubrum*. In fact, he got the species wrong. It was correctly identified many years later by Charles Thom as *Penicillium notatum*.

The mold was originally named *Penicillium* because, under a microscope, its spore-bearing arms were thought to look like tiny paintbrushes. The Latin for a writer's paintbrush is *penicillum*, the same word from which *pencil* comes. In fact, what the mold cells of *Penicillium notatum* much more closely and spookily resemble is the hand bones of a human skeleton. There is a picture of it here:

http://botit.botany.wisc.edu/Toms_fungi/nov2003.html.

Stilton, Roquefort, Danish Blue, Gorgonzola, Camembert, Limburger, and Brie all contain penicillin.

Is a virus a germ?

Yes, *germ* is an informal term for any biological agent that causes illness to its host and so covers both viruses and bacteria.

Viruses and bacteria are quite different. Viruses are microscopic parasites too small to have cells or even their own metabolism. Their growth is entirely dependent on their host. Each infected host cell becomes a factory capable of producing thousands of copies of the invading virus. The common cold, smallpox, AIDS, and herpes are viral infections and can be treated by vaccination but not antibiotics.

Bacteria are simple but cellular, the most abundant of all organisms. There are approximately ten thousand species living in or on the human body: a healthy human will be carrying ten times as many bacterial cells as human cells, and they account for about 10 percent of dry body weight. The vast majority are benign, and many are beneficial. Bacterial illnesses include tetanus, typhoid fever, pneumonia, syphilis, cholera, food poisoning, leprosy, and tuberculosis, and they are treatable with antibiotics.

The word *germ* comes from the Latin *germen*, meaning "sprout" or "bud." It was first used to describe a harmful microorganism in 1871 and it wasn't until 1875 that Robert Koch finally demonstrated that anthrax was caused by a particular species of bacteria.

Thirty-five years earlier, Ignaz Semmelweis, a Hungarian doctor, had set up the first hygienic hospital ward in Vienna General Hospital. He noticed that the death rate of poor women attended by the nurse midwives was three times less than that of the wealthier women attended by the doctors. He concluded that this was a matter of cleanliness—the doctors used to go directly from the morgue to the obstetrics ward without washing their hands. When he presented his findings, his fellow doctors rejected his theory, unable to believe in what they could not see.

In recent years, however, hygiene itself has come under scrutiny. There does seem to be evidence that indiscriminate use of antibacterial agents might have damaging side effects, allowing those bacteria that do survive to mutate into even more virulent strains. Also, our immune system, deprived of bacteria and parasites that it has struggled against for thousands of years, has a tendency to overreact, leading to a sharp upswing in allergic diseases such asthma, diabetes, and rheumatoid arthritis.

Despite this, infectious diseases still kill more people than anything else and 80 percent of those diseases are transmitted by touch.

Most hygienists recommend that washing our hands regularly with good old-fashioned soap and water is the best and safest way to stay healthy.

What causes stomach ulcers?

It's not stress or spicy food.

Contrary to decades of medical advice, it turns out that stomach and intestinal ulcers are not caused by stress or lifestyle but by bacteria.

Ulcers are still relatively common, afflicting one in ten people. They are painful and potentially lethal. Napoleon and James Joyce both died from complications connected with stomach ulcers.

In the early 1980s, two Australian pathologists, Barry Marshall and Robin Warren, noticed that a previously unidentified bacterium colonized the bottom part of the stomachs of people who suffered from gastritis or ulcers. They cultivated it, gave it a name (*Helicobacter pylori*), and began to run trials. They found that when the bacteria were eliminated, the ulcers healed.

Even today, most people still think that ulcers are caused by stress. The medical explanation was that stress diverted blood from the stomach, which reduced the production of its protective mucus lining. This gradually left the tissue beneath vulnerable to stomach acid and the result was an ulcer.

What Marshall and Warren were proposing—that a common physiological condition, akin to a blister or a bruise, might actually be an infectious disease—was unprecedented in modern medicine.

Marshall decided to become his own experiment. He drank a Petri dish full of the bacteria, and soon came down with a severe case of gastritis. He tested himself for the bacteria—his stomach was teeming with them—and then cured himself with a course of antibiotics. The medical establishment had been proved wrong.

In 2005 Marshall and Warren were rewarded for their tenacity and vision, winning the Nobel Prize in Physiology or Medicine.

Helicobacter pylori is present in half the human population, and in almost everyone in developing countries. It is usually contracted in early childhood and can stay in the stomach for life. It only leads to ulcers in 10 to 15 percent of those infected.

We still don't know why this should be, but we do know how to treat it.

What are guinea pigs used for?

Lunch.

Guinea pigs, or cavies, are almost never used for vivisection these days, but Peruvians consume an estimated 65 million of them each year. They are also eaten in Colombia, Bolivia, and Ecuador. The best bits are the cheeks, apparently.

Ninety-nine percent of laboratory animals are mice and rats, and more rabbits and chickens are used as "guinea pigs" than guinea pigs are.

Rats and mice are easier to manipulate genetically and can be made to model a greater range of human conditions than guinea pigs, which were much more popular victims of medical research in the nineteenth century. In 1890 the antitoxin for diphtheria was discovered using guinea pigs; it saved the lives of millions of children.

One area where they are still used today is in the study of anaphylactic shock. They are also useful in nutritional research because guinea pigs are the only mammals (apart from primates) that cannot synthesize their own vitamin C and have to absorb it through their food.

Ordinary guinea pigs weigh on average one half to one and a half pounds, but researchers at La Molina National University in Peru have developed guinea pigs that weigh more than two pounds, which they hope will catch on in the export market. The meat is low in fat and cholesterol and tastes like rabbit.

In Peru, the animals are kept in the kitchen because of the ancient Andean belief that they need smoke, and folk doctors in the Andes use guinea pigs to detect illness in people—they believe that when the rodent is pressed against a sick person, it will squeak when near the source of disease. In the cathedral of the city of Cuzco, Peru, there's a painting of the Last Supper in which Jesus and the disciples are shown about to eat roast guinea pig.

In 2003, archaeologists in Venezuela discovered the fossilized remains of a huge guinea pig–like creature that lived eight million years ago. *Phoberomys pattersoni* was the size of a cow and weighed fourteen hundred times more than the average pet guinea pig.

Nobody really knows where the expression "guinea pig" comes from but the most likely suggestion was that they reached Europe as part of the triangle slave trade routes that linked South America to the Guinea coast of West Africa.

What was the first animal in space?

The fruit fly.

The tiny astronauts were loaded on to an American V2 rocket along with some corn seeds, and blasted into space in July 1946. They were used to test the effects of exposure to radiation at high altitudes.

Fruit flies are a lab favorite. Three-quarters of known human disease genes have a match in the genetic code of fruit flies. They also go to sleep every night, react in a similar way to general anaesthetics and, best of all, reproduce very quickly. You can have a whole new generation in a fortnight.

Space is defined as starting at an altitude of 62 miles. After fruit flies, we sent first moss, then monkeys.

The first monkey in space was Albert II in 1949, reaching 83 miles. His predecessor, Albert I, had suffocated to death a year earlier, before reaching the 62-mile barrier. Unfortunately, Albert II also died, when the parachute on his capsule failed on landing.

It took until 1951 for a monkey to return safely from space, when Albert VI and his eleven mice companions managed it (although he died two hours later).

Generally, pioneering space monkeys were not distinguished by their longevity, with the honorable exception of Baker, the squirrel monkey, who survived his 1959 mission by twenty-five years.

The Russians preferred dogs. The first animal in orbit was Laika on *Sputnik 2* (1957), who died of heat stress during the flight. At least ten more dogs were launched into space before the first man, Yuri Gagarin, made it up there in 1961. Six of the dogs survived.

> SPACE ISN'T REMOTE AT ALL. IT'S ONLY AN HOUR'S DRIVE AWAY IF YOUR CAR COULD GO STRAIGHT UPWARDS.
>
> FRED HOYLER

The Russians also sent the first animal into deep space in 1968. It was a Horsefield's tortoise, and it became the first living creature to orbit the moon (as well as the world's fastest tortoise).

Other animals in space have included chimps (who all survived), guinea pigs, frogs, rats, cats, wasps, beetles, spiders, and a very hardy fish called the mummichog. The first Japanese animals in space were ten newts in 1985.

The only survivors of the *Columbia* space-shuttle disaster in 2003 were some nematode worms from the shuttle's lab found among the debris.

Which has the most neck bones: a mouse or a giraffe?

They both have seven neck vertebrae, as do all mammals except for manatees and sloths.

Because two-toed sloths have only six neck vertebrae, they find it hard to turn their heads.

Birds, who need to turn their heads a lot to preen, have many more neck vertebrae than mammals. Owls have fourteen; ducks, sixteen; but the record holder is the mute swan, with twenty-five.

Owls can't turn their head 360°, as some people claim, but

they do manage 270°. This is made possible by the extra vertebrae and specialized muscles that allow the bones to move independently of one another.

It compensates for the fact that owls can't move their eyes. If they want to change their view, they have to swivel their head.

An owl's eyes are forward-facing to increase their binocular vision, which is the ability to see things in three dimensions. This is essential for hunting at night. Their eyes are also very large, to capture as much light as possible. If we had eyes on the same scale, they'd be the size of grapefruits.

Owls' eyes are tubular rather than spherical to create an even larger retina. A tawny owl's eyes are one hundred times more sensitive to light than ours. They can still see a mouse on the ground if the light level is reduced to a single candle 500 yards away.

Who was the first man to circumnavigate the globe?

Henry the Black.

An unfamiliar name to almost everyone, Enrique de Malaca was Magellan's slave and interpreter.

Ferdinand Magellan himself never completed his circumnavigation. He was killed in the Philippines in 1521, when he was only halfway around.

Magellan first visited the Far East in 1511, arriving from Portugal across the Indian Ocean. He found Henry the Black in a slave market in Malaysia in 1511 and took him back to Lisbon the way he had come.

Henry accompanied Magellan on all his subsequent voyages, including the around-the-world attempt, which set off in 1519. This went in the other direction, across the Atlantic and the Pacific oceans, so when it arrived in the Far East in 1521, Henry became the first man to have been around the world.

No one knows where Henry the Black was born—he was

probably captured and sold into slavery by Sumatran pirates as a child—but when he arrived in the Philippines, he found the locals spoke his native language.

After Magellan's death, the expedition continued on its way, successfully completing the circumnavigation under Juan Sebastián Elcano, the Basque second-in-command.

Henry the Black was not with them. Elcano had refused to honor the promise made in Magellan's will to release Henry from slavery, so he escaped and was never seen again.

Juan Sebastián Elcano gets the credit for being the first man to travel around the world in a single trip.

He returned to Seville in September 1522. Five ships had set sail four years earlier but only the *Victoria* made it back. It was full of spices, but just eighteen of the original crew of 264 had survived: scurvy, malnutrition, and skirmishes with indigenous peoples had accounted for the rest.

The Spanish king awarded Elcano a coat of arms depicting the globe and carrying the motto "You first circumnavigated me."

Henry the Black is a national hero in several Southeast Asian nations.

Who was the first to claim that the earth goes around the sun?

Aristarchus of Samos, born 310 B.C., a whole eighteen hundred years before Copernicus.

Not only did Aristarchus suggest the earth and planets traveled around the sun, he also calculated the relative sizes and distances of the earth, moon, and sun and worked out that the heavens were not a celestial sphere, but a universe of almost infinite size. But no one paid much attention.

Aristarchus was most famous in his lifetime as a mathematician not an astronomer. We don't know much about him, except that he studied at the Lyceum at Alexandria and is later mentioned by the Roman architect Vitruvius as a man who was "knowledgeable across all branches of science." He also invented a hemispherical sundial.

Only one of his works has survived, *On the Sizes and Distances of the Sun and Moon.* Unfortunately, it doesn't mention his sun-centered theory. The reason we know about it at all is due to a single remark in one of Archimedes' texts, which mentions Aristarchus' theories only to disagree with them.

Copernicus was certainly aware of Aristarchus because he credits him in the manuscript of his epoch-making *On the Revolutions of the Heavenly Spheres.* However, when the book was printed in 1514, all mentions of the visionary Greek had been removed, presumably by the publisher, nervous of it undermining the book's claims for originality.

Who invented the Theory of Relativity?

It wasn't Einstein. The theory of relativity was first stated by Galileo Galilei in his *Dialogue Concerning the World's Two Chief Systems* in 1632.

To understand relativity we need to understand the theory that it replaced. This was the theory of absolute rest postulated by Aristotle in the fourth century B.C. which stated that rest was the natural state of any object and that an object would return to this state if left to its own devices.

The theory of relativity says that the motion of all objects is relative to the motion of each other, and that to define one as being "at rest" is simply a matter of convention. It follows from this that the speed of an object cannot be stated absolutely—only as relative to something else.

Galileo, the Italian astronomer and philosopher, was also one of the founders of modern physics. He is most famous for his support of the Copernican (or Aristarchan) theory, that the earth went around the sun.

The Catholic Church rounded smartly on him, but Galileo did not rot in a rat-infested cell for his principles. He began his sentence in the luxurious home of the Archbishop of Siena before being taken back to a comfortable house arrest in his villa near Florence. It wasn't until 1992 that the Catholic Church finally admitted that Galileo's views on the solar system were correct.

While Galileo may have been right about this, he was perfectly capable of making mistakes: his favorite argument for a moving earth was that this movement caused the tides. He observed that the Mediterranean is more tidal than the Red Sea, and attributed this to the water being sloshed about by the earth's spin—which he said acted more strongly on the Mediterranean because it is aligned East–West.

This argument was refuted by the eyewitness testimony of seafarers, who pointed out that there were two tides a day, not one as Galileo had assumed. Galileo refused to believe them.

Albert Einstein realized that Galileo had also made a mistake in his theory of relativity, or rather that the theory broke down in special circumstances.

Einstein's 1905 work, *On the Electrodynamics of Moving Bodies,* was the first to talk about the Special Theory of Relativity, which describes the strange properties of particles moving at close to the speed of light in a vacuum.

The General Theory of Relativity, which applied the special theory to large-scale phenomena like gravity, was published ten years later in 1915.

What shape did Columbus think the earth was?

a. Flat
b. Round
c. Pear-shaped
d. An oblate spheroid

Columbus himself never said the world was round—he thought it was pear-shaped and about a quarter of its actual size.

Despite his later reputation, his voyage of 1492 wasn't intended to discover a new continent but to prove that Asia was much closer than anyone imagined. He was wrong.

Columbus never actually set foot on mainland America—the closest he came was the Bahamas (probably the small island of Plana Cays)—but made his crew swear an oath that, if asked, they would say they'd reached India. He died in Valladolid in 1506 and remained convinced to the end that he'd reached the coast of Asia.

There is a remarkable degree of uncertainty about Columbus. Most of the evidence points to him being the son of a Genoese weaver called Domenico Columbo, but there are enough inconsistencies for him to be claimed as Sephardic Jewish, Spanish, Corsican, Portuguese, Catalan, or even Greek.

He spoke the Genovese dialect (not Italian) as his first tongue and learned to read and write in Spanish (with a marked Portuguese accent) and Latin. He even wrote a secret diary in Greek.

We don't know what he looked like, as no authentic portrait survives, but his son claimed he was blond until the age of thirty, whereupon his hair turned completely white.

We don't even know where he is buried. We do know his corpse had its flesh removed, as was the style for the great and the good in the sixteenth century, and that his bones were interred first in Valladolid, then in the Carthusian monastery in Seville, then in Santa Domingo,

THE FACT THAT SOME GENIUSES WERE LAUGHED AT DOES NOT IMPLY THAT ALL WHO ARE LAUGHED AT ARE GENIUSES. THEY LAUGHED AT COLUMBUS, THEY LAUGHED AT FULTON, THEY LAUGHED AT THE WRIGHT BROTHERS. BUT THEY ALSO LAUGHED AT BOZO THE CLOWN.

CARL SAGAN

Cuba, then Havana, then, and apparently finally, in Seville Cathedral in 1898.

However, a casket with his name on it remains in Santa Domingo, and now Genoa and Pavia have also made competing claims to hold bits of him. DNA tests are under way, but it seems likely that the final resting place of Columbus—or Columbo, or Colón (as he preferred)—will remain as contentious as the rest of his life and achievements.

What shape did medieval people think the earth was?

Not what you think.

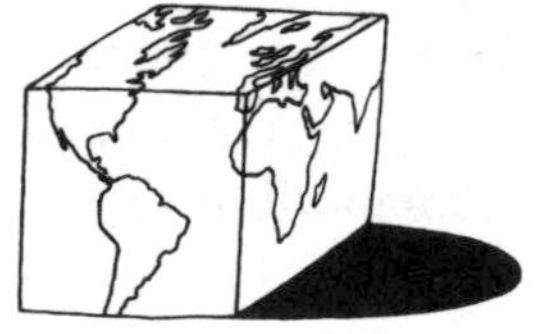

Since around the fourth century B.C. almost no one, anywhere, has believed that the earth is flat. However, if you did want to show the earth as a flat disc, you'd end up with something very similar to the United Nations flag.

Belief in a flat earth may not even have actually originated until the nineteenth century. The guilty text was Washington Irving's semifictional *The Life and Voyages of Christopher Columbus* (1828), which incorrectly suggests that Columbus's voyage was made to prove the world was round.

The idea of a flat earth was first seriously put forward in 1838 by the eccentric Englishman Samuel Birley Rowbotham, who published a sixteen-page paper entitled: "Zetetic Astronomy: A Description of Several Experiments Which Prove That the Surface of the Sea Is a Perfect Plane and That the Earth Is Not a Globe" ("Zetetic" derives from the Greek *zetein,* meaning "to search, or inquire").

More than a century later, a member of the Royal Astronomical Society and devout Christian named Samuel Shenton rebranded the Universal Zetetic Society as the International Flat Earth Society.

The NASA space program of the 1960s, culminating in the lunar landings, should have buried the issue. But Shenton was undeterred. Looking at photographs of a spherical earth taken from space, he commented: "It's easy to see how a photograph like that could fool the untrained eye." The *Apollo* landings were, apparently, a Hollywood hoax, scripted by Arthur C. Clarke. Membership shot up.

Shenton died in 1971 but not before choosing his successor as president of the society. The odd but charismatic Charles K. Johnson took over and made the society a rallying point for a heroic, homespun anti–Big Science movement. By the early 1990s, membership had surged to more than thirty-five hundred.

Johnson, who lived and worked in the vast flatness of the Mojave Desert, proposed a world in which we live on a disc, with the North Pole at its center, surrounded by a 150-foot-high perimeter wall of ice. The sun and moon are both 32 miles in diameter, and the stars are "about as far away as San Francisco is from Boston."

Johnson's desert hideaway burned down in 1995, destroying all the society's archives and membership lists. Johnson died in 2001, by which time the society had shrunk to a few hundred members. It exists today solely as a Web forum, www.the-flatearthsociety.org, with around eight hundred registered users.

Who first discovered that the world was round?

Not who, what. Bees worked it out first.

Honeybees have evolved a complex language to tell one another where the best nectar is, using the sun as a reference point. Amazingly, they can also do this on overcast days and at night, by calculating the position of the sun *on the other side of the world.* This means they can actually learn and store information, despite having a brain 1.5 million times smaller than our own.

A bee's brain has about 950,000 neurons. A human brain has between 100 and 200 billion.

Honeybees have an in-built "map" of the sun's movements across the sky over twenty-four hours and can modify this map to fit local conditions very quickly—all decisions about where to fly are made within five seconds.

The honeybee is also more sensitive to the earth's magnetic field than any other creature. They use this for navigation and for making the honeycomb panels of their hives. If a strong magnet is put next to a hive under construction, a strange cylindrical comb results, unlike anything found in nature.

The temperature of a beehive is the same as that of a human body.

Bees evolved about 150 million years ago in the Cretaceous period, roughly at the same time as flowering plants. The honeybee family, *Apis*, didn't appear until 25 million years ago. They are really a form of vegetarian wasp.

Bees smell with their antennae. Queen honeybees give off a chemical called queen-substance, which prevents worker bees developing ovaries.

It takes the entire lifetimes of twelve bees to make enough honey to fill a teaspoon. Bees will travel as much as 7.5 miles per trip, several times a day. A single bee would have to travel about 46,600 miles to make a pound of honey, which is almost twice around the world.

Why do bees buzz?

To communicate.

Bees use their buzzing much as they use their movements, or "dancing": to pass on information. Ten distinct sounds have been identified, and some have been linked to specific activities.

The most obvious of these uses is fanning, to cool the hive. It is loud and steady at about 250 beats per second, and is amplified by the hive itself. Bees also buzz more loudly to signal danger (anyone who has approached a hive will have noticed the change in tone) followed by a sequence of 500 beats per second pulses to sound the all clear and calm the hive.

The queen bee has a particularly rich range of sounds. When a new queen hatches she makes a high-pitched chirrup called "piping" or "tooting." Her sisters (still curled up inside their cells) answer with a croaklike call called "quarking." This is a big mistake: there can only be one queen. Using the quarks as a guide, the hatched queen picks each off in turn, tearing open their cells and either stinging them to death or ripping their heads off.

Bees use their legs to hear: sound "messages" in the hive are communicated through the intensity of the vibration. However, recent research into bees' antennae suggest that as well as the chemical receptors they use to smell, the antennae are covered in eardrumlike plates, which might be ears.

This would explain why other workers touch the dancing bee's thorax with their antennae rather than the waggling abdomen during the "waggle dance"—they are hearing the directions to the nectar rather than seeing them. After all, it's dark in a hive.

How bees buzz is more controversial. Until recently, the main theory was that they used the fourteen breathing holes along their sides (called "spiracles") rather as a trumpeter controls the sound of his instrument with his lips.

Entomologists at the University of California have ruled out this theory by carefully blocking the spiracles. The bees still buzzed.

The latest hypothesis is that buzzing is partly caused by the vibration of the wings, with some amplification from the thorax. Clipping a bee's wings doesn't stop the buzzing, though it does change its timbre and intensity.

Which has the largest brain in comparison to its size?

a. Elephants
b. Dolphins
c. Ants
d. Humans

> ANTS ARE SO MUCH LIKE HUMAN BEINGS AS TO BE AN EMBARRASSMENT. THEY FARM FUNGI, RAISE APHIDS AS LIVESTOCK, LAUNCH ARMIES INTO WAR, USE CHEMICAL SPRAYS TO ALARM AND CONFUSE ENEMIES, CAPTURE SLAVES, ENGAGE IN CHILD LABOR, EXCHANGE INFORMATION CEASELESSLY. THEY DO EVERTHING BUT WATCH TELEVISION.
>
> LEWIS THOMAS

The ant.

An ant's brain is about 6 percent of its total body weight–if we were to apply the same percentage to humans, our heads would have to be nearly three times as large, making us all look rather like the Mekon or Morrissey.

An average human brain weighs 3.5 pounds, which is a little more than 2 percent of body weight. An ant's brain weighs approximately 0.3 milligrams.

Although an ant's brain has only a fraction of the neurons of a human brain, a colony of ants is a superorganism. An average-sized nest of forty thousand ants has about the same number of brain cells as a person.

Ants have been around for 130 million years and there are about 10,000 trillion of them at large as we speak. The total mass of ants on the planet is slightly heavier than the total mass of human beings.

There are about eight thousand known species of ant. Ants account for about 1 percent of all the insects on earth. The total number of insects in the world has been calculated at one quintillion (or 1,000,000,000,000,000,000).

Ants sleep for only a few minutes a day and can survive for nineteen days underwater. A wood ant can manage for twenty-four days without its head. A single ant cannot live alone outside the colony, head on or not.

Ants appear to have photographic memories to help them navigate. They seem to take a series of snapshots of landmarks. Scientists do not understand how ants' tiny brains can store so much information.

Ants are not stronger than people. Though ants can lift many times their own weight, this is only because they are small. The smaller an animal is, the stronger its muscles are in relation to its body mass. If people were the same size as ants, they would be equally strong.

How much of our brains do we use?

One hundred percent.

Or 3 percent.

It's commonly said we only use 10 percent of our brain. This usually leads to discussions of what we might do if only we could harness the other 90 percent.

In fact, all of the human brain is used at one time or another. On the other hand, a recent paper by Peter Lennie of the New York University Center for Neural Science indicates that the brain should ideally have no more than 3 percent of neurons firing at any one time, otherwise the energy needed to "reset" each neuron after it fires becomes too much for the brain to handle.

The central nervous system consists of the brain and the spinal cord and is made of two kinds of cells: neurons and glia.

Neurons are the basic information processors, receiving input and sending output between one another. Input arrives through the neuron's branchlike dendrites; output leaves through the cablelike axons.

Each neuron may have as many as ten thousand dendrites, but it only has one axon. The axon may be thousands of times longer than the tiny cell body of the neuron itself. The largest axon in a giraffe is 15 feet long.

Synapses are the junctions between axons and dendrites, where electrical impulses are turned into chemical signals. The synapses are like switches, linking neurons to one another and making the brain into a network.

Glia cells provide the structural framework of the brain; they manage the neurons and provide a housekeeping function, removing debris after neurons die. There are fifty times more glia than neurons in the brain.

There are about three million miles of axons, one quadrillion (1,000,000,000,000,000) synapses, and up to 200 billion neurons in a single human brain. If the neurons were spread out side by side they would cover nearly 30,000 square yards: the size of four football fields.

The number of ways information is exchangeable in the brain is greater than the number of atoms in the universe. With such astonishing potential, whatever percentage of our brains we use, we could all, clearly, do a little better.

What color is your brain?

So long as you're alive, it's pink. The color comes from the blood vessels. Without fresh oxygenated blood (as when it's removed from the body) the human brain appears gray.

To confuse things, about 40 percent of the living brain is made of so-called gray matter and 60 percent of white matter. These terms are not accurate descriptions of the colors you see, but thinly sliced, and in section, they are clearly two different kinds of brain tissue.

Using brain scans, we have begun to understand what functions they each perform. Gray matter contains the cells where the actual processing of information is done. It consumes about 94 percent of the oxygen used by the brain.

The white matter is a fatty protein called *myelin*, which sheathes and insulates the dendrites and axons that extend out from the cells. It is the brain's communication network, linking different parts of the gray matter together and linking the gray matter to the rest of the body.

A good analogy is the computer. The gray matter is a processor, the white matter is the wiring. What we call intelligence requires both to work together at high speed.

Now it gets even more interesting. Recent studies at the Universities of California and New Mexico scanned the brains of men and women with identical IQs. The results were surprising: the men had six and a half times more gray matter than women, and women had nearly ten times more white matter than men.

The women's white matter was found in a high concentration in the frontal lobes, whereas the men had none. This is significant, as the frontal lobes are believed to play a key role in emotional control, personality, and judgment.

So, all the various "Mars and Venus" theories of gender difference might soon find a physiological justification. Men's and women's brains do seem to be differently wired and configured. The output (intelligence) is the same, but the way it is produced is very different.

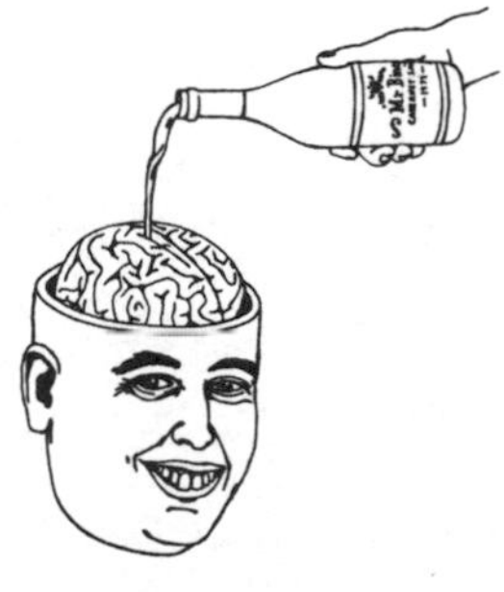

What effect does alcohol have on brain cells?

Good news. Alcohol doesn't kill brain cells. It just makes new cells grow less quickly.

The idea that alcohol destroys brain cells dates back at least as far as the temperance campaigners of the early nineteenth century, who wanted all alcoholic drinks banned. It has no basis in scientific fact.

Samples from alcoholics and nonalcoholics show no significant difference in either the overall number or the density of neurons between the two groups. Many other studies have shown that moderate drinking can in fact help cognition. A study in Sweden showed that *more* brain cells are grown in mice that are given alcohol.

Alcohol abuse does cause serious damage, not least to the brain, but there is no evidence that these problems are to do with the death of cells—it's more likely that alcohol interferes with the working processes of the brain.

A hangover comes from the brain shrinking due to dehydration, causing the brain to tug on its covering membrane. It's the membrane which is sore. The brain itself feels nothing, even if you stick a knife in it.

The philtrum is the vertical groove on your upper lip that nobody knows the word for. It allows you to drink beer from the bottle by letting the air in.

If you were to open a beer can in zero gravity all the beer would come out at once and float around in spherical droplets.

Astronomers have recently discovered a massive amount of alcohol in our region of the Milky Way. The giant cloud of methanol measures 288 billion miles across. Although the alcohol we like to drink is grain alcohol (otherwise known as ethyl alcohol or ethanol) and methanol would poison us, the discovery goes some way to supporting the theory that the universe is here so that we can drink it.

WHAT IS SAID WHEN DRUNK HAS BEEN THOUGHT OUT BEFOREHAND.

FLEMISH PROVERB

What do dolphins drink?

They don't drink at all.

Dolphins are like animals in a desert, without any access to fresh water. They get liquid from their food (which is mainly fish and squid) and by burning their body fat, which releases water.

Dolphins are whales—the killer whale is the largest member of the dolphin family. Their name is a reversal of the original Spanish, *asesina-ballenas*, meaning "whale killer." They were so called because packs of them sometimes hunt and kill much larger whales.

Pliny the Elder didn't help their reputation. According to him, an orca "cannot be properly depicted or described except as an enormous mass of flesh armed with savage teeth."

Dolphins have up to 260 teeth, more than any other mammal. Despite this, they swallow fish whole. Their teeth are used solely to grasp prey.

Dolphins sleep by shutting down one half of their brain and the opposite eye at a time. The other half of the brain stays awake, while the other eye watches out for predators and obstacles, and remembers to go to the surface to breathe. Two hours later, the sides flip. This procedure is called "logging."

Dolphins have been working for the U.S. Navy since the Vietnam War, where they saw extensive service. The U.S. Navy currently employs about a hundred dolphins and thirty other assorted sea mammals. Six sea lions have recently been posted to join the Task Force in Iraq.

After Hurricane Katrina, a story circulated that thirty-six U.S. Navy–trained attack dolphins had escaped and were roaming the sea armed with toxic dart guns. The story seems to have been a hoax; apart from anything else, military dolphins aren't trained for attack, only for finding things.

What was James Bond's favorite drink?

Not the vodka martini.

A painstaking study at www.atomicmartinis.com of Fleming's complete oeuvre has shown that James Bond consumed a drink, on average, every seven pages.

Of the 317 drinks consumed in total, his preferred tipple was whisky by a long margin—he drinks 101 in all, among them fifty-eight bourbons and thirty-eight Scotches. He's pretty fond of champagne (thirty glasses), and in one book, *You Only Live Twice* (1964), which is mostly set in Japan, Bond tries sake. He likes it: he has thirty-five of them.

Bond only opts for his supposed favorite, vodka martini, nineteen times, and he drinks almost as many gin martinis (sixteen—though most of these are bought for him by other people).

The famous "shaken, not stirred" line appears for the first time in *Diamonds Are Forever* (1956) but isn't used by Bond himself until *Dr. No* (1959). Sean Connery was the first screen Bond to utter "shaken, not shtirred," in *Goldfinger* (1964), and it occurs in most of the films thereafter. In 2005 the American Film Institute voted it the ninetieth greatest movie quote of all time.

James Bond's personal martini recipe, taken from the first book, *Casino Royale* (1953), is: "Three measures of Gordon's, one of vodka, half a measure of Kina Lillet. Shake it very well until it's ice cold, then add a large thin slice of lemon peel."

This is the only time he drinks a gin and vodka mix. He calls it the Vesper, after Vesper Lynd, the double agent and love interest in the novel. She is also the girl who drinks most in all the novels and stories.

Why does Bond insist on shaken martinis? Strictly speaking, a shaken gin martini is called a Bradford. Purists frown on them because the intake of air caused by the shaking oxidizes—or "bruises"—the aromatic flavorings in the gin. But there's no such problem with vodka, and the action of shaking makes the drink colder and sharper.

Ian Fleming himself preferred his martinis shaken, and made with gin. On his doctor's orders he switched from drinking gin to bourbon later in life, which may explain his hero's predilection. Fleming and Bond were both men who knew what they liked.

What shouldn't you drink if you're dehydrated?

Alcohol is fine. So are tea and coffee.

Virtually any fluid will help to hydrate you, although you should steer clear of seawater.

There's no scientific basis for the curious idea that fluids other than water cause dehydration. As a diuretic (something that makes you pass water), caffeine does cause a loss of water, but only a fraction of what you're adding by drinking the coffee. Tea, coffee, squash, and milk for children are all equally good at replacing fluids.

Ron Maughan, professor of Human Physiology at the University of Aberdeen Medical School, has looked at the effects of alcohol, considered to be another diuretic, and found that, in moderation, it too has little impact on the average person's state of fluid balance.

His results, published in the *Journal of Applied Physiology*, showed that alcoholic drinks with an alcohol content of less than 4 percent, such as light beer and lager, can be used to stave off dehydration.

Seawater, on the other hand, is an emetic, so, if you drink it, you'll throw up. If you do manage to keep any of it down, then all the water in your body's cells will move toward the highly concentrated salty fluid, by osmosis, in an attempt to dilute it.

This will leave your cells dehydrated, and in severe cases can lead to spasms, the breakdown of brain functions, and liver and kidney failure.

What contains the most caffeine: a cup of tea or a cup of coffee?

A cup of coffee.

Dry tea leaves contain a higher proportion of caffeine by weight than coffee beans. But an average *cup* of coffee contains about three times as much caffeine as an average cup of tea, because more beans are needed to make it.

The amount of caffeine in coffee and tea depends on several factors. The higher the temperature of the water, the greater the caffeine extracted from beans or leaves. Espresso, which is made with pressurized steam, contains more caffeine, drop for drop, than brewed coffee. The amount of time that water is in contact with coffee beans or tea leaves affects the caffeine content. Longer contact equals higher levels of caffeine.

> IF THIS IS COFFEE, PLEASE BRING ME SOME TEA; IF THIS IS TEA, PLEASE BRING ME SOME COFFEE.
>
> ABRAHAM LINCOLN

Also important are the variety of coffee or tea, where it is grown, and the roast of the coffee and cut of the tea leaf.

The darker the roast of coffee, the lower the caffeine content. With tea, the tips of the plant contain a higher concentration than the larger leaves.

Paradoxically, an average 1 fluid ounce of espresso contains about the same amount of caffeine as a 5 fluid ounces cup of Liptons. So a single-shot cappuccino or latte won't give you much more of a caffeine hit than a cuppa. A cup of instant coffee, on the other hand, contains only half the caffeine of a filter coffee.

Why was the dishwasher invented?

Not to make doing the dishes easier.

Its main purpose was to reduce the number of breakages caused by servants, rather than to act as a labor-saving device.

The first practical mechanical dishwasher was invented in 1886 by Josephine Garis Cochran (1839–1913) of Shelbyville, Illinois. She was the daughter of a civil engineer and, on her mother's side, the great-granddaughter of John "Crazy" Fitch, the inventor of the steamboat. A prominent socialite, married to a merchant and politician, her main problem in life was worrying about the maids chipping her precious china (it had been in the family since the seventeenth century).

This enraged her and, so the story goes, one night she dismissed the servants, did the dishes on her own, saw what an impossible job it was, and vowed, if no one else would, to invent a machine to do it instead. When her husband, William, died in 1883, leaving her in debt, she got serious.

With the help of an engineer friend, she designed the machine in her woodshed. It was crude and cumbersome but effective. There was a smal foot-pedal-driven version and a large steam-driven one. The latter, able to wash and dry two hundred dishes in two minutes, was the sensation of the 1893 Chicago World's Fair, and won first prize for the "best mechanical construction for durability and adaptation to its line of work." At $250 each, however, the machines were too expensive for home use, but enough were sold to hotels and restaurants to keep *Cochran's Crescent Washing Machine Company* in business until her death in 1913.

Other mechanical dishwashers had been developed (and patented) in the United States between 1850 and 1865 (all of them, it seems, by women) but none of them really worked. A hand-cranked wooden machine was invented and patented in 1850 by Joel Houghton. In 1870 Mary Hobson obtained a

> HOUSEWORK CAN KILL YOU, IF YOU DO IT RIGHT.
>
> ERMA BOMBECK

dishwasher patent, but even then it contained the word "improved." The electric dishwasher first appeared in 1912; the first specialized dishwasher detergent (Calgon), in 1932; the first automatic dishwasher, in 1940, but it didn't reach Europe until 1960.

How was Teflon discovered?

Despite persistent claims to the contrary, Teflon was not discovered as a by-product of the space program.

Teflon is the trade name of polytetrafluoroethylene (PTFE), or fluoropolymer resin, discovered serendipitously by Roy Plunkett in 1938 and first sold commercially in 1946.

While experimenting with chlorofluorocarbons (CFCs) used in refrigeration, Plunkett found that a sample had frozen overnight into a whitish, waxy solid with unusual properties: it was extremely slippery as well as inert to virtually all chemicals, including highly corrosive acids.

His employers, DuPont, soon found a range of uses for the new material, initially in the Manhattan Project (the code name for the development of nuclear weapons in 1942–46) and subsequently in cookware.

No one has been able to find a precise source for the space program myth, except that the *Apollo* missions all depended on Teflon for cable insulation.

Other myths about Teflon include the belief that Teflon-coated bullets are better at piercing body armor than other kinds; actually the Teflon coating is there to reduce the amount of wear on the inside of the rifle barrel, and has no bearing on the effectiveness of the bullet.

Teflon does, however, have the lowest friction rating of any known solid material, which is why it works so well as a non-stick surface for frying pans.

If it's so slippery, how do they get it to stick to the pan? The process involves sandblasting to create tiny scratches on the pan's surface, then spraying on a thin coat of liquid Teflon, which flows into the scratches. This is baked at high heat, causing the Teflon to harden and get a reasonably secure mechanical grip. It's then coated with a sealant and baked again.

Which organization invented Quaker Oats?

Not the Quakers.

The Quaker Oats Company, started in Pennsylvania in 1901, was named after the Quakers because there were a lot of them in Pennsylvania and they had a reputation for honesty.

However, Quaker Oats, now part of the huge PepsiCo corporation, has no affiliation at all with the Quakers (or Religious Society of Friends) and, unlike the chocolate companies Cadbury's, Fry's, and Rowntree, was not founded by Quakers, or established on Quaker principles.

This has caused some distress among the Society of Friends.

In the 1950s researchers from Quaker Oats, Harvard University, and the Massachusetts Institute of Technology conducted experiments to try to understand how nutrients from cereals traveled through the body.

Parents of educationally subnormal children at the Walter E. Fernald State School (formerly known as the Massachusetts School for Idiotic Children) were asked to let their children become members of a special science club. As part of the club, the children were put on a diet high in nutrients and taken to baseball games.

What was not made clear, however, was that the food the children were given was laced with iron and radioactive calcium so its path could be traced in the body. The parents sued the Quaker Oats Company, who agreed to pay out $1.85 million to more than one hundred participants in 1997.

The cheery character on the front of the box is sometimes said to be William Penn, the founder of Pennsylvania in 1682, and an influential Quaker. The Quaker Oats Company, perhaps wishing to improve relations with the Society, has emphatically denied this.

It was painted by Haddon Sundblom in 1957, the artist who also created Coca-Cola's iconic Santa Claus images in the 1930s. Sundblom's last commission was a Christmas cover for *Playboy* in the early 1970s.

It is often alleged that the Society of Friends got the nickname "Quakers" following the trial for blasphemy in 1650 of George Fox, the founder of the movement, who suggested during sentencing that the judge should "tremble at the word of the Lord." However, the sect already had the reputation for "trembling" in religious ecstasy, and this seems a more likely source.

What shouldn't you do twenty minutes after eating?

Swim, is the answer your parents would have given, but there's no evidence that normal swimming after normal eating is risky.

Swimming pools are not particularly dangerous places—according to government statistics you are much more likely to injure yourself taking off a pair of tights, chopping vegetables, walking the dog, or pruning the hedge.

> THE CHIEF DANGER IN LIFE IS THAT YOU MAY TAKE TOO MANY PRECAUTIONS.
>
> ALFRED ADLER

And keep well clear of cotton swabs, cardboard boxes, vegetables, aromatherapy kits, and loofahs. All of these things are becoming more dangerous.

The idea behind the popular injunction against swimming after eating—frequently posted at pools to this day—is that blood will be diverted from other muscles to the stomach to assist in digesting food, leaving your limbs with insufficient blood, thus leading to paralyzing cramps. (In less sophisticated versions, the weight of the food in your gut sinks you.)

Even if you overeat before swimming, the most likely result is a stitch in the side or a touch of nausea. There is nothing intrinsically dangerous about the combination of food and water.

A greater risk is dehydration from not drinking, or weakness caused by fasting.

On the other hand, the Royal Society for the Prevention of Accidents (RoSPA) advocates common sense, arguing that there's at least a theoretical risk of regurgitation, which might be more dangerous in water than on land.

The 2002 RoSPA report revealed the following causes of accidents for one year in the United Kingdom:

Sneakers	71,309
Tights	12,003
Cardboard boxes	10,492
Indoor swimming pools	8,795
Cotton swabs	8,751
Trousers	8,455
Twigs	8,193
Aromatherapy	1,301
Loofahs and sponges	942

How does television damage your health?

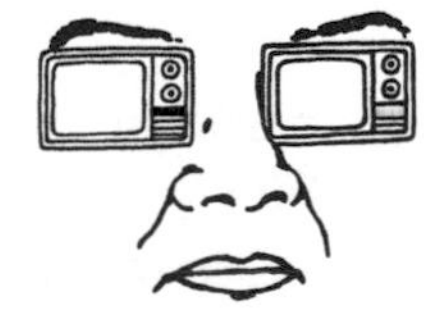

Not by sitting too close to one.

Until the late 1960s, cathode-ray-tube television sets emitted extremely low levels of ultraviolet radiation, and viewers were advised to sit no nearer than six feet from them.

Children were at greatest risk. Their eyes are so good at accommodating changes in distance that they were able to sit and watch at a much closer range than most adults.

Almost forty years ago, the Radiation Control for Health & Safety Act compelled all manufacturers to use leaded glass for their cathode-ray tubes, rendering television sets perfectly safe.

The real damage caused by television is the lazy lifestyle it creates. Obesity rates among children in the United Kingdom have tripled in the last twenty years, and this has been linked to television. The average U.K. child aged between three and nine years old spends fourteen hours a week watching television and just over an hour playing sport or doing outdoor activities.

A 2004 study in the journal *Pediatrics* concluded that children who watched two to three hours' television a day had a 30 percent higher chance of developing attention deficit disorder (ADD).

In 2005 the research company Nielsen revealed that the average U.S. home tuned in to eight hours of television per day. This is 12.5 percent higher than ten years ago, and the highest level since television viewing figures were first measured in the 1950s.

The American Academy of Pediatrics estimates that by the time they reach the age of seventy, Americans will have spent an average of eight whole years watching television.

How much sleep should you have every night?

It is, apparently, dangerous to have eight hours' sleep a night.

Adults who sleep eight hours a night or more die younger than those who sleep only six to seven hours a night.

A six-year study involving 1.1 million people published by Professor Daniel Kripke at the University of California in 2004 showed that a significantly larger number of people who slept eight or more hours (or less than four hours) a night died during the six-year study.

The average Briton gets between six and seven hours' sleep a night, which is one and a half hours less every night than our grandparents did. In 1900 a normal night's sleep was nine hours.

There is evidence to suggest that sleep deprivation leads to short-term loss of IQ, memory, and the ability to reason.

Leonardo da Vinci spent almost half his life asleep. Like Einstein, he took short naps during the day, in his case fifteen minutes every four hours. The great lexicographer Dr. Johnson rarely got up before noon. The French philosopher Pascal also spent much of his day dozing in bed.

On the other hand, the famously long-lived elephant sleeps for only two hours a day. Koalas sleep for twenty-two hours a day but only live ten years. Ants, as noted earlier, sleep for only a few minutes a day.

The average person takes seven minutes to fall asleep. Normal healthy sleepers wake up between fifteen and thirty-five times every night.

There are currently eighty-four recognized sleep disorders, including insomnia, excessive snoring, narcolepsy (falling asleep during the day), apnea (ceasing to breathe while asleep), and restless leg syndrome. The United Kingdom has twenty-five sleep clinics, all of which are overwhelmed with patients.

Twenty percent of all U.K. motorway accidents are caused by drivers falling asleep. The best way to stop this happening is to trap a lock of your hair in the sunroof.

The second-best way is to eat an apple. This stimulates digestion and provides slow-release energy, which is more effective than the short-term hit of coffee.

What will be the biggest killer in the world by 2030?

a. Tuberculosis
b. AIDS
c. Malaria
d. Tobacco
e. Murder

According to the World Health Organization, tobacco is currently the second major cause of death in the world. It is responsible for the death of one in ten adults worldwide, about five million deaths each year, while cancer is currently killing seven million people a year.

If figures continue to rise at current levels, tobacco—and a range of smoking-related diseases—will become the world's biggest killer by 2030, killing ten million people a year.

Around 1.3 billion people are regular smokers. Half of them—that is, 650 million people—will eventually be killed by tobacco.

Developing countries will suffer the most. Eighty-four percent of smokers currently reside in middle- to low-income countries, where smoking has been steadily on the increase since 1970.

In contrast, smoking levels among men from the United States declined from 55 percent in the 1950s to 28 percent in the 1990s. In the Middle East—where half the adult males smoke—tobacco consumption increased 24 percent between 1990 and 1997.

The economic consequences of smoking in the developing world are just as disastrous as the implications for health. In places like Niger, Vietnam, and Bangladesh, impoverished households are spending one-third more on tobacco products than on food.

It was not until the late 1940s that modern science linked disease to tobacco and, in the United Kingdom, it wasn't until the Royal College of Physicians report in 1964 that the government fully accepted the link between smoking and cancer. It was another seven years before warnings appeared on cigarette packets.

Despite thirty years of mounting evidence, one in four U.K. adults (13 million people) continue to smoke regularly (although 70 percent of those are trying to give up).

In 2004 the Himalayan Kingdom of Bhutan not only banned smoking in public, but also banned tobacco sales, the first country ever to do so.

Is the answer to depression just to "walk it off"?

Yes. It's at least as effective as drugs.

Recent research involving subjects aged twenty-four to forty-five found that half an hour's exercise three to five times a week has the same (or better) effect on depression than drugs, regularly reducing symptoms by nearly 50 percent.

According to *Science News*, placebos are more effective at curing depression than either drugs or herbal remedies. In a series of trials carried out between 1979 and 1996, Seattle psychiatrist Dr. Arif Khan found that St. John's Wort completely cured 24 percent of cases, the antidepressant drug Zoloft cured 25 percent of cases, but the sugar-pill placebos effected a complete cure in 32 percent of patients.

In a more recent study comparing the antidepressants Prozac and Efexor with placebos, the drugs won with a 52 percent cure rate, but the placebos still scored impressively with 38 percent. But as soon as the deception was revealed, the patients' condition worsened rapidly.

I GOT THE BLUES THINKING OF THE FUTURE, SO I LEFT OFF AND MADE SOME MARMALADE. IT'S AMAZING HOW IT CHEERS ONE UP TO SHRED ORANGES AND SCRUB THE FLOOR.

D. H. LAWRENCE

Many commentators believe that the context of the treatment—a clinical trial with lots of professional attention being paid to the participants—was an important factor. The conclusion seems to be that a combination of drugs and personal care produces the quickest and longest-lasting cure.

Meditation also seems to work. In a research project involving Tibetan monks recommended by the Dalai Lama, Richard Davidson, professor of neuroscience at the University of Wisconsin–Madison, asked the monks to meditate on "unconditional loving-kindness and compassion."

The result was an extraordinary pattern of gamma brainwaves, usually very difficult to detect. The implication seems to be that, if trained to do so, the brain can produce its own dopamine—the chemical whose lack causes depression.

Using drugs leads your brain to stop producing its own dopamine almost completely.

By training yourself to be positive you can make yourself cheerful again. This may also be why placebos work: belief is a powerful thing.

Which country has the world's highest suicide rate?

Lithuania, which in 2003 boasted an astonishing 42 suicides per 100,000 of population. This is more than 1,500 people: more than are killed by traffic accidents and twice as many as a decade ago.

To put it in an international context, Lithuanian suicides outstrip the British figure by six to one, the United States' by five to one, and are almost three times the world average. Nobody knows why, but it is interesting that seven of the top ten suicide nations are Baltic states or other former members of the Soviet Union. Perhaps it's because Lithuania also has the world's highest density of neurologists.

Across the world, including the Baltic, the people most likely to commit suicide are men (young and old) living in rural areas.

This makes sense: anyone who's spent time on a struggling farm knows that alcohol, isolation, debt, the weather, and the inability to ask for help (known by psychologists as "helpless male" syndrome), combined with proximity to firearms and dangerous chemicals, make a lethal combination.

The exceptions are China and southern India, where young women in rural areas are most at risk. The respective rates are 30 and 148 per 100,000. In China this is thought to be because young brides are often left isolated by their new husbands, who immediately leave to work in the city. In India, self-immolation accounts for a third of all suicides by teenage girls.

Suicide, generally, is on the rise—accounting for a million deaths a year, or one every forty seconds. That's half of all violent deaths: more people now kill themselves than die in wars.

On the other hand, Sweden, for a long time plagued with the "so boring, everyone kills themselves" tag, is no longer even in the top twenty.

The precise historical basis of the Swedish suicide myth is lost in the fog of postwar reconstruction, but many Swedes blame Dwight D. Eisenhower, president of the United States (1953–61), who used their (at that time) high suicide rate to undermine the cheerful, dangerously anticapitalist egalitarianism of Swedish social democracy.

Was Hitler a vegetarian?

No.

It's a good story. The twentieth century's worst dictator, with the blood of tens of millions on his hands, was too fastidious, or sentimental, or cranky to eat meat. It's regularly trotted out—illogically—as a good argument against vegetarianism. Unfortunately, it's not true.

Various biographers, including those who knew the dictator intimately, record his passion for Bavarian sausages, game pie, and (according to his chef) stuffed pigeon.

He was, however, plagued by chronic flatulence, for which his doctors regularly recommended a vegetarian diet (a remedy that will surprise many vegetarians). He also received regular injections of a high-protein serum derived from pulverized bull's testicles. That's a long way from a mushroom timbale or lentil bake.

There is no evidence in his speeches or writings that he was ideologically sympathetic to vegetarianism, and not one of his lieutenants was a veggie. In fact, he was far more likely to have criminalized vegetarians along with Esperanto speakers, conscientious objectors, and other detested "internationalists."

Nor was he an atheist. Here he is in full, unambiguous flow in *Mein Kampf* (1925): "I am convinced that I am acting as the agent of our Creator. By fighting off the Jews, I am doing the Lord's work." He was to use the same form of words in a Reichstag speech in 1938.

Three years later he told General Gerhart Engel: "I am now, as before, a Catholic and will always remain so."

Far from being a godless state, Nazi Germany enthusiastically worked with the Catholic Church. Infantry soldiers each wore a belt with *Gott mit uns* (God is with us) inscribed on the buckle, and blessings of troops and equipment were regular and widespread.

Which nation invented the concentration camp?

If you still think it's Germany, you must have been living in a cave.

The usual answer is Britain, because of their use of internment camps for families in the Second Boer War of 1899–1902.

In actuality, the concept is Spanish. In their struggle to retain Cuba in 1895, they first came up with the idea of "concentrating" civilians in one place to make them easier to control. That struggle ended in defeat for Spain, and their troops began to withdraw from the island in 1898. The United States stepped into the vacuum, exerting a military influence on the island until Castro's revolution of 1959.

The British translated the Spanish term, *reconcentratión*, when faced with a similar situation in South Africa. The camps had been made necessary by the British policy of burning down Boer farms. This created a large number of refugees. The British decided to round up all the women and children left behind by the Boer troops, to stop them resupplying the enemy.

In total, there were forty-five tented camps for Boer women and children and sixty-four for black African farm laborers and their families.

Despite the humane intentions, conditions in the camps quickly degenerated. There was very little food, and disease spread rapidly. By 1902, 28,000 Boers (including 22,000 children) and 20,000 Africans had died in the camps—twice as many as the soldiers killed in the fighting.

Shortly after this, the Germans also established their first concentration camps in their attempts to colonize Southwest Africa (now Namibia).

Men, women, and children of the Herero and Namaqua peoples were arrested, imprisoned, and forced to work in camps. Between 1904 and 1907, 100,000 Africans—80 percent of the Herero and 50 percent of the Namaqua—died through violence or starvation.

The U.N. now considers this the first genocide of the twentieth century.

In what year did World War II end?

In 1990.

Although actual hostilities came to an end with the Japanese surrender signed on September 2, 1945, the cold war got in the way of a fomal legal settlement. Peace treaties were signed with Italy, Romania, Hungary, Bulgaria, and Finland in 1950. All the Allies except the U.S.S.R. signed a treaty with Japan in 1951. Austria waited until 1955 to regain its sovereignty. Germany, however, was divided between the Western powers and the U.S.S.R., and no peace treaty was signed with what emerged as the German Democratic Republic in 1949.

So, the first celebration of German reunification, on October 3, 1990, marks the official end to World War II.

The United States has formally declared war just eleven times: twice against Germany, twice against Hungary (1917, in its guise as Austria-Hungary, and 1942) and once each against Romania (1942), Bulgaria (1942), Italy (1941), Japan (1941), Spain (1898), Mexico (1898), and the United Kingdom (1812).

The Vietnam War and the two Iraq campaigns were not formal declarations of war, but "military engagements authorized by Congress." Under the 1973 War Powers Act, the president gained authority to deploy troops (within certain limits of size and time) without a formal declaration. Formal declarations are disliked because they lend legitimacy to unrecognized or unpopular regimes.

WAR IS GOD'S WAY OF TEACHING AMERICANS GEOGRAPHY.

AMBROSE BIERCE

The Korean War was neither formally declared nor approved by Congress and despite hostilities ending in 1953, a peace treaty has never been signed with North Korea.

The longest war fought by the United States was the forty-six-year campaign against the Apache nation, which ended in 1886 with Geronimo's surrender at Skeleton Canyon, New Mexico.

Who was the most dangerous American in history?

J. Edgar Hoover? J. Robert Oppenheimer? George W. Bush?

It was probably Thomas Midgely, a chemist from Dayton, Ohio, who invented both CFCs and lead in gasoline.

Born in 1889, Midgely trained as an engineer. Early in his career he discovered by chance that adding iodine to kerosene slightly reduced knocking in engines. But slightly was not good enough for him. So he taught himself chemistry from scratch and, over six years, worked through the entire periodic table looking for the *perfect* solution. In 1921 he found it.

By then, the company he worked for had merged with General Motors, which eagerly began adding his completely "knock-free" answer to fuel for car engines. It was tetraethyl lead. Ethyl gasoline transformed the modern world. But it was also toxic, and pumped billions of tons of lead into the atmosphere over seven decades, poisoning thousands of people–including Midgely himself (though he always denied it).

Some think it was Midgely's guilt over lead gasoline that motivated him to develop a safe alternative to the noxious chemicals, like sulfur dioxide and ammonia, that were used in refrigeration. His discovery of dichlorofluoromethane–the first of the Freons–took three days. CFCs seemed like the perfect solution: inert, nontoxic, beneficial. Unfortunately, we now know they destroy the ozone layer and, since 1987, their production has been banned internationally.

By any standard, Midgely was an extraordinary man. He held 171 patents, loved music, and wrote poetry. But his inventions were lethal. At fifty-one he contracted polio and lost the use of his legs. In a final irony, the harness he designed to help him get in and out of bed got tangled one morning and in the ensuing struggle, America's most dangerous man inadvertently strangled himself. He was fifty-five.

How many dog years equal one human year?

It's not seven.

No reliable authority can be found to help us make simple cross-species age comparisons.

Some twelve-year-old cats and dogs have a much higher level of physical capability than even the most sprightly eighty-four-year-old human and there does seem to be significant variation between different breeds.

The best that can be done is to apply a widely accepted approximate formula which suggests that kittens and puppies mature much faster than babies, with the rate of aging slowing down significantly after two years.

Therefore, a one-year-old cat might be roughly sixteen in human years, while a four-year-old could be compared to a man or woman of thirty-two, an eight-year-old to a sixty-four-year-old, and so on.

How long is a day?

That depends.

A day is a single rotation of the earth about its axis. It is never exactly twenty-four hours long.

Astonishingly, it can be as much as fifty whole seconds longer or shorter. This is because the speed of the earth's rotation is continually changing as the result of friction caused by tides, weather patterns, and geological events.

Over a year, an average day is a fraction of a second shorter than twenty-four hours.

Once atomic clocks had recorded these discrepancies, the decision was made to redefine the second, hitherto a set fraction of the solar day—i.e., an eighty-six-thousand-and-four-hundredth of a day.

The new second was launched in 1967 and defined as: "the duration of 9,192,631,770 periods of the radiation corresponding to the transition between the two hyperfine levels of the ground state of the caesium-133 atom." Accurate, but not easy to say when tired at the end of a long day.

This new definition of a second means that the solar day is gradually drifting away from the atomic day. As a result, scientists have introduced a "leap second" into the atomic year, to bring it into line with the solar year.

The last leap second added (the seventh since Coordinated Universal Time (UTC) was established in 1972) was on 31 December 2005, on the instruction of the International Earth Rotation Service based at the Paris Observatory.

That's good news for astronomers and those of us who want our watches to correspond to the movement of the earth around the sun, but bad news for computer software and all technology based on satellites.

The idea was vigorously opposed by the International Telecommunication Union who made a formal proposal to abandon the leap second by December 2007.

One compromise might be to wait until the discrepancy between UTC and GMT reaches an hour (in about 400 years time) and adjust it then. In the meantime, the debate about what constitutes the "real" time continues.

What's the longest animal?

Not the blue whale. Sorry.

Or the lion's mane jellyfish.

The bootlace worm, *Lineus longissimus*, reaches lengths of just under 200 feet, almost twice as long as a blue whale and a third longer than the longest lion's mane jellyfish, the previous record holder.

You could drape a bootlace worm from one end of an Olympic swimming pool to the other and still have some to spare.

Bootlace worms, also known as ribbon worms, belong to the Nemertea worm family (Nemertea comes from the Greek *Nemertes*, a sea nymph). There are more than a thousand species, most of them aquatic. They are long and thin: even the longest may be only a few millimeters in diameter.

Many sources claim the bootlace worm only reaches 100 feet in length, which is not quite as long as the lion's mane jellyfish. But the latest information reveals that their capacity to stretch is extraordinary. Several have been found that are 165 feet long when fully extended.

MAN CANNOT MAKE A WORM, YET HE WILL MAKE GODS BY THE DOZEN.

MICHEL DE MONTAIGNE

Fossil evidence shows they have been around for at least 500 million years.

Bootlace worms have no hearts—their blood is pumped by their muscles—and they are the simplest organisms to have a separate mouth and anus.

They are voracious carnivores, shooting out a long thin tube, which is sticky or armed with poisonous hooks, to skewer and stun small crustaceans. This can be three times as long as the worm's own body.

Most ribbon worms lurk in the murk of the ocean bottom, but some are incredibly brightly colored.

Nemerteans can regenerate if damaged. But some bootlace species actually reproduce by fragmenting into small pieces, each of which becomes a new worm.

What happens if you cut an earthworm in half?

You get two halves of a dead worm, usually. Sometimes the head end survives, but you can't get two worms from one.

Some species of worm can regenerate amputated tails, depending on how many body segments they've lost, and some species jettison tails to escape predators, but the headless part will always die, as will the head if it hasn't retained sufficient body. The death throes of the severed sections can go on for hours and could easily be mistaken for lively wriggling.

The "both ends become a worm" idea seems to have started as a way of shutting up small children. Sadly, nobody ever gets around to telling you that it isn't true once you've grown up.

The smooth band a third of the way along an earthworm isn't the join from which the new worm grows. It is called the *clitellum* and is responsible for secreting the sticky, clear mucus that covers the worm.

There is a freshwater flatworm called a *planaria* or "cross-eyed worm," which also has an extraordinary ability to regenerate itself when damaged. The American geneticist and Nobel laureate T. H. Morgan (1866–1945) found that a piece of planaria 1/279th of its original size could regenerate into a full-sized planaria, and a planaria split lengthwise *or* crosswise will regenerate into two separate individuals.

What's the loudest thing in the ocean?

Shrimps.

Though the blue whale produces the loudest noise of any individual animal in the sea or on land, the loudest natural noise of all is made by shrimps.

The sound of the "shrimp layer" is the only natural noise that can white out a submarine's sonar, deafening the operators through their headphones.

Below the layer they can hear nothing above it and vice versa. Hearing from below can only be accomplished by raising a mast up through it.

The noise of the collected shrimps amounts to an earsplitting 246 decibels, which even adjusting for the fact that sound travels five times faster in water, equates to about 160 decibels in air: considerably louder than a jet taking off (140 dB) or the human threshold of pain. Some observers have compared it to everyone in the world frying bacon at the same time.

The noise is caused by trillions of shrimps snapping their single oversized claw all at once. Snapping shrimps, members of the various *Alpheus* and *Synalpheus* species, are found in shallow tropical and subtropical waters.

But it's even more interesting than it sounds. Video shot at 40,000 frames per second shows clearly that the noise occurs 700 microseconds after the claw has snapped shut. The noise comes from burst bubbles, not the shutting of the claw itself, an effect known as cavitation.

It works like this. A small bump on one side of the claw fits neatly into a groove on the other side. The claw is shut so rapidly that a jet of water traveling at 62 mph squirts out, fast enough to create expanding bubbles of water vapor. When the water slows down and normal pressure is restored, the bubbles collapse, creating intense heat (as high as 20,000°C), a loud pop, and light—this last being a very rare phenomenon called sonoluminescence, where sound generates light.

Shrimps use this noise to stun prey, communicate, and find mates. As well as ruining sonar, the sharp, hot intense noise makes dents in ships' propellers.

Why are flamingos pink?

Because they eat a lot of blue-green algae.

Flamingos do eat shrimps, but the color of the birds comes from the algae. Despite the name, blue-green algae can be red, violet, brown, yellow, or even orange.

Flamingos are named for their bright color. Like *flamenco*, the word comes from the Latin for "flame." The red and white flag of Peru was inspired by them.

There are four species of flamingo. They are at least ten million years old and once ranged over Europe, America, and Australia. Now they live in isolated pockets of Africa, India, South America, and southern Europe.

All species are monogamous. They lay only one egg a year, which is balanced on a mound of soil. Both parents take turns to incubate it, and both produce bright red, highly nutritious "milk" from their throats, which the chicks feed on for their first two months. Flamingos are one of only two kinds of bird to produce milk: the other is pigeons. In captivity, flamingos that are not parents will spontaneously produce milk if they hear the cries of chicks.

After leaving the nest, flamingos live in vast crèches. Though these may contain more than thirty thousand birds, the young flamingo is fed only by its parents, who recognize it by its cry. A family of flamingos is called a "pat."

Flamingos eat with their heads upside down. Unlike other birds, they filter their food in the same way as whales and oysters. Their beaks are lined with rows of plates that sift items from the water. The lesser flamingo (*Phoeniconaias minor*) has such a dense filter it can strain single-celled plants less than two hundredths of an inch in diameter. The flamingo's tongue acts as a pump, pushing water through its beak four times a second.

Pliny the Elder recommended eating flamingo tongue as a tasty delicacy.

Flamingos sleep on one leg, with one half of their body at a time—like dolphins—while the other remains alert for predators.

Flamingos can live for fifty years. They inhabit inhospitable lakes that have high levels of salt and soda, where the water is undrinkable by other animals and nothing grows. Their main predators are zookeepers.

What color is a panther?

There is no such thing as a panther.

The word probably comes from the Sanskrit for whitish-yellow, *pandarah*, which was originally applied to the tiger.

The Greeks borrowed the word and adapted it as *panthera*, meaning "all beasts." They used it to describe mythological as well as real animals.

In medieval heraldry, the panther was portrayed as a gentle, multicolored beast that had a very sweet smell.

Scientifically speaking, all four of the largest species of big cat are panthers.

The lion is *Panthera leo;* the tiger, *Panthera tigris;* the leopard, *Panthera pardus;* and the jaguar *Panthera onca.* They are the only cats that can roar.

The animals that most people think of as panthers are, in fact, either black leopards (in Africa or Asia), or black jaguars (in South America).

Neither animal is completely black. Close examination shows that their spots are still faintly visible on their skin. They carry a genetic mutation that means the black pigment in their fur dominates the orange.

Rare white panthers are in fact albino leopards or jaguars.

In the United States, when people say "panther" they mean a black puma. Despite many unproven reports and supposed sightings, no one has ever found one.

What makes an animal see red?

The myth that bulls are infuriated by the color red has been around since at least 1580, when the bestselling writer of the time, John Lyly, noted that: "He that commeth before an Elephant will not wear bright colors, nor he that commeth to a Bul, red."

The fact is that, like rats, hippos, owls, and aardvarks, bulls are color-blind. It is the movements of the bullfighter's cape that cause the bull to charge; the color is merely for the benefit of the crowd.

Dogs can distinguish between blue and yellow, but can't tell green from red. At traffic lights, guide dogs decide whether it is safe to cross by listening to the traffic. Hence the peeping sounds on modern pedestrian crossings.

The creatures that have really strong views on red are chickens.

Poultry farmers know only too well the practical problems of a chicken "seeing red." When one of them bleeds, the others peck at it obsessively.

This cannibalistic behavior, if unchecked, can lead to a killing spree and a rapid reduction in the farmer's flock.

The traditional solution is to trim the chickens' beaks with a hot knife so they are blunt and cause less damage. However, in 1989 a company called Animalens launched red-tinted contact lenses for egg-laying chickens. The early results were promising—because everything looked red, the chickens fought less and needed less feed because they weren't so active, but still laid the same number of eggs.

The egg industry operates on a tiny profit margin of about 1.6 percent. There are 250 million egg-layers in the United States, 150 million of them on just fifty farms. Red contact lenses for chickens promised a tripling in profits.

Unfortunately, fitting the lenses was fiddly and labor-intensive.

Deprived of oxygen, the chickens' eyes degenerated rapidly, causing pain and distress. Falling foul of the animal rights lobby, Animalens withdrew the product.

What color were the original Oompa-Loompas?

a. Black
b. Gold
c. Multicolored
d. Orange

In the first edition of Roald Dahl's classic 1964 children's novel *Charlie and the Chocolate Factory*, the tireless, loyal Oompa-Loompas were black, not orange.

Dahl described them as a tribe of three thousand black pygmies imported by Mr. Wonka from "the very deepest and darkest part of the African jungle where no white man had been before," to replace the sacked white workers in his factory. They lived on chocolate, whereas before they had only eaten "beetles, eucalyptus leaves, caterpillars and the bark of the bong-bong tree."

Although it was well received at the time, Dahl's description of the Oompa-Loompas, with its overtones of slavery, veered dangerously close to racism, and by the early 1970s his U.S. publishers, Knopf, insisted on changes. In 1972 a revised edition of *Charlie and the Chocolate Factory* appeared. Out went the black pygmies, and in came Oompa-Loompas looking like small hippies with long "golden-brown hair" and "rosy-white skin."

Later, Dahl's illustrator Quentin Blake depicted them as multicolored futuristic punks with Mohawk hairdos. The two Hollywood films in 1971 and 2005 made the Oompa-Loompas look like orange elves.

Dahl hated the 1971 film, not least because the (uncredited) screenwriter David Seltzer (later to write *The Omen*) had Wonka spouting poetic quotations that weren't in the book.

The film's title was changed to *Willy Wonka & the Chocolate Factory* allegedly because "Charlie" had become U.S. street slang for an African American.

What color were Robin Hood's tights?

Red.

The earliest Robin Hood stories were ballads dating from the fifteenth century.

In the longest and most important of these, *A Gest of Robyn Hode*, Robin and his "mery men" wear "a good mantell of scarlet and raye," a kind of striped bright red wrap.

In other ballads, Robin wears red or scarlet while his men wear green. This reflects his status as leader—scarlet was the most expensive cloth in medieval England, dyed using kermes, the dried bodies of the female shield louse (*Kermes ilicis*).

This also explains the name Robin—associated with the robin redbreast—and that of one of his closest associates: Will Scarlet.

It is only in later versions that "Lincoln Green" becomes the color for the outlaws' gear but even this may not have been green.

Lincoln was the capital of the medieval English dyeing industry. "Lincoln Green" was green (blue dye made from woad was overdyed with yellow) but "Lincoln Grain" was scarlet, dyed with kermes, known as "graine."

The early Robin Hood stories are obsessed by clothing. As well as Robin being named after his headgear, mantles, kirtles, coats, breeches, shirts, and six different colors of cloth are mentioned in the *Gest*, and at one point Robin plays at being a draper, selling the King 123 feet of green cloth.

This has prompted the idea that the ballads may have been written for the Livery Guilds, companies of merchants involved in manufacturing. Many of them were founded at the time the *Gest* was written (ca. 1460); their preferred style of uniform was a colored hood.

At least one historian has suggested that the real point of the Robin Hood stories is not the traditional "forest versus town" or "rich versus poor" battle, but the victory of the merchant adventurer over the failing, corrupt nobility.

Robin Hood, dressed in expensive red cloth, was really the champion of the emerging middle classes rather than the poor.

What rhymes with orange?

There are two rhymes for orange in English, although both are proper nouns: Blorenge and Gorringe.

The Blorenge is a hill outside Abergavenny in Wales, and Gorringe is a splendid English surname.

The best view of Abergavenny is from the top of the Blorenge, a 1,833-foot-tall hill owned by the South East Wales Hang-gliding and Paragliding Club, who bought it from the Coal Authority in 1998.

Distinguished Gorringes include: General George Frederick Gorringe (1865–1945), the unpopular British World War I commander; Harry Gorringe, the first-class Australian cricketer; and Henry Honeychurch Gorringe, the man who brought Cleopatra's Needle from Egypt to New York's Central Park.

In 1673 New York was called New Orange (so the New Orange became the Big Apple). The city was founded by the Dutch in 1653 as New Amsterdam, taken by the English in 1664 and renamed New York, and retaken by the Dutch in 1673 and named New Orange.

It lasted less than a year. Under the Treaty of Westminster in 1674 the city was ceded to the English, and New York became its permanent name.

The word *orange* is a good example of what linguists call wrong word division. It derives from the Arabic *naranj* and arrived in English as *narange* in the fourteenth century, gradually losing the initial *n.* The same process left us with *apron* (from *naperon*) and *umpire* (from *noumpere*).

Sometimes it works the other way around, as in *nickname* (from an *eke-name*, meaning "also-name") or *newt* (from an *ewt*).

Orange was first used as the name for a color in 1542.

What color are carrots?

Carrots didn't reveal their inner orangeness for almost five thousand years.

The earliest evidence of carrots being used by humans dates from 3000 B.C. in Afghanistan. These original carrots were purple on the outside and yellow on the inside.

The ancient Greeks and Romans cultivated the vegetable, but mostly for medicinal purposes: the carrot was considered a powerful aphrodisiac.

Galen, the famous second-century Roman physician, on the other hand, recommended carrots for expelling wind. He was the first to identify them as separate from their close relative the parsnip.

As Arab traders spread carrot seed through Asia, Africa, and Arabia carrots blossomed into different shades of purple, white, yellow, red, green, and even black.

The very first orange carrot was grown in sixteenth-century Holland, patriotically bred to match the color of the Dutch Royal House of Orange.

> YOU ASK "WHAT IS LIFE?" THAT IS THE SAME AS ASKING, "WHAT IS A CARROT?" A CARROT IS A CARROT AND WE KNOW NOTHING MORE.
>
> ANTON CHEKHOV

By the seventeenth century, the Dutch were the main European producers of carrots and all modern varieties are descended from their four orange ones: Early Half Long, Late Half Long, Scarlet, and Long Orange.

There is currently a vogue for nonorange carrots: white, yellow, dark red, and purple varieties are available in the shops. In 1997 Iceland developed a chocolate-flavored carrot as part of their child-focused Wacky Veg range. It was withdrawn after eight months.

According to the United Nations, in 1903 there were 287 varieties of carrot but these now number just 21, a fall of 93 percent.

Some breeds of carrot contain a protein that stops ice crystals growing. This natural carrot antifreeze can be extracted and used to preserve body tissues for medical use and improve the shelf life of frozen food.

Do carrots help us see in the dark?

Not really.

Carrots are a good source of vitamin A, a deficiency of which can lead to night blindness, where the eye adapts very slowly to changes in light.

The retina of the eye is made up of light-sensitive cells called rods and cones. Cones pick up detail and color, but need plenty of light to function (like a slow film emulsion). The rods can't distinguish color at all but need less light (like a fast emulsion) so are used for night vision. They contain a light-sensitive chemical called rhodopsin, the key ingredient of which is vitamin A.

The easiest way to treat night blindness is to increase the intake of vitamin A, most commonly found in carotene. Carrots contain carotene, but even better are apricots, dark-leaved vegetables such as spinach, and blueberries.

But improving defective night vision is very different from making normal night vision better. Eating lots of carrots won't help you see any better in the dark—all it will do, over time, is to turn your skin orange.

During World War II, Group Captain John Cunningham (1917–2002) gained the nickname "Cats Eyes Cunningham." His 604 squadron operated at night. The British government encouraged rumors that he was able see in the dark because he ate so many carrots.

This was deliberate disinformation designed to cover up the fact that he was testing the newly developed (and top secret) airborne radar system.

It seems highly unlikely the Germans were taken in, but it helped persuade a generation of British children to eat the one vegetable that remained in constant supply through the war.

The government started to overdo the carrot propaganda. Carrots became "these bright treasures dug from the good British earth." A 1941 recipe for Carrot Flan—"reminds you of Apricot Flan—but has a deliciousness all of its own"—fooled no one. And carrot jam and marmalade failed to find their way onto the British breakfast table.

The Portuguese are fond of carrot jam, though. In 2002 this led to the European Union's redefining the carrot as a fruit.

What do bananas grow on?

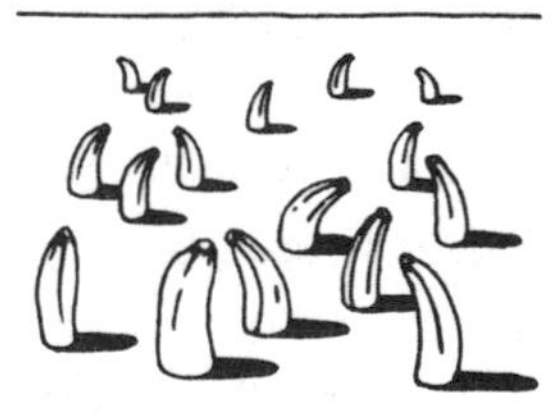

There is no such thing as a banana tree.

The banana plant is actually a giant herb and the bananas are its berries.

An herb is defined as "a plant with a fleshy not a woody stem, which, after the plant has bloomed and set seed, dies down to the ground." This is not always true: sage, thyme, and rosemary have woody stems (though they are not covered with true bark).

As the definition says, after flowering, the part of the herb above the ground dies. With bananas, this gives rises to a strange effect. After the stem dies, another one grows, slightly further along the root. Over a few years, the banana plant will appear to have "walked" a couple of yards.

Bananas are native to Malaysia and have been cultivated for ten thousand years. Wild bananas, which can still be found in Southeast Asia, contain large stony seeds and a small amount of flesh. They are pollinated by bats.

The banana in your local supermarket is a cultivated variety, chosen by farmers for its fleshy pulp and lack of seeds. Domestication has produced plants that are sweet and tasty but sterile: they cannot reproduce without human help.

Most banana plants have not had sex for ten thousand years. Almost every banana we eat has been propagated by hand, from a sucker of an existing plant, whose genetic material has not changed in one hundred centuries.

As a result, bananas are extremely susceptible to disease. Many species have already succumbed to fungal infections like black Sigatoka and Panama disease, which are impervious to fungicides. Unless a genetically modified version can be developed soon, all bananas may become extinct.

This is a serious problem. Bananas are the most profitable export crop in the world. The industry is worth $12 billion a year and supports 400 million people, many of them living well below the poverty line.

Most bananas come from hot countries, but Europe's largest producer is Iceland. The bananas are grown in large greenhouses heated by geothermal water, just two degrees below the Arctic Circle.

Fyffe's, the banana multinational that buys the entire crop of Belize each year, is Irish.

Where do Panama hats come from?

Ecuador.

They first appeared in Europe and North America in the early nineteenth century, where they were called "panama" hats because they were exported through shippers based in Panama.

In England, they were chosen as perfect summer headgear by the royal family, and quickly became indispensable accessories for sporting and outdoor social occasions. When Queen Victoria died in 1901, the black band was added in her honor.

In the Americas, the hats were standard issue for the men digging the Panama Canal. President Theodore Roosevelt visited the site in 1906 and was photographed wearing one. The panama's fame was assured.

The hat's origins are ancient: ceramic figures wearing curious headpieces have been discovered on the Ecuadorian coast and date back to 4000 B.C. Some archaeologists believe that the weaving skills needed to make a panama were acquired through contact with the Polynesian people of the Pacific, famous for their woven flax. The first Spaniards were so unnerved by the material's translucent quality that they believed it was vampire skin.

The modern hats date back to the sixteenth century and are made from the woven fibers of the ten-foot-tall panama-hat palm, the *jipijapa* or *toquilla* (its scientific name is *Carludovica palmata*). They are mostly produced in the town of Cuenca, although the finest examples come from the towns of Montecristi and Biblian.

The time it takes to make a panama hat varies enormously. The *toquilla* can be harvested only five days a month, during the moon's final quarter, when the palm fiber holds less water, making it lighter and easier to weave. A skilled weaver can extract a fiber that is as fine as silk. A low-grade hat can be knocked out in a matter of hours, whereas a top-quality, or *superfino*, hat can take five months to finish and sell for thousands of dollars.

In 1985 the Conran Foundation nominated the panama hat as one of the "100 best designs ever" for an exhibition at the V&A.

Ecuador is named after the Spanish word for "equator." As well as hats, it is the world's largest exporter of bananas and balsa wood for model aircraft.

What is coffee made from?

Coffee seeds, *not* beans.

Coffee is really a fruit. What we call coffee beans are, botanically speaking, seeds. Coffee trees produce delicate white, jasminelike blossoms, which last only a few days. The flowers give way to fruit called coffee cherries, which turn bright red when ripe. The skin of the cherry is bitter but the flesh is intensely sweet with a grapelike texture. Inside various further layers are two bluish-green seeds.

The word *bean* once meant only the seed of the broad bean. This later expanded to include members of the *Phaseolus* family such as the haricot bean and the runner bean, and the related genus *Vigna*, which includes mung and adzuki beans and black-eyed peas. The term is now applied to other related plants such as soybeans, peas, lentils, vetches, and lupins.

I NEVER DRINK COFFEE AT LUNCH. I FIND IT KEEPS ME AWAKE FOR THE AFTERNOON.

RONALD REAGAN

The coffee tree is an evergreen that grows twenty feet tall but is pruned to eight to ten feet. Coffee pickers can pick 100 to 200 pounds of coffee cherries per day. Only 20 percent of this weight is the actual seed. It takes about 2,000 *Arabica* cherries to produce a pound of roasted coffee. Since each cherry contains two beans, your one pound of coffee is derived from 4,000 coffee beans.

In 5 to 10 percent of any coffee crop, the cherry will contain only a single seed. This is called a peaberry, and it has a distinctly different, stronger flavor than normal.

In common English usage, the word *beans* also refers to seeds or other organs of other plants. For example: castor beans (from which castor oil is made); cocoa beans (which resemble bean seeds), and vanilla beans (which resemble the pods). Botanically, none of these are beans, either.

Which of the following are berries?

a. Strawberry
b. Raspberry
c. Peach
d. Watermelon

A berry is defined as "a fleshy fruit containing several seeds."

Strictly speaking, strawberries, raspberries, and blackberries are not berries but aggregated drupes—a drupe being a fleshy fruit containing a single stone or pit.

Peaches, plums, nectarines, and olives are drupes. The world's largest drupe is the coconut, which, because of its hard flesh, is called a dry drupe.

Strawberries, raspberries, and blackberries are called aggregated drupes because each individual fruit is actually a cluster of miniature drupes—the characteristic bumpy bits which make up blackberries and raspberries.

Each one of these drupelets contains a single tiny seed—these are the bits that get stuck in your teeth when you eat a blackberry.

Tomatoes, oranges, lemons, grapefruit, watermelons, kiwi fruit, cucumbers, grapes, passion fruit, papaya, peppers, and bananas are all berries.

Blueberries are also berries. They are variously known as bleaberries, bilberries, whortleberries, huckleberries, hurtleberries, myrtleberries, and trackleberries.

Which of the following are nuts?

a. Almond
b. Peanut
c. Brazil nut
d. Walnut

Nuts are defined as a simple dry fruit with one seed (very occasionally two) in which the seed-case wall becomes very hard at maturity.

True nuts include walnuts, butternuts, hickory, pecan, chestnut (but not conkers), beech, oak acorns, tan oak, hazel, filbert, hornbeam, birch, and alder.

Peanuts, almonds, pistachios, Brazils, cashews, coconuts, horse chestnuts, and pine nuts are not nuts. So the legendary health warning on a packet of peanuts ("may contain nuts") is, strictly speaking, untrue.

> IF YOU DON'T MIND SMELLING LIKE PEANUT BUTTER FOR TWO OR THREE DAYS, PEANUT BUTTER IS DARN GOOD SHAVING CREAM.
>
> BARRY GOLDWATER

Brazil nuts are not nuts but seeds. The wooden pods they come in (up to twenty-four to a pod) grow right at the top of the tree, 150 feet above the ground, and are lethal if they fall on you. In Brazil, the pods are called *ouricos*, "hedgehogs."

Almonds are the stone of a once fleshy drupe.

Peanuts, also known as groundnuts, earthnuts, goobers, goober peas, pindas, pinders, Manila nuts, and monkey nuts, are actually a type of pea which grows underground.

They are native to South America but now widely cultivated, notably in Georgia. Some people are so severely allergic to peanuts that eating a tiny amount (or even inhaling peanut dust) can be fatal; these people may or may not also be allergic to true nuts.

Pistachios are deadly dangerous. They are classified under Class 4.2. of the International Maritime Dangerous Goods code: Flammable Solids (Substances Liable to Spontaneous Combustion). Fresh pistachios, if stacked under pressure, can burst into flames and cause a cargo fire.

Pistachios continue to absorb oxygen and excrete carbon dioxide even after harvesting. This can be a serious problem when transporting them by sea. If there is inadequate ventilation, seamen entering the hold of a cargo ship can die from carbon dioxide poisoning or from lack of oxygen.

Pistachios have been eaten by humans for at least nine thousand years. According to Muslim legend, the pistachio was one of the foods brought to earth by Adam when he came down from Heaven.

Who goes gathering nuts in May?

No one. There are no nuts to gather in May. The children's song is a corruption of the phrase "Here we go gathering knots of may." It refers to the ancient custom of picking bunches (knots) of flowers on May Day to celebrate the end of winter, or "to go a-maying."

May, the blossom of the hawthorn, is the only British flower to be named after the month in which it blooms. The may tree is the origin of both the maypole and the phrase "Ne'er cast a clout before May is out"—which refers not to the ending of the month, but to the opening of the flowers.

Though the may tree is closely associated with May Day, it blossoms in the middle of the month not at the beginning of it. This is due to the change to the Gregorian calendar in 1752. Before this, May Day would have occurred eleven days later, exactly the time when the may tree breaks into flower.

It is considered extremely unlucky to bring hawthorn flowers inside the house, a superstition more widely believed for may than for any other species of plant in the British Isles.

There are many possible reasons for this but the most convincing is to do with its smell. Hawthorn flowers have a heavy, complicated scent, the distinctive element of which is triethylamine, which is also one of the first chemicals produced by a dead human body when it starts to decay.

In some areas it is still referred to as "the smell of the Great Plague" and people who know say it reminds them of the smell of gangrene. In the old days, bodies were laid out at home for up to a week before burial, and everybody would have been familiar with the smell of death. Hawthorn brought inside the house would have instantly triggered the association.

On the other hand, triethylamine is also the smell of sex: specifically of semen; hence its positive association with wild springtime romps *outside* in the fields.

As well as may, hawthorn is also known by scads of bizarre vernacular names including "bread-and-cheese," "arzy-garzies," and "aglets." *Aglet* is also the word for the little metal or plastic tip on the end of a shoelace.

What's inside a coconut?

Not milk, but coconut water. Coconut milk has to be made by boiling the white coconut meat with water and straining it. Boil this down further and you get coconut cream.

Coconut is the only plant to produce such a seed liquid. As the coconut grows, the seed inside changes into a sweet, spongy mass called the coconut apple. From this the young plant shoot emerges out of one of the three holes at the end.

Fresh coconut water is an excellent hangover cure. It is completely sterile, full of vitamins and minerals, and has the same balance of salts as human blood (the technical term for this is isotonic).

Because of this it can be used in place of a saline drip and is being commercially exploited as a sports drink, particularly in Brazil, where it is now a 75-million-dollar industry. Coconut water also ferments quickly and can be made into wine or vinegar.

Coconut oil is used to treat AIDS. Far from being the world's most dangerously fatty oil, it is now being marketed as the healthiest. It is rich in lauric acid, the saturated fat found in mother's milk, and full of antiviral and antibacterial properties. It's also been shown to reduce cholesterol, as it doesn't enter the bloodstream but travels straight to the liver.

Some less well known uses for the coconut palm: Daimler-Chrysler now use the husk (or coir) to make biodegradable seats for their trucks (springier than plastic foam); the root is liquefied to make mouthwash; and a flour made from the shell is used to clean jet engines. The first car body to be made of coconut is already on the drawing board.

The coconut palm has been heralded as the world's most useful tree for more than three thousand years. In early Sanskrit texts it was referred to as *kalpa vriksha*—the tree that fulfils all needs.

You could survive on a desert island by eating and drinking only coconut.

What did Captain Cook give his men to cure scurvy?

a. Limes
b. Lemons
c. Sauerkraut
d. Rum and blackcurrant

Cook never carried fresh limes or lemons onboard. The closest he got to a remedy was barrels of sauerkraut and a concentrated fruit-juice mixture called rob. Both had been boiled to preserve them on the long voyage and so had lost most of their vitamin C.

Cook had been dead for twenty years before the supply of lemon juice to British sailors became standard practice.

Scurvy was a huge problem on long voyages. Magellan lost most of his crew to it crossing the Pacific. Now we know it is a combination of a lack of vitamins C and B, causing the body's cells to break down, but in the eighteenth century it was treated with more superstition than knowledge. Many sailors believed that the touch of earth would cure it.

The breakthrough came with the publication of Edinburgh physician James Lind's *Treatise on Scurvy* in 1754, which advocated the use of citrus fruit and fresh vegetables.

The legend is that Cook's enlightened approach kept his ships free of the disease. The truth seems to be that Cook simply ignored it. The journals of his fellow officers indicate that it was widespread on all three voyages, although there were few deaths.

ESKIMO/INUIT PEOPLE DON'T SUFFER FROM SCURVY BECAUSE WHALE BLUBBER IS A RICH SOURCE OF VITAMIN C.

When, in 1795, the Admiralty finally ordered ships to be supplied with citrus fruit (on Lind's recommendation), it was lemon, not lime, juice that was supplied. This had a dramatic effect on the disease.

By the 1850s, lemons were being replaced by limes for economic reasons (limes were grown by British businessmen in the colonies; lemons were grown by Johnny Foreigner in the Mediterranean). Scurvy returned with a vengeance as, ironically, limes contain very little vitamin C.

The first recorded use of the term *lime juicer* (later *limey*) for a Brit was in 1859. Vitamin C wasn't identified and named until the 1930s. Its chemical name is ascorbic acid. *Ascorbic* means "anti-scurvy."

Who discovered Australia?

You still hear "Captain Cook" trotted out at dinner parties (though very rarely at Australian ones).

Let's take it from the top: he wasn't a captain, for a start, he was Lieutenant Cook on the *Endeavour's* first voyage (1768–71). And he wasn't the first European to see the continent—the Dutch beat him by 150 years—or even the first Englishman to land there. That was William Dampier, who in 1697 was also the first to record a "large hopping animal."

Dampier (1652–1715) was a sea captain, navigator, explorer, cartographer, scientific observer, pirate, and buccaneer. Alexander Selkirk—the model for *Robinson Crusoe*—was a member of his crew. He circumnavigated the world three times, invented the first wind map, and is cited more than one thousand times in the *OED*, introducing words like *avocado, barbecue, breadfruit, cashew, chopsticks, settlement,* and *tortilla* into English.

In recent years, there has been a lot of lobbying in favor of the Chinese as the continent's first foreign visitors. There is some archaeological evidence that the great Ming Dynasty admiral Zheng He (1371–1435) landed near Darwin in 1432.

Without having to swallow the whole "Zheng He discovered the entire world" theory cooked up by Gavin Menzies in his bestselling *1421: The Year the Chinese Discovered America*, there seems to be a good chance that this extraordinary fifteenth-century voyager (he was a Muslim and a eunuch) did reach the northern coast of Australia.

After all, Indonesian fishermen, crazed for the local sea cucumbers (which they traded with the Chinese), had managed it many years before the earliest recorded Europeans.

Some of the northern Aboriginal peoples, like the Yolngu,

even learned to sail and fish from these visitors from overseas, picking up words, tools, and the usual bad habits (alcohol and tobacco) along the way.

The real discoverers are, of course, the Aboriginal peoples who reached Australia more than fifty thousand years ago. They have been present on the continent for 2,000 generations, in comparison to just eight generations of Europeans.

That is long enough for them to have witnessed dramatic changes in their environment. The landscape of the Australian interior thirty thousand years ago would have been one of green vegetation, brimming lakes, and snow-capped mountains.

What does "kangaroo" mean in Aboriginal?

It doesn't mean "I don't know," despite the endless websites and trivia books that tell you otherwise, citing it as a hilarious early example of cultural misunderstanding.

The real story is much more interesting. In eighteenth-century Australia there were at least 700 Aboriginal tribes speaking as many as 250 different languages.

Kangaroo or *gangaru* comes from the Guugu Ymithirr language of Botany Bay, where it means the large gray or black kangaroo, *Macropus robustus.*

As the English settlers moved into the interior, they used this word to refer to any old kangaroo or wallaby.

The Baagandji people lived 1,400 miles from Botany Bay and didn't speak Guugu Ymithirr. They heard the English settlers using this unfamiliar word and took it to mean "an animal that no one has ever heard of before."

Since they had never seen them before, they (quite reasonably) used the word to describe the settlers' horses.

What is "pom" short for?

a. Port of Melbourne
b. Prisoners of Her Majesty
c. Prisoner of Old Mother England
d. Permit of Migration
e. Pomegranates

Most of these are easy to discount because they are acronyms. Folk etymologists seem to be drawn to acronymic explanations, which are almost never right.

Fondness for acronyms is a military habit, dating from World War I (an early example is AWOL, or "Absent Without Leave," though even this wasn't consistently pronounced as a word at the time). Acronyms didn't get into general circulation until World War II.

There are almost no examples of words of acronymic origin before 1900. Indeed, the very word *acronym* wasn't coined until 1943.

In the case of *pom*, most reliable authorities agree it is a shortening of *pomegranate*.

In his 1923 Australian novel, *Kangaroo*, D. H. Lawrence wrote: "'Pommy' is supposed to be short for pomegranate. Pomegranate, pronounced invariably pommygranate, is a near enough rhyme to immigrant, in a naturally rhyming country. Furthermore, immigrants are known in their first months, before their blood 'thins down,' by their round and ruddy cheeks. So we are told."

The term is first recorded in 1916, suggesting that it dates to the latter stages of the nineteenth century and not to the original convict ships.

Michael Quinion in *Port Out, Starboard Home* (2000) also accepts pomegranate, citing H. J. Rumsey's 1920 introduction to a book called *The Pommie or New Chums in Australia*, in which the word is sourced to children's rhyming slang of the 1870s.

The older term "Jimmy Grant" used for "immigrant" became "Pommy Grant," which was irresistible as the fierce Australian sun turned their new chums skin pomegranate red.

What's the biggest rock in the world?

It's not Ayers Rock.

Mount Augustus, or Burringurrah, in a remote part of Western Australia, is the largest single rock in the world, more than two and a half times bigger than Uluru, or Ayers Rock, and one of the natural world's least known but most spectacular sites.

It rises 2,815 feet out of the surrounding outback, and its ridge is more than 5 miles long.

Not only is it bigger and higher than Uluru, its rock is much older. The gray sandstone that is visible is the remains of a sea floor laid down 1,000 million years ago. The bedrock beneath the sandstone is granite dated to 1,650 million years ago. The oldest sandstone at Uluru is only 400 million years old.

The rock is sacred to the Wadjari people and is named after Burringurrah, a young boy who tried to escape his initiation. He was pursued and speared in the leg, and then beaten to death by women wielding clubs. The shape of the rock reflects his prostate body, lying on its stomach with its leg bent upward toward his chest and a stump of the spear protruding from it.

A final sting in the tail for Ayers Rock snobs: Mount Augustus is a monolith—a single piece of rock. Uluru isn't. It's just the tip of a huge underground rock formation that also pokes out at Mount Conner (Attila) and Mount Olga (Kata Tjuta).

What were boomerangs used for?

Knocking down kangaroos? Think about it. Boomerangs are designed to come back. They are lightweight and fast. Even large ones are unlikely to give a 180-pound adult male kangaroo much more than a sore head, and if it did knock them down, you wouldn't need it to return.

In fact, they weren't clubs at all. They were used to imitate hawks in order to drive game birds into nets strung from trees—a kind of wooden, banana-shaped bird dog.

Nor are they exclusive to the Aboriginal peoples. The oldest returning throwing stick was found in the Olazowa Cave in the Polish Carpathians and is more than eighteen thousand years old. Researchers tried it out, and it still worked.

This suggests there was already a long tradition of using them—the physical properties have to be so exact to make a successful boomerang that it's unlikely to be a one-off.

The oldest Aboriginal boomerangs are fourteen thousand years old.

Various types of throwing woods were used in Ancient Egypt, from 1340 B.C. In Western Europe a returning throwing stick called a *cateia* was used by the Goths to hunt birds from around A.D. 100.

In the seventh century, the Bishop of Seville described the *cateia:* "There is a kind of Gallic missile consisting of very flexible material, which does not fly very long when it is thrown, because of its heavy weight, but arrives there nevertheless. It only can be broken with a lot of power. But if it is thrown by a master, it returns to the one who threw it."

Australian Aboriginals probably became adept with the boomerang because they never developed the bow and arrow. Most Aboriginal peoples used both boomerangs and non-returning throwing sticks (known as *kylies*).

The first recorded use of the word *bou-mar-rang* was in 1822. It comes from the language of the Turuwal people of the George's River near Sydney.

The Turuwal had other words for their hunting sticks, but used *boomerang* to refer to a returning throwing stick. The Turuwal belong to part of the Dharuk language group. Many of the Aboriginal words used in English are from Dharuk languages, including wallaby, dingo, kookaburra, and koala.

Did cannibals cook their victims whole in large pots?

Producing a watertight metal pot large enough to hold a person requires industrial technology that was new, even to the West, in the nineteenth century. In reality, you were much more likely to be butchered and roasted in small joints, or else smoked and salted for snacking on later.

The word *cannibal* comes from a misrecording of the name for the Central American Carib tribe by Columbus in 1495. He reported finding a recently abandoned "Canib" feast of human limbs simmering in small cauldrons and roasting on spits.

Other explorers reported cannibalism in South America, Africa, Australia, New Guinea, and throughout the Pacific. Captain Cook was in no doubt that the Maori ate enemies taken in battle. During his second voyage, his lieutenant, Charles Clerke, grilled a portion of head at the behest of a Maori warrior and records that he "devour'd it most ravenously, and suck'd his fingers ½ a dozen times over in raptures."

William Arens's influential *The Man-Eating Myth* (1979) argued that these stories were racist lies invented to justify Western colonialism. It resulted in a period of "cannibal denial" among anthropologists.

However, more recent discoveries have led most historians and anthropologists to accept that cannibalism was practiced by many tribal cultures, mostly for ritual purposes, sometimes for food.

The last society to admit to ritual cannibalism, the Fore tribe of New Guinea, stopped in the mid-1950s after an outbreak of *kuru*, a brain disease contracted through eating human brain and spinal tissue.

There is also archaeological evidence. Collections of butchered human remains have even been found in France, Spain, and Britain. Some of the British remains date from 30 B.C. to A.D. 130, suggesting that the Romans' belief that the ancient Britons ate people was justified.

In October 2003 the inhabitants of a Fijian village announced that they would be making a formal apology to the family of the Rev. Thomas Baker, an English missionary killed and eaten by their ancestors in 1867. They'd even tried to eat his boots, but these proved too tough and were returned to the Methodist Church in 1993.

Which religion curses people by sticking pins into dolls?

There is no tradition of sticking pins in dolls to harm people in voodoo (known as *vodun* in Benin; *voudou* in Haiti; and *vudu* in the Dominican Republic).

The magical practices of voodoo are complex and originated in West Africa before being exported to the Caribbean and America.

Healing is at the heart of most of the rituals. The closest thing to a voodoo doll is a wooden figure called a *bocheo* (literally "empowered figure") that contains small peg holes. Twigs are inserted into the appropriate hole, and used to channel healing energy.

The voodoo doll of popular myth derives from a *European* figure called a

ONE IS ALL FOR RELIGION UNTIL ONE VISITS A REALLY RELIGIOUS COUNTRY. THEN, ONE IS ALL FOR DRAINS, MACHINERY, AND A MINIMUM WAGE.

ALDOUS HUXLEY

poppet (from the Latin *pupa* for "doll"), traditionally used in witchcraft. It originated in ancient Greek dolls used as protective effigies called *kolossoi*. The poppet doll, made from clay, wax, cotton, corn, or fruit, became a symbol of the life of the subject—whatever was done to the doll would happen to the person.

King James I mentions them in his *Demonology* (1603):

"To some others at these times he [the Devil] teacheth, how to make Pictures of wax or clay: that by the roasting thereof, the persons that they bear the name of, may be continually melted or dried away by continual sicknesse."

It was the early colonists and slave owners who projected forbidden European "black magic" practices on to voodoo, adding their suspicions of cannibalism, zombies, and human sacrifice to spice up their stories. It was these that captured the popular imagination and stimulated the appetites of early filmmakers and dime-store novelists, fixing the idea of voodoo as dark and fearful.

The idea of sticking pins into people and meditating on suffering is not entirely foreign to Christianity. Some of the more grisly Counter-Reformation images of the Crucifixion leave little to the imagination.

Voodoo has made its peace with Christianity: the two traditions coexist quite happily. A common Haitian saying is that "Haitians are 80 percent Catholic and 100 percent Voodoo."

What are you doing when you "do the Hokey Pokey"?

You may be performing a sinister parody of the Roman Catholic Latin mass.

The theory goes that in the days when the priest celebrated the Mass facing the altar the congregation mimicked his gestures and the words as they misheard them behind his back. Thus the words *hokey pokey* are a corruption of the Latin phrase: *Hoc est enim corpus meum* (This is my body).

It may also be related to *hocus pocus*, the old conjuror's phrase dating from the early seventeenth century. By the end of the eighteenth century this had been contracted to make a new word, *hoax*.

Whatever the origin, *hokey-pokey* came to mean "nonsense" and attached itself to early ice cream street vendors who sold it as "Hokey-pokey penny a lump." Ice cream with toffee in it is still called Hokey-pokey in New Zealand and Australia.

In Britain, a dance with lyrics called "The Cokey Cokey," was copyrighted in 1942 by Jimmy Kennedy of "Teddy Bear's Picnic" fame. It seems to have been appropriated by a G.I. named Larry Laprise (a.k.a. The Hokey Pokey Man) who carried it back to the United States, where he and two friends adapted it for the après-ski crowd at a nightclub in Sun Valley, Idaho. His group, the Rain Trio, recorded the song as "The Hokey Pokey" in 1949 and it became a dance floor favorite.

Kennedy always claimed that his version was based on a traditional Canadian folk song, but it also seems to bear a striking resemblance to a Shaker song from Kentucky called "The Hinkum-Booby": *I put my right hand in, I put my right hand out, I give my right hand a shake, And I turn it all about.*

Whoever wrote it, and despite its possible religious (or Satanic) resonances, the dance has become a firm favorite with foreign language teachers trying to get students to remember the names of their body parts in other languages.

How many Wise Men visited Jesus?

Somewhere between two and twenty.

It has generally been assumed that there were three of them because they brought three gifts, but it is quite possible that there were four and one forgot to get a present until after the shops were closed and had to come in on the frankincense.

In the Gospel of St. Matthew the number of wise men is never mentioned. Besides, Jesus seems not to have been a baby but a young child, living in a house not a stable.

Most scholars agree that the Magi were Zoroastrian astrologer-priests, but their number varies from two to twenty. It wasn't until the sixth century that three was settled on as the standard.

The Church has now started to backtrack on this. In February 2004 the General Synod of the Church of England agreed on a revision to the Book of Common Prayer. Their committee decided that the term *magi* was a transliteration of the name used by officials at the Persian court, and that they could well have been women.

"While it seems very unlikely that these Persian court officials were female, the possibility that one or more of the Magi were female cannot be excluded completely," the report concluded. "'Magi' is a word which discloses nothing about numbers, wisdom, or gender. The visitors were not necessarily wise and not necessarily men."

Where does Santa Claus come from?

Depending on your age, the answer is likely to be the North Pole, Lapland, or Coca-Cola. None of them is right: Santa, like Saint George, is Turkish.

Saint Nicholas—the real Santa—lived and performed miracles in what is now the sun-baked town of Demre in southwestern Turkey. His most famous miracles usually involved children. In one, he restored to life three children who'd been chopped up by the local tavern owner and kept in a brine tub.

Being kind to children explains his suitability as a Christmas saint, but Saint Nick is also the patron saint of judges, pawnbrokers, thieves, merchants, bakers, sea travelers, and, oddly, murderers.

Italian sailors stole Saint Nicholas's miraculously myrrh-exuding bones in 1087. Turkey is still demanding their return.

In the rest of Europe, the benign Saint Nicholas fused with older, darker mythological types—in eastern Germany he is known as Shaggy Goat, Ashman, or Rider. In Holland he is Sinterklass, attended by the sinister Black Peters.

The jolly Coca-Cola Santa existed well before Haddon Sundblom's famous advertising images of the 1930s. His illustrations, and those of Thomas Nast in the 1860s, were based on New Yorker Clement Clarke Moore's 1823 poem "A Visit from Saint Nicholas" (better known as "The Night Before Christmas").

Moore was an unlikely author—his day job was as a professor of Hebrew and Oriental Languages—but the poem's importance in fueling the Santa myth would be hard to exaggerate. It moves the legend to Christmas Eve and, instead of the dour Saint Nick, describes a rotund, twinkly-eyed, white-bearded elf, with fur-trimmed red clothes, reindeer with cute names, a sledge that landed on rooftops, and a sack full of toys. It became one of the most popular children's poems of all time.

It's not clear when the North Pole and the factory of elves became attached to the story, but it was established enough by 1927 for the Finns to claim that Santa Claus lived in Finnish Lapland, as no reindeer could live at the North Pole because there was no lichen.

Santa's official post office is in Rovaniemi, capital of Lapland. He receives 600,000 letters a year.

As if in revenge for his secular success, the Vatican demoted Saint Nicholas's saint's day (December 6) from obligatory to voluntary observance in 1969.

What do Bugs Bunny, Brer Rabbit, and the Easter Bunny have in common?

They are all hares, not rabbits.

Bugs Bunny and Brer Rabbit are both modeled on North American Jack Rabbits, which are long-eared, large-legged hares.

Bugs Bunny, who won an Oscar in 1958 for *Knighty Knight*, made his screen debut in 1938 in *Porky's Hare Hunt.* Mel Blanc, the voice of Bugs Bunny, loathed carrots: nevertheless he still had to chew them during recordings as no other vegetable produced the desired crunch.

The origins of Brer Rabbit are in the story-telling traditions of African American slaves, who told tales about the hare being more wily than the fox. Robert Roosevelt, uncle of President Theodore and a friend of Oscar Wilde, was the first person to write down the stories but it wasn't until 1879 that the Uncle Remus stories, transcribed by Joel Chandler Harris, became national classics.

The insufferably cute Easter Bunny is also a modern American invention. It's a commercial sanitization of the hare as fertility-rebirth-moon symbol. In Saxon culture, the hare was sacred to Eostre, the goddess of spring, which is where we get the word *Easter.*

Few animals have such rich mythological associations. From Ancient Egypt and Mesopotamia through to India, Africa, China, and Western Europe, hares have been portrayed as sacred, evil, wise, destructive, clever, and, almost always, sexy.

Maybe it's because they are so fast—they can run at 48 mph and leap 8 feet in the air. Or maybe it's their astonishing fertility: a female hare (doe) can produce forty-two leverets in a single year. Pliny the Elder believed eating hare would make you sexually attractive for up to nine days.

Hares and rabbits are not rodents but lagomorphs (which derives from the Greek for "hare-shaped"). Lagomorphs are peculiar in being able to close their nostrils and choosing to eat their own droppings.

They do this for the same reasons cows chew the cud—to extract the maximum amount of nutrients and energy from their food. Unlike cows, hares and rabbits don't get to stand around for hours ruminating.

The familiar spring ritual of boxing hares is not a male dominance contest but a doe fighting off unwanted suitors.

What were Cinderella's slippers made from?

Squirrel fur.

Charles Perrault, who wrote the familiar version of the story in the seventeenth century, misheard the word *vair* (squirrel fur) in the medieval tale he borrowed and updated for the similar-sounding *verre* (glass).

Cinderella is an ancient and universal story. A Chinese version dates back to the ninth century and there are more than 340 other versions before Perrault's. None of the early versions mentions glass slippers. In the original Chinese story "Yeh-Shen," they're made of gold thread with solid gold soles. In the Scottish version "Rashie-Coat" they're made of rushes. In the medieval French tale, adapted by Perrault, her shoes are described as *pantoufles de vair*—slippers of squirrel's fur.

> DID YOU KNOW THAT SQUIRRELS ARE THE DEVIL'S OVEN MITTS?
>
> MISS PIGGY

One source says the *vair/verre* error occurred before Perrault, and he merely repeated it. Others think glass slippers were Perrault's own idea and that he intended them all along.

The *OED* states that *vair*, in use in English as well as French since at least 1300, comes from the Latin *varius*, "*parti-colored*," and refers to fur from a species of squirrel that is "much used for trimming or lining garments."

Snopes.com states that Perrault could not have misheard *vair* as *verre* because *vair* "was no longer used in his time." This seems extremely doubtful—the word was continuously in use in English until at least 1864.

Perrault was an upper-class Parisian author who rose to become director of the Académie Française. His *Tales of Mother*

Goose (1697), originally devised as Court entertainment and published under the name of his seventeen-year-old son, were immediately popular and opened up a new literary genre: the fairy tale. Apart from "Cinderella," his famous versions of classic tales include "Sleeping Beauty," "Little Red Riding Hood," "Bluebeard," and "Puss-in-Boots."

As well as polishing up "Cinderella"—adding the mice, the pumpkin, and the fairy godmother—Perrault reduced their peasant bloodthirstiness. In the medieval original, the ugly sisters cut off their toes and bunions to try on the slipper, and after the Prince marries Cinders, the King takes revenge on them and the wicked stepmother by forcing them to dance themselves to death wearing red-hot iron boots. Much of this bloodthirstiness was later reinstated by the Brothers Grimm.

In *Three Contributions to the Theory of Sex*, Freud claimed slippers were a symbol for the female genitals.

Where do loofahs come from?

Trees.

Not from the sea—that'll be sponges you're thinking of—loofahs grow on trees. They are a kind of gourd and are regarded as a tasty snack throughout Asia.

Smooth loofah (*Luffa aegyptiaca*) is a rampant, fast-growing annual vine that produces pretty yellow flowers and strangelooking fruits that are edible when immature and useful when fully grown. The vine can grow more than 30 feet long and scrambles over anything in its path.

Probably native to tropical Africa and Asia, it is grown throughout most of Asia and is cultivated commercially in the United States for export to Japan.

The immature fruits, 3 to 6 inches in length, can be stir-fried whole or sliced, or they can be grated and used in soups and omelettes. Any fruits longer than 4 inches need to be peeled because the skin becomes bitter.

Allowed to mature on the vine until they start turning brown and their stems go yellow, loofahs are easy to peel for use as back scrubbers, skin exfoliators, or general kitchen pot scrubs.

What's the strongest wood?

Balsa.

It's the strongest wood in the world when measured in three categories of stiffness, bendability, and compressibility—stronger than oak or pine.

Although it is the softest of woods, it is not, botanically, a softwood but a hardwood. *Hardwood* is a botanical term that describes broad-leaved, mostly deciduous trees that are angiosperms (flowering plants such as balsa) as opposed to coniferous gymnosperms (nonflowering plants such as pine).

It is also light, of course, though it is not the lightest in the world—the lightest practical wood is a New Zealand native, the small whau tree (pronounced "phow"), which is used by Maori fishermen to make floats.

Balsa is Spanish for "raft." Balsa wood is mothproof.

What do you get if you suck your pencil?

Nothing bad, apart from being told not to.

Pencils don't contain lead and never have done. They contain graphite, one of the six pure forms of carbon, which is no more poisonous than the wood it's wrapped in. Even the paint is now lead-free.

The confusion comes from the fact that

sharpened lead was used for more than two thousand years to draw on papyrus and paper.

The only deposit of pure, solid, graphite ever found was uncovered by accident in Borrowdale, Cumbria, in 1564. It was protected by strict laws and armed guards and mined for just six weeks a year.

The so-called black lead it produced was cut into thin square sticks to make the first pencils. English pencils were adopted quickly across Europe. The first recorded use was by the Swiss naturalist Konrad Gessner in 1565.

> EVEN WHAT CAN APPEAR TO BE THE MOST COMMON, SMALL, AND SIMPLE OF OBJECTS, CAN REVEAL ITSELF TO BE ON ITS OWN TERMS AS COMPLEX AND AS GRAND AS A SPACE SHUTTLE OR A GREAT SUSPENSION BRIDGE.
>
> HENRY PETROSKI

Henry David Thoreau, author of *Walden*, was the first American to successfully fire graphite with clay to make a pencil lead but the big commercial breakthrough came in 1827, when Joseph Dixon of Salem, Massachusetts, introduced a machine that mass-produced square graphite pencils at the rate of 132 per minute.

By the time he died in 1869, the Joseph Dixon Crucible Company was the world leader, producing 86,000 round-cased pencils a day. Today (now called Dixon Ticonderoga) it is still one of the world's leading pencil makers.

Roald Dahl wrote all his books using a yellow Dixon Ticonderoga medium pencil. The traditional yellow pencil goes back to 1890 when Josef Hardmuth manufactured the first one at his Prague factory and named it after Queen Victoria's famous yellow diamond, Koh-i-Noor (she'd called his luxury line "the Koh-i-Noor of pencils"). Other manufacturers copied it. In North America, 75 percent of all pencils sold are yellow.

The average pencil can be sharpened seventeen times and can write 45,000 words or a straight line 35 miles long.

The rubber attached to the end of a pencil is held in place by a device known as a ferrule. The patent was first granted in 1858, but they were unpopular in schools because teachers believed they encouraged laziness.

The "rubber" in most pencils is actually made from vegetable oil, with a very small amount of rubber binding it together.

Have you ever slid down a banister?

No, you haven't.

Banisters are the thin struts that support the fat bit you slide down, which is properly called a balustrade or handrail.

With a stone staircase, banisters are called balusters, and, strictly speaking, *baluster* is the correct word for the struts on any kind of staircase. The word *banister* (or, worse, *bannister*) is a corruption of the original word. Though in common usage since at least 1667, Victorian dictionaries railed and blustered about the use of the word *banister* as improper and vulgar, but it is now deemed acceptable.

The word *newel post*—the bit with a knob on top that stops you from sliding off the end of the balustrade—has also changed its meaning. It was originally the central pillar of a spiral staircase and comes from the Latin *nux* (a nut), passing into the Romance languages as *nucale* (i.e., something kernel-like), and then into Old French as *nouel*, which became the English *newel*. In due course, it came to mean any pillar-shaped bit associated with stairs, and eventually just the one at the end.

In modern French, a language with many fewer words than English, the word *noyau* serves the multiple purpose of meaning a newel post; the stone or pit of a fruit; the kernel of a nut; and the nucleus of an atom.

Where was the log cabin invented?

Probably in Scandinavia, four thousand years ago.

The development of metal tools during the Bronze Age made them possible. As a quick-to-build, durable, warm form of building, they were used widely across northern Europe.

The ancient Greeks may also have a claim, because although the ancient coniferous forests have now receded from the Mediterranean, there is a theory that the Minoans' and Mycenaeans' one-room house or *megaron* was originally made from horizontal pine logs.

It was through the Swedish and Finnish settlements in Delaware in the 1630s that the log cabin reached America, its spiritual home. British settlers, incidentally, constructed their homes of wooden planks, not logs.

A museum in Hodgenville, Kentucky, proudly displays the famous log cabin in which Abraham Lincoln was born, though it was, in fact, built thirty years after his death. This is uncomfortably close to the old schoolboy howler: "Abe Lincoln was born in a log cabin he built with his own hands."

Despite this ludicrous fakery, the U.S. National Park Service solemnly tells tourists not to use flash photography, in case they damage the historic logs.

Where did Stone Age people live?

Put away that cliché.

"Cavemen" isn't a good description of Stone Age or palaeolithic people. It's part of the couldn't-care-less-about-anything-much-before-the-Romans school of history teaching, much favored in the late nineteenth century. It's not used by modern historians or archaeologists at all.

Palaeolithic humans were nomadic hunter-gatherers who occasionally used caves. There are 277 sites that have been identified in Europe—among them Altamira, in Spain; Lascaux, in France; and Creswell Crags, in Derbyshire, England. They left paintings and evidence of fires, cooking, rituals, and burials, but they were not designed as permanent dwelling places.

The earliest European cave art has been dated to forty thousand years ago, although the precise age is notoriously difficult to establish. Paint isn't organic, so can't be carbon-dated.

The most persuasive explanation of its function relates it to more recent cave painting among hunter-gatherer people in southern Africa and Australia. Here the paintings were the work of shamans, who entered the dark and often remote caves in order to connect with the spirit world. Another theory suggests they were simply palaeolithic teenage graffiti.

In northern China, an estimated 40 million people currently live in cave homes known as *yaodong*. As the human population of the entire planet in 8000 B.C. was probably only five million, there are eight times as many cavemen now than there were people of any kind then.

People who live in caves are called troglodytes, from the Greek for "those who get into a hole."

Other places where there have been troglodyte dwellings in modern times include Cappadocia, in Turkey; Andalucia, in southern Spain; New Mexico, in the United States; and the Canary Islands.

This may be the beginning rather than the end of a trend. Research from the University of Bath has demonstrated that an underground home uses 25 percent less energy than a normal house.

What was the first animal to be domesticated?

a. Sheep
b. Pig
c. Reindeer
d. Horse
e. Dog

Around fourteen thousand years ago, palaeolithic hunter-gatherers on what is now the Russian/Mongolian border learned to lure reindeer away from their huge migratory groups and breed them to create their own small herd.

Reindeer were like walking corner-shops, offering meat, milk, and fur for clothing. It is possible that they trained dogs at the same time to help them domesticate the reindeer.

Today, there are about three million domesticated reindeer, most of them in the wastes of Lapland, which stretches across Sweden, Norway, Finland, and Russia.

The Lapps, who herd them, prefer to call themselves the Sami. Perhaps they don't know that *Sami* is ancient Swedish for "chavs."

Caribou is the North American name for reindeer. It comes from *xalibu* (one who digs) in the Mi'Maq (or Micmac) language of eastern Canada. Reindeer/caribou use their large feet to dig through to the lichen beneath the snow. Lichen provide two-thirds of a reindeer's food.

Reindeer are nomadic and travel up to 3,000 miles a year, the mammal travel record. They're fast, too, reaching speeds of 48 mph on land and 6mph in water. Because of a clicking tendon in their feet, a herd of migrating reindeer sounds like a castanet convention.

Here are the estimated dates for domestication of the major animals:

Reindeer	ca.12000 B.C.
Dogs (Eurasia, North America)	ca.12000 B.C.
Sheep (SW Asia)	8000 B.C.
Pig (SW Asia, China)	8000 B.C.
Cattle (SW Asia, India, N Africa)	6000 B.C.

Domestication is different from taming. It implies selective breeding. Elephants can be tamed, but not domesticated.

What was odd about Rudolph the Red-Nosed Reindeer?

He was a girl.

Despite being called Rudolph and referred to as "him," like all Santa's reindeer he must in fact have been female. Male reindeer lose their antlers at the beginning of the winter. Females keep their antlers until they give birth in the spring.

Reindeer/caribou are the only female deer to have antlers. They are shed and regrow every year. They are shorter and simpler than those of the males but still grow at a rate of more than an inch a day, making them the fastest-growing tissue of any mammal.

The other possibility is that Rudolph was a eunuch. The Sami sometimes castrate male reindeer, thus enabling them to keep their antlers, and to carry especially heavy loads.

Where do turkeys come from?

Despite being native to North America, the domesticated turkeys that graced the tables of the Pilgrim Fathers had traveled out with them from England.

Turkeys first reached Europe in the 1520s, brought back from their native Mexico first to Spain and then sold throughout the continent by Turkish merchants. They quickly became a favorite food for the richer classes.

By 1585, turkey had become a Christmas tradition in England. Norfolk farmers set to work to produce a heavier-breasted, more docile version of the wild bird. The Norfolk Black and the White Holland were both English breeds reintroduced to America, and most domestic turkey now consumed in the United States derives from them.

From the late sixteenth century, English turkeys walked the 100 miles from Norfolk to Leadenhall Market in London each year. The journey would take three months and the birds wore special leather boots to protect their feet.

A flock of one thousand turkeys could be managed by two drovers carrying long wands of willow or hazel with red cloth tied on the ends. Traffic jams were caused by the vast flocks entering London from Norfolk and Suffolk in the weeks before Christmas.

Turkeys have nothing to do with Turkey. They were called "Turkie cocks" in England because of the traders who supplied them. Maize, also originally from Mexico, was once called "turkie corn" for the same reason.

In most other countries—including Turkey—they were named after India, perhaps because the Spanish returned with it from the Indies (as America was called).

Only the Portuguese got close to the truth, calling the turkey a *peru*. The Native American word for "turkey" was *furkee*, according to the Pilgrim Fathers, although no one seems to know which Algonquin language it comes from. In Choctaw they are called *fakit*, based on the sound the bird makes.

Even science seemed unsure what to call the turkey. The Latin name *Meleagris gallopavo* translates literally as the "guinea-fowl chicken-peacock," which looks like linguistic spread betting.

A male turkey is called a stag, gobbler, or tom. The female is always a hen. Turkeys are the largest birds able to give birth without sex: the offspring of such virgin births are male, and invariably sterile.

Most languages write the turkey's gobble as "glu glu" or "kruk kruk." In Hebrew, however, they go "mekarkerim."

Who was born by Immaculate Conception?

Mary.

This catches out a lot of non-Catholics. The Immaculate Conception refers to the birth of the Virgin Mary, not the virgin birth of Jesus.

It is commonly confused with the doctrine of the Virgin Birth, by which Mary became pregnant with Jesus through the Holy Spirit.

Under the doctrine of the Immaculate Conception, Mary was granted immunity from all suspicion of sin at the moment she was conceived.

Unfortunately, the Bible doesn't make any reference to this happening. It only became an official Catholic dogma in 1854.

Many theologians believe the doctrine to be unnecessary, because Jesus redeemed everyone anyway.

The Virgin Birth is a core doctrine of the Church but that doesn't mean it is beyond controversy. It is explicitly mentioned in Luke and Matthew's Gospels but not by the earlier Gospel of Saint Mark, or the even earlier letters of Saint Paul.

Saint Paul, in his letter to the Romans, states clearly that Jesus "was made of the seed of David, according to the flesh." We also know that the earliest Jewish Christians, called Nazarenes, didn't believe in the virgin birth, either.

The supernatural elements of Jesus' life story became exaggerated as the new religion gradually absorbed pagan ideas to broaden its appeal.

The virgin birth wasn't a part of Jewish tradition. But Perseus and Dionysus in Greek mythology, Horus in Egyptian and Mithra, a Persian deity whose cult rivaled Christianity in popularity, were all "born of virgins."

Was Jesus born in a stable?

No.

Not according to the New Testament. The idea that Jesus was born in a stable is an assumption made only because Saint Luke's Gospel says he was "laid in a manger."

Nor is there any biblical authority for the presence of animals at the Nativity. Of course, we're all familiar with the scene from the crib we see in churches and schools, but it was one thousand years before it was invented.

Saint Francis of Assisi is credited with making the first crib, in 1223 in a cave in the hills above Greccio. He placed some hay on a flat rock (which can still be seen), put a baby on top, and added carvings of an ox and an ass (though no Joseph, Mary, Wise Men, Shepherds, angels, or lobsters).

How many sheep were there on Noah's Ark?

Seven. Or fourteen.

The relevant passage in the King James Bible appears in Genesis 7:2, where God tells Noah: "Of every clean beast thou shalt take to thee by sevens, the male and his female: and of the beasts that are not clean by two, the male and his female."

"Unclean" beasts are the extensive range of creatures that Jews were (and are) forbidden to eat, including pigs, camels, rock badgers, chameleons, eels, snails, ferrets, lizards, moles, vultures, swans, owls, pelicans, storks, herons, lapwings, bats, ravens, cuckoos, and eagles.

"Clean" (edible) animals include sheep, cattle, goats, antelopes, and locusts.

So there were at least seven sheep on the Ark, not two as taught in Sunday school. But the passage is slightly ambiguous: does it mean seven males and seven females, or seven altogether?

Those who know say that seven of each would be a disaster: fights would break out between the rams. A more practical solution would be one ram and six ewes.

However, the Douay-Rheims Bible, the authoritative Catholic translation of the Latin Vulgate published in 1609, is quite clear on the matter: "Of all clean beasts, take seven and seven, the male and the female." So it looks like there were fourteen sheep on the Ark.

Medieval rabbis spent a good deal of time debating whether fish were left to fend for themselves in the Flood, or whether Noah dutifully brought them onboard the ark in an aquarium. In the mid-sixteenth century, Johannes Buteo calculated that Noah's Ark would have had a usable space of 350,000 cubic cubits, of which 140,000 must have been taken up by hay.

But the flood really happened. More than 500 different flood myths exist in cultures all over the world.

Human beings evolved during the last Ice Age. Toward the end of it, as the temperature rose, there were vast catastrophic rises in sea level caused by the melting ice caps. The story of Noah is thought to describe the disappearance of the Tigris-Euphrates Delta under the Persian Gulf.

The sudden shortage of land could no longer support hunter-gathers, and for the first time, human beings were forced to turn to farming.

Aborigines, whose culture and oral tradition reaches back to the last Ice Age, can name and locate mountains that have been under the sea since the ice caps melted eight thousand years ago.

> EVERY SCIENTIFIC TRUTH GOES THROUGH THREE STAGES. FIRST, PEOPLE SAY IT CONFLICTS WITH THE BIBLE. NEXT THEY SAY IT HAD BEEN DISCOVERED BEFORE. LASTLY THEY SAY THEY ALWAYS BELIEVED IN IT.
>
> LOUIS AGASSIZ

Who's the oldest man in the Bible?

Enoch, Methuselah's father, who's still alive. He's 5,387 years old, give or take a week. Methuselah lived to a measly 969.

Methuselah is famous for being the oldest man who ever lived but, according to the Bible, he was not that much older than his own grandfather, Jared, who lived to be 962. The direct line of Adam's descendants up until the Flood (with their ages) is as follows: Adam (930); Seth (912); Enos (905); Cainan (910); Mahalaleel (895); Jared (962); Enoch (365 not out); Methuselah (969); Lamech (777); Noah (950).

Though all of these characters were abnormally old, all but one of them died in a perfectly normal way. The exception is the mysterious Enoch, who was a stripling of just 365 when God took him. Enoch never died at all: a distinction not even granted to Jesus Christ. In the New Testament, Saint Paul reiterates the story of Enoch's immortality in his Epistle to the Hebrews.

"By faith Enoch was translated that he should not see death; and was not found, because God had translated him: for before his translation he had this testimony, that he pleased God" (Hebrews 11:5).

The French philosopher Descartes believed it ought to be possible for all human beings to live as long as the biblical Patriarchs—around a thousand years—and was convinced he was on the brink of cracking the secret when he died in 1650, aged fifty-four.

> MY DOCTOR TOLD ME THAT JOGGING COULD ADD YEARS TO MY LIFE. I THINK HE WAS RIGHT. I FEEL TEN YEARS OLDER ALREADY.
>
> MILTON BERLE

Where were the first modern Olympics held?

At Much Wenlock, Shropshire, in 1850. The games were held there annually and inspired Baron Coubertin to organize the Athens Olympiad of 1896:

"Much Wenlock is a town in Shropshire, a county on the borders of Wales, and if the Olympic Games that modern Greece has not yet been able to revive still survive today, it is due not to a Greek, but to Dr. W. P. Brookes."

Brookes believed a rigorous program of physical training would help make people better Christians by keeping them out of the pubs. His knowledge of the ancient Olympics inspired him to found the Much Wenlock Society for the Promulgation of Physical Culture in 1841.

The first of the annual Brookes's Olympian Games was held in 1850 with small cash prizes for running, long jump, football, quoits, and cricket. Other events were gradually added, such as a blindfold wheelbarrow race, a pig race, and a medieval tilting contest. Winners were crowned with laurel wreaths and medallions inscribed with Nike, the Greek goddess of victory.

The fame of the Wenlock Olympics quickly spread, attracting entries from all parts of Britain. They were even noticed in Athens and King George I of the Hellenes sent a silver medal to be awarded as a prize.

With visions of reviving the ancient games on an international scale, Brookes founded the National (British) Olympic Association in 1865 and staged its first games at the Crystal Palace in London. Without sponsors, it was snubbed by the leading sportsmen of the day.

In 1888 Brookes began a correspondence with Baron Coubertin. In 1890 the Baron came to see the Wenlock Games for himself, planting an oak that still stands in the village. He returned home determined to re-establish the ancient games, founding the International Olympic Committee in 1894.

Through his wealth, prestige, and political connections, Coubertin succeeded where Brookes had failed. He staged the first international revival of the games in Athens in the summer of 1896.

Dr Brookes had died the previous year, aged eighty-six. The Wenlock Games are still held annually in his honour.

Why is a marathon 26 miles and 385 yards long?

For the convenience of the British royal family.

At the first three modern Olympics, the marathon was run over a distance of roughly 26 miles, varying from games to games. In 1908 the Olympic Games were held in London, and the starting line was put outside a window at Windsor Castle from which one half of the royal family could watch, with the finish in front of the royal box in the White City stadium, where the other half of the family was waiting. This distance was 26 miles and 385 yards: the standard length of a marathon ever since.

The origin of the 26-mile run dates to a Greek messenger called Pheidippides, who ran this distance from Marathon to Athens to relate the victory of the Athenians over the Persians in 490 B.C. According to popular legend, he delivered the message and then dropped dead.

It's a heroic tale, but it doesn't hold water. Very few marathon runners die after the event, and professional ancient Greek couriers were regularly required to run twice as far.

This version of the story first appears in the work of the Roman historian Plutarch (circa A.D. 45–125) more than five hundred years later. He calls the runner Eucles. It seems to have become confused with the much older story of Pheidippides recorded by Herodotus, who was born six years after the battle, and whose account is the nearest we have to a contemporary one.

According to him, Pheidippides ran from Marathon to Sparta (153 miles) to ask for help in beating off the Persian attack. The Spartans were busy with a religious festival, so he ran all the way back and the Athenians had to fight the Persians on their own. They won a resounding victory, losing 192 men to the Persians' 6,400. Pheidippides didn't die.

Ultra-running is the discipline that covers any running event that's longer than a marathon. In 1982 the American Ultrarunning Association ran the authentic Pheidippides route (as agreed by a consortium of Greek scholars) and established it as the International Spartathlon in 1983. The first winner was a modern legend: the Greek long-distance runner, Yannis Kouros.

Kouros currently holds every world record from 125 to 1,000 miles. In 2005 he retraced Pheidippides's complete route, running from Athens to Sparta and back.

What does the Queen say to someone she's knighted?

Not a lot.

According to the official website of the British monarchy, www.royal.gov.uk:

"[A]fter his name is announced, the knight-elect kneels on a knighting-stool in front of The Queen, who then lays the sword blade on the knight's right and then left shoulder. After he has been dubbed, the new knight stands up (contrary to popular belief, the words 'Arise, Sir–' are not used), and The Queen then invests the knight with the insignia of the Order to which he has been appointed (a star or badge, depending on the Order). By tradition, clergy receiving a knighthood are not dubbed, as the use of a sword is thought inappropriate for their calling."

The actual meaning of the English word *accolade* is "the

salutation on the bestowal of knighthood." It comes from Latin *ad* (to) and *collum* (neck)—hence, "an embrace round the neck."

There also used to be a ceremony associated with the removal of a knighthood: degradation. The last public degradation was in 1621, when Sir Francis Mitchell was found guilty of "grievous exactions" and had his spurs broken and thrown away, his belt cut, and his sword broken over his head. Finally, he was pronounced to be "no longer a Knight but Knave."

Unlike Lord Kagan (jailed for theft in 1980), Baron Jeffrey Archer of Weston-super-Mare was never knighted and so hasn't faced degradation following his own "grievous exactions." He keeps his peerage but has inspired reforms—so far not carried out—that will make it impossible for a convicted criminal to serve in the House of Lords.

Who was the first King of England?

Alfred the Great's grandson.

King Aethelstan (924–39) was the first true king of all England. His grandfather, Alfred the Great, was only King of Wessex, even though he did refer to himself rather optimistically as "King of the English."

When Alfred came to the throne, England was still made up of five separate kingdoms. During Alfred's life, Cornwall came under his control, but Mercia, Northumbria, and East Anglia fell to Viking invaders.

After a period hiding in the Somerset levels (where he *didn't* burn any cakes), Alfred fought back against the Danes, eventually restoring his old kingdom. But in the treaty he made following his defeat of the Viking warlord Guthrum at Edington in 878, he chose to give half the country (everything east of a line from London to Chester) to the enemy. This was known as the Danelaw. In return, Guthrum agreed to convert to Christianity.

Alfred was keen to ensure that any future Scandinavian

raiders wouldn't find it quite so easy and set about creating a network of defended towns to protect his territory.

It worked. By his grandson's reign, Wessex's control of England was complete. At the battle of Brunanburh in 937, Aethelstan defeated the kings of Scotland, Strathclyde, and Dublin to establish the Anglo-Saxon kingdom of England.

No one is sure where Brunanburh is: Tinsley Wood near Sheffield seems the best guess.

The last king of "England"—that is, the last king to rule England and nothing else—was Harold Godwinson or Harold II. William, his successor, was already Duke of Normandy, and the English crown controlled substantial portions of France until Calais was finally surrendered in 1558.

How many wives did Henry VIII have?

We make it two.

Or four if you're a Catholic.

Henry's fourth marriage to Anne of Cleves was annulled. This is very different from divorce. Legally, it means the marriage never took place.

There were two grounds for the annulment. Anne and Henry never consummated the marriage; that is, they never had intercourse. Refusal or inability to consummate a marriage is still grounds for annulment today.

In addition, Anne was already betrothed to Francis, Duke of Lorraine when she married Henry. At that time, the formal act of betrothal was a legal bar to marrying someone else.

All parties agreed no legal marriage had taken place. So that leaves five.

The pope declared Henry's second marriage to Anne Boleyn illegal, because the king was still married to his first wife, Catherine of Aragon.

Henry, as head of the new Church of England, declared in turn that his *first* marriage was invalid on the legal grounds that a man could not sleep with his brother's widow. The king cited the Old Testament, which he claimed as "God's Law," whether the pope liked it or not.

Depending on whether you believe the pope or the king, this brings it down to either four or three marriages.

Henry annulled his marriage to Anne Boleyn just before he had her executed for adultery. This was somewhat illogical: if the marriage had never existed, Anne could hardly be accused of betraying it.

He did the same with his fifth wife, Catherine Howard. All the evidence suggests she was unfaithful to him before and during their marriage. This time, Henry passed a special act making it treasonable for a queen to commit adultery. Once again, he also had the marriage annulled.

So that makes four annulments, and only two incontestably legal marriages.

Apart from Henry's last wife, Catherine Parr (who outlived him), the lady who got off lightest was Anne of Cleves. After their annulment, the king showered her with gifts and the official title of "beloved sister." She visited court often, swapping cooks, recipes, and household gadgets with the man who had never been her husband.

Index